GORDON FORBES

A Handful of Summers

A FIRESIDE BOOK · PUBLISHED BY SIMON & SCHUSTER INC.
NEW YORK · LONDON · TORONTO · SYDNEY · TOKYO

A Fireside Book
Published by Simon & Schuster Inc.
Simon & Schuster Building
Rockefeller Center
1230 Avenue of the Americas
New York, New York 10020
FIRESIDE and colophon are registered trademarks
of Simon & Schuster Inc.
Originally published in Great Britain
by William Heinemann Ltd., 1978

Manufactured in the United States of America

10 9 8 7 6 5 4 3 2 1 Pbk.

Library of Congress Cataloging in Publication Data

Forbes, Gordon.
A handful of summers.

(A Fireside Sports Classic)
Reprint. Originally published: London :
Heinemann, 1978.
"A Fireside Book."
1. Forbes, Gordon, 1934– . 2. Tennis
players—South Africa—Biography. I. Title.
II. Series.
[GV994.F67A34 1988] 796.342'092'4 [B] 87-35604

ISBN 0-671-66183-3 Pbk.

For Jeannie,
For Abie and the others whose lunacies
raised the laughter,
And for the game that we play—
For tennis itself.

Contents

Acknowledgements

The author would like to thank Peter Ustinov, Owen and Jenny Williams, Ron Bookman, Gladys Heldman, Kate and Marshall Lee, Jacques Sellschop, Jane Fraser, the Segal girls, Pat Tayler, Allie Inglis, Margo Blanchett, Jenny Archibald, Jane and Burt Boyar, Frances Forbes, Ed Fernberger, Russ Adams, Arthur Cole, C. M. Jones, H. Harris and The Press Association Ltd. The author is also very grateful to the two tennis publications, World Tennis and Tennis S.A.

The two lines of poetry on page 112 are reprinted by permission of Faber & Faber Ltd, from the *Collected Poems* 1909–1962 by T. S. Eliot.

A Handful of Summers

"In the middle of a lifetime
Of Days and Nights
And the unexpected seasons that
Sly changes ring;
Go back down the years
And recall if you can
All the warm temperate times;
You may find with surprise
That they're all squeezed in
To a headful of thoughts
And a handful of summers."

G.F. Diary Notes—1968

Introduction

Wimbledon—1976

Staircase number one at the All England Club leads you into a section of the stadium just above the members' enclosure. Climb the stairs on finals day and there, suddenly, in the sun, the soft old centre court, lying waiting, all green; waiting; for two o'clock. It is venerable, that court, and it lives. Heaven knows why, but it does. Perhaps the shades of green do it; or the canvas awnings, or the smell of the place. England and cut grass. From the stand at the top of staircase one, you get a perfect, almost end-on view of the court.

I arrived early, and sat there with my chin in my hands, allowing memories to wash over me; of this Wimbledon, and of others past. The soft, sad nudges of good times spent, of chances gone; and of dreams, half-dreamed. You could see right into the players' enclosure from the stand at the top of staircase one. In 1954 I had watched Drobny and Rosewall take the court. They wore blazers and baggy shorts that tipped up at the back when they bowed towards the Royal Box. Good God! The inordinate thrill of that very first Wimbledon!

At two, there came a crash of applause and Nastase and Borg appeared, superbly fitted out. Beautifully-cut tennis gear. They took their bow, arranged their paraphernalia, and began to play; easy, expert strokes. Exclusive and aloof. There is no doubt at all that Borg is one of the game's great athletes. There is a simplicity about the way he plays—a marvellous logic that carves away all complications. And Nastase! Who can add to the screeds already written about the charm and roguery of Nastase? I sat there, engrossed in the tennis—this new tennis with its indefinable air of style and grandeur. I sensed the hero-worship for the young Swede and the pure glamour of Nastase. The aura of theatre! And I found myself thinking suddenly of the older days when tennis tournaments had been simpler and more personal things; when there were no Las Vegas Spectaculars, no money prizes, nor the fascinations created by money, nor any of its motivations; when the spirit of the game had been much more the thing, and getting into the next round meant no increased winnings, but only the excitement of a victory, and a small step nearer to some private and much-beloved ambition, longed for with unimagined longings.

This book is about tennis when it was a game played in white; about an extraordinary band of players who travelled the world playing tennis for fun and the few pocketfuls of loose change that could, by sly and devious means, be extracted from the thrifty amateur officials.

This book is a story about tennis and me when we were both a little younger.

I've wanted to write it for years. The diaries which I kept during my playing days are dotted with the random beginnings of books.

"There I was, in Rome," I find scribbled, "locked in combat with the dreaded Italian, Pietrangeli. Slow courts, Pirelli balls, foreign language, boiling sun. Suddenly, at six-five in the first set the umpire called out 'New balls' in Italian, which I, at that time, thought meant 'Boiled eggs'.

"'What's happening?' I asked. 'Are we stopping for a snack?'" One never knows with Italians, you see!

It rambles on about the agonies of the grass-court player, bogged down on the damp clays of Rome.

There were many such beginnings.

This one, perhaps, will lead to something more coherent.

1

Diary Notes—1942

Yesterday was Saturday, so in the afternoon we all went into town. Joseph opened the first gate for us, and my father threw him a penny. My father says a penny is a lot of money for a little black boy. We looked back and saw him waving to us through the dust. Jack and I opened the other four gates, and Jean slept in the back. At the tennis club it was so hot that we climbed the trees by the side of the courts and just sat there. My father says it's a damn shame that the club has only nineteen members. My mother won all her matches quite easily.

The spring that year must have been a rainy one. By midsummer, I remember, the wheat was waist-high and ripening. If you lay flat on your back in the wheat field, you saw the stalks and ears stark against the white sky and if you turned your cheek to the soil you could smell earth smells and summer. Dreams came drifting. Then, if one of the big, black, floppy-tailed birds loped over you with his tail just brushing the wheat husks, you could leap up and chase him. And sometimes catch his frantic tail in a huge dive that brought you and him down in a tumble amongst the wheat stalks. You could look at him while you held him, see his frightened eyes and feel his little heartbeats and smile at him so strangely close to you, when before, he was just a flapping bird, far away. Then, having scolded him for being a fat and clumsy bird, you could throw him up and laugh at him paddling away.

We did that, Jack and I, those far-off summers—roamed the wheatlands and the river banks on summer days soft with heat and the hum of river insects; while all the time, in the north, the towering thunderheads reared up, solid and white and soft-grey as marble. You could find dozens of interesting things in the rivers. Wagtails' nests and lazy carp and fat turtles that widdled when you held them up. Everything smelt of muddy water.

My father was less enthusiastic than we were about the birds that swarmed in the wheat. Finches mainly. "Cheeky little devils," he would say, and let fly with a few charges of number nine. We would crouch behind him, waiting, and when the twin echoes died away, we would dash ahead to collect the victims. Sometimes we'd collect as many as thirty; gather them up into little heaps, broken little bundles of feathers, the bright finch-eyes clouding over, the cheekiness gone. After the gunshots the little black boys would instantly arrive. They clicked excitedly at the little heaps, and then, settling on their haunches, they plucked the birds and grilled them on open coals, turning them over with pointed sticks.

In dry summers, the clouds piled up but wouldn't rain. The wheat would wilt and the older people would look at the sky and mutter that the weather had changed. Farming people often get pessimistic about the weather, because their lives are ruled by the seasons.

Diary Notes: Summer 1942

Sometimes on Sundays there are tennis parties on our court. Some of the ladies wear long dresses and serve underarm. Uncle Harry is nearly eighty. Today he was playing with Aunt Ellie, also old. When volleys come to her, she hoots and makes excuses. She missed an easy shot, and called out, "Oh tut! There was hair in my eye. That makes it forty love."

And Uncle Harry said:

"Yes, and if there had been hare in your mouth, it would have been game."

We were farming folk—a close-knit little family of six, held together by a name. Our farm is on the edge of the Karroo, hot in summer, bitter in winter, and only sometimes, at dusk and in autumn, sublime. On the edge of the Karroo, the mountains begin—dreary, old mountains, unless you knew them well. We knew them well. Climbed them over and over, with the little troop of black blokes at our heels. Joseph, Absalom, Walk-Tall and the rest of the gang, tapering down to Webbcorn, who was only about a foot and a half high.

Joseph was our right-hand man—Jack's and mine, that is. He was shiny black with white teeth and eyes, and a permanent grin. In addition to being our friend, he was, being a black boy, at our beck and call night and day, because, in those days, that was the scheme of things in South Africa and we, as children, knew no other world. He was also the vanguard for many of our more uncertain adventures—like testing the ice in winter to see whether it would take our weight, or test-sailing our experimental rafts, boats or canoes, which often broke up and capsized due to our lack of experience in building floating things. We also used him for such things as leading the way on pitch dark nights, lighting fuses to our various explosive devices, climbing to hawks' nests on slender-looking poplars, pushing his hand into holes which looked as though they might contain:

starlings' eggs; baby crabs; sandmartins;
hedgehogs; molesnakes
or big green frogs.

It was also requested of Joseph to be the first down the tree slide for a speed test, or to find out whether the willow fronds would take the weight of a boy swinging out over the river pools and back. Thus, when Jack returned from the mountain one day to announce with great excitement that the black eagle had finally laid its eggs, I was not surprised, when in answer to my question: "How do we get at them?" he replied briefly: "We lower Joseph."

I might add at this point that Joseph had not yet been consulted—nor was he, until we three, equipped with a coil of rope, normally used for the wool-bale hoist, stood atop the lonely cliff that the black eagles liked. Lying on our stomachs in a row, we peered over the edge.

"There they are," said Jack, with deep satisfaction. "The eyrie of the great black eagles, rarest of birds except only for the golden eagles of the West."

He was given to these impressive bits of oratory (the factual accuracy of which was unimportant), on what he considered to be special occasions. I was too excited to enquire as to the exact whereabouts of the "West", or what golden eagles were like. Thirty feet below us on a meagre rock ledge lay the great nest, and in its centre nestled the two marvellous, freckled, creamy eggs. Below the nest, the cliff fell vertically for a full hundred feet before burying itself in a mass of scrub and broken rock. The two eagles wheeled and screamed above us, riding the up draughts with their huge wings. Jack regarded them.

"Stupid birds," he said, "we'll leave one for you." Then turning to me. "Gordon! Pass the rope!"

Together we uncoiled the rope and tied one end to the stem of a mountain tree.

"Now we tie the other end to Joseph," said Jack, completely in command. "And you and I simply lower him over the edge. Joseph, you will have the excitement of actually GETTING THE EGG."

Joseph's grin disappeared and the whites of his eyes showed rounder. He shook his head, whistled through his teeth and muttered to himself in Xhosa while we looped the rope around a second tree, then formed a sort of bosun's chair for him.

He never complained.

He firmly believed that we were the children of a great white god and that if we considered it wise to lower him over a cliff, no harm could possibly befall him.

"Tie plenty of knots," instructed Jack, though he himself was doing the knotting. "We don't want anything to come loose or slip."

With a final whistle, Joseph disappeared over the edge while we grimly paid out rope, running it around the second tree as a device for braking. The rope seemed to pay out forever. At last a yell floated up from below.

"He's there," said Jack. "Have a look. I'll hold the rope."

I peered over the edge. Joseph was on the ledge beside the nest, his grin back in place, holding an egg up to me. He looked surprisingly small.

"He's got it," I cried.

"He mustn't break it," said Jack.

"Don't break it!" I shouted. "We'll pull you back."

In ten minutes the egg was in our hands, far bigger than we had ever supposed, a full four inches across the long diameter. I will never forget the feel of it, satin smooth yet rough as we fondled it, nor the thrill of that achievement. Joseph was the complete hero. The precious egg was ours at last. It would be the ninety-third species in our collection. Our aim was one hundred, and there were still the herons and the blue hawks and kestrels, not counting the nightjars and the snipe.

Diary Notes: Summer 1945

Today I forgot to unload the air-gun before I carried it into the house, and Jack left the shed gate open so that the cows got into the vegetables and ate all my mother's cabbages and lettuce and then made steaming heaps in the kitchen yard. That meant cleaning up the heaps and then two hours of tennis straight after lunch when it was boiling hot. We started out making Joseph collect the balls for us, but my father soon stopped that.

"You fetch your own damn balls," he said, "and don't stop playing until I tell you to."

Jack was furious.

On Saturday morning we have to re-plant, and Jack has to write out a hundred times, "I must not let the cows get into the cabbages."

Forcing us to play tennis for hours at a time was a punishment, devised by my father, which in his opinion killed two birds with one stone. It gave us time to ruminate over our sins while at the same time teaching us "something useful". My father was obsessed with utilising spare time for "something useful". Given half a chance he would recite in an earnest voice:

"The heights by great men reached and kept
Were not attained by sudden flight:
But they, while their companions slept,
Toiled upwards in the night."

The words impressed us only later in life. At that time, we were much more interested in "Sudden Flights", than "Toiling in the night".

Memories that lie in the mind like old photographs, to be unpacked, dusted, examined and replaced—

Of The War Games We Invented:

"Joseph!" Jack's stern voice. "You black guys are the German army in Tobruk. Gordon and I will bombard you. You will lose ground, then counter-attack and finally be completely annihilated—all of you dead or dying."

Joseph, quite used to being surrounded, swarmed, bombarded, shot down, imprisoned, routed, sunk or sacked, merely nodded and began entrenching himself, beckoning to the others to do the same.

"Right, Gordon," said Jack. "I am Montgomery. You are my second-in-command. The divisions move out at dawn. Good luck!"

Of Pastimes Which We loved:

I closed the lid of the box containing our egg collection and turned to Jack.

"We have ninety-six different kinds," I said, "and the herons have nested in the poplar bush."

We'd wanted a heron's egg for months, but they nested on the very tops of the poplars where even Joseph couldn't climb.

"He'll get killed if the branch breaks," muttered Jack, as we inspected the nest from below. "And it will for sure."

"Perhaps," I said wistfully, "it will hold Webbcorn."

Webbcorn immediately rolled his eyes over backwards and disappeared into the undergrowth.

"Not even Webbcorn," said Jack, "although I suppose we could all stand underneath him in case the branch breaks, and catch him in a quilt. Like firemen, you see."

We all digested this new idea.

"Why don't we tip the nest and catch the eggs in a quilt?" I said.

"Brilliant," said Jack. "Cut and trim three long bamboos. Lash bamboos tightly together. Place end of third bamboo to underside of nest. Poke gently to tilt." Jack was a great one for instruction manuals.

With laborious care, the bamboos were cut, tied and hoisted. They collapsed, were re-tied, re-hoisted and, finally, placed against the underside of the nest.

"Right," said Jack, grunting under their weight. "I'll tip it, and you and Joseph catch the eggs in the eiderdown. Ready?"

Blue eggs spilled from the tilted nest. One hit a branch and broke, splattering us with egg. A second hit Joseph between the eyes and two more fell obediently into our stretched out eiderdown, where we pounced on them with a shout of delight—the operation had taken us a full day.

"Joseph," said Jack, recounting the story to our father, "was severely damaged by falling bombs."

Of Reconnaissance Cruises On Hostile Waters:

Jack raised an eye above the gunwale of our home-made canoe and scanned the horizon as we nosed around the little headland of reeds.

"Enemy shipping!" he whispered, his voice almost a scream. "Point blank range." In a frenzy of whispers, the old .22 rifle was brought to bear.

Forty yards away the convoy of spurwing geese began their raucous cries of alarm just prior to their flying off.

"They're diving!" whispered Jack, "fire at will! Shoot, shoot, shoot!"

A pair of geese came into line along my sights and I pulled the trigger. The birds rose with a tremendous clamour and clatter of wings, but one fat one lay flopping on the water.

"Heavy casualties," cried Jack. "Good shooting, guns. Joseph! Prepare to take survivors on board!"

Effects of the war again. All the farm wildlife had to adopt the role of "The Enemy". Certain of the enemy were open game, and free to be hunted. Other species were rigidly protected (our father's laws) and could only be taken prisoner. The big hawks, and vultures, which attacked the lambs were the "Luftwaffe", while predators such as jackals and lynx were "Panzers". These had to be fired at on sight. There were to be no prisoners.

Diary Notes: Summer 1943

Uncle Harry forgets things. He put .22 bullets into the same pocket as his pipe tobacco, and then stuffed his pipe and lit it. There was a great bang and his pipe flew to pieces and there was a hole in the brim of his hat.

Jack and I laughed when he told the story and he glared at us and said that it wasn't so damn funny.

In inventing games we would go to great lengths to remain what we considered to be authentic. Foraging in the loft above the shearing shed one day (ours was a sheep farm), Jack came upon a canvas bag full of blasting powder. It consisted of fat granules that looked like graphite and which went off with colossal bangs when you placed them upon an anvil and gave them a whack with a hammer. Also in the bag was a coil of dynamite fuse. It was a tremendous discovery and opened a completely new field of enterprise. We began blowing up things almost immediately.

With the graphic BBC war accounts each evening at six, we were seldom short of inspiration. We built several Moehne dams across the irrigation furrow and devastated those. Whole squadrons of German tanks were destroyed, the Reichstadt was razed, the Kiel Canal blocked, the Siegfried line badly mauled, Tobruk relieved for the fifth time and several fortresses sabotaged. We even mined the fierce red rooster that used to sneak up behind us and peck our ankles. We blew him up by planting a charge beneath his favourite roosting spot, and had the satisfaction of seeing him run around in dizzy circles for some time, squawking blue murder before realising that he was not badly hurt and that he still had his undercarriage.

Then we became more sophisticated and spent a week building a cannon which I called a mortar, but which Jack insisted was a siege gun, and planned a naval action. As the *Graf Spee* had been gloriously sunk by the Royal Navy, I can't imagine why we didn't choose her as our victim. Perhaps it was because we had just been to see Tyrone Power in *The Black Swan*, or perhaps because building an actual iron-clad dreadnought was beyond our capabilities.

Once a month we were allowed to go to the pictures. The Town Hall was converted into a cinema, and on a piece of white canvas draped across the stage, people like Loretta Young and Clark Gable and Dan Dailey did extravagant things in black and white, often rudely interrupted by sudden breakdowns and blackouts. We watched, riveted. God, how marvellous were Betty Grable's legs in our smelling-of-dust-and-polish little hall.

But the naval action:

We built a galleon out of willow and painstakingly rigged her out to the last detail before conveying her, one morning, to the launching site and floating her out onto the dam.

The cannon was brought to bear. The scene was set. Joseph and the minions stood in a straight line behind us, having been told that they were deckhands.

"Load with grape," said Jack in a naval sort of voice.

"Loaded with grape, sir," I replied mechanically.

"Double the charge."

"Charge doubled, sir."

"All cannon to bear."

"All cannon to bear, sir."

"Aim."

"Cannon aimed, sir."

Slowly the ominous muzzle of the piece was raised, lowered fractionally, then steadied. Twenty yards away the galleon rode the dam surface, graceful as a swan, her sails just filling, her rows of deck ordinance clearly visible.

"Steady on target," said Jack in a flat voice.

"Steady on target," I echoed.

"Fire!"

"Firing now!"

I lowered the glowing twig to the primer. With a great roar the gun exploded, turning a back somersault and ending up with its smoking muzzle pointing directly at the deckhands who disappeared, instantly, into the bullrushes. A cloud of black smoke rolled out over the dam, and a pair of startled moorhens trod water frantically for safer places. Slowly the smoke cleared.

"Good God," breathed Jack, as our galleon came into view, "a direct hit."

A row of black heads rose up out of the rushes. Jack was right. Never before had a naval operation produced such spectacular results. The galleon was ravaged, crippled, drifting helplessly. Large rents showed in her balsa frame, her aftermast trailed to starboard and her sails were in tatters. To our infinite delight, instead of riding the breeze, she now drifted in tight helpless circles and seemed to be making water fast.

"By George, sir," said Jack, quickly reassuming his naval voice. "I think we have her. Well done, guns! She's drifting. Steering shattered." He raised his voice to the deckhands. "Cutlasses, lads. Cutlasses and pistols. Prepare to board!"

"Boarding party at the ready, sir!" I echoed.

In these games of action, it was always Jack who took command, and the rest of us automatically became whatever was needed, singly or collectively, in the way of seconds-in-command, troops, sergeants, messengers, platoons, anything in fact that the action required. Now, with the dreaded and deadly pirate ship *Black Hawk* brought to book, I was as eager as he to deliver the *coup de grace*.

"We'll swarm 'em, men!" Jack went on. "Show no mercy. Never again shall Silver live to ravage the seas."

"You silly damn fools!" The voice of my father brought the whole thrilling action to an abrupt halt. "Don't you know that if you overload that cannon you'll blow your bloody heads off?"

He approached through the willows, hiding his smiles, and we hung our heads. The double charge of black powder had been Jack's idea, because, as he said, we'd taken a full week to build the pirate galleon, and we wanted a "good show". As it was, the violence of the blast had half-scared the wits out of me.

My father stopped beside us and surveyed the overturned cannon, our black faces, the cloud of smoke dispersing gently over the water and the shattered galleon.

"A direct hit, I see," he said. "Very impressive. Now put away that cannon for two weeks as punishment for overloading her. Then get on to the court and play two sets of tennis. You will play two sets on every day that the cannon is out of action."

We received the news in silence. The cannon had been built by us at great cost in time and ingenuity and had become our most prized possession. It had a twelve-inch barrel of three-quarter-inch waterpipe, a strong wooden carriage and little levers for horizontal and vertical adjustment. A cumbersome muzzle-loader, it was nonetheless our main armament in any emergency, since, during the war, ammunition for any of the other farm firearms was unobtainable.

Reluctantly we stowed the cannon away and went after our rackets.

Diary Notes: 1946

It's the middle of winter. In the evenings we sit around the fire and read out loud. This week it's Robin Hood; so the guns are put away and it's longbows. Dry quince wood is the best, and heavy baling twine, and there is a wild river bush that makes good arrows. Quivers out of buckskins. The black boys are the merry men, and are armed with quarterstaffs, but Joseph, who is Will Scarlett, demands a bow. We'll have to make him one. Jack, of course, is Robin, and I'm Little John. The part in the book we like best is when Robin has the Sheriff at his mercy, and the Sheriff calls out:

"Thou art a coward, Robin of Locksley. Had I but a sword, you would mock me no more." And Robin throws him a sword, saying:

"Take then thy sword, Good Sheriff," and beats him again.

Yesterday in the greenwood (the belt of poplars that grows along the river) our activities got so exciting that Webbcorn, who was Guy of Gisborne, was captured, gagged and bound to a tree overhanging the water. We then forgot about him completely, and only remembered him again as we sat down to supper that evening.

"Oh Lord!" said Jack, "Webbcorn's still tied up," so we had to take a torch and go down into the dark woods to release him. My father was furious. Three hours of tennis, and sixpence for Webbcorn as compensation. "Remember, NO BREAKS," said my father the next day as we began to play.

Jack watched him go, then muttered after him: "Had I but a sword, you would mock me no more!"

The compulsory practice sessions enforced on us by our father used to last for two hours each day. Thus, when people say to me, "But what made you become a tennis player?", the answer is fairly straightforward. If you are forced to stand on a tennis court for two hours each day, you might as well practise. We did, anyway. And in those long-ago sessions on the rough farm court, we eased the boredom by inventing a world of make-believe, and "becoming" the great players whom we'd heard of, but had never seen. Our entire childhood depended a great deal on make-believe.

My brother, Jack, the eldest and leader of the gang, had first choice of whom he wanted to be. Usually it was Perry or Budge or Riggs or Kramer. But on inventive days he would sometimes announce that he was "Kukuljevic".* Having done so, he would suddenly become aloof and merciless, and leave us to make our selections with some trepidation.

Now none of us was quite certain who Kukuljevic was, but the name conjured visions of a truly fearful opponent. My father believed that it was Kukuljevic who had invented the "topspin service" as he called it.

Having said that he was "Kukuljevic", Jack would arrange his face in a fierce and evil way, and serve a selection of spins, wild and frightful, which he called "Kukuljevic twists". Occasionally these "twists" would bounce in the service court, and once, to our profound delight, one of them gave a huge sideways bound, scattering the gravel surface of the court and leaving an oval mark which we all inspected reverently, while Jack strutted about saying:

"*That* must be *it*. I've done it. *That* must be the 'Kukuljevic Twist'."

Speaking from experience, I now submit, without question, that a good tennis shot, struck while one is representing the personage of Budge, Kramer, Parker, Rosewall or Hoad, is infinitely more grand and satisfactory than the same tennis shot, no matter how good, struck while one is anonymous.

In the evenings, my father would tell us stories of the genius of the great players of that time. Perry could do *this*, Bromwich *that*, Tilden *something else*, Alice Marble *still another unbelievable thing*. He had a way of making their deeds seem so marvellous that we'd be out at first light, giving them a try.

*A Yugoslav Davis Cup player who had once toured South Africa and whose service, a left arm American twist, had filled my father with such awe that he often talked about him.

Tennis stories became for us heady draughts quite early in our lives. Raptly we listened to them, savoured them, re-enacted them and stored them away in our memories. Favourite amongst the early ones was that which told of some great player, we never quite discovered whom, who amongst his rackets carried one which was pitch black all over. At match point, either for or against him, he would with marvellous haughtiness stop the game, walk to the umpire's stand, draw out the black racket ("like drawing a blade" we would say to ourselves) and with this mighty weapon, deal with the situation. He captivated us absolutely, long before we realised the traumas and tensions of that most scary of situations, the match point.

How often since then, with match points of varying intensities at hand, have I not thought wistfully of that black racket and fervently wished for some such visible strength to draw upon.

Diary Notes: Summer 1946

Our father makes us play tennis. Our mother shows us how. She is a very gentle lady; teaches us school, how to mix the mash that makes the chickens lay, and how to make butter. Softens the cross words of my father. He has just announced two very scary bits of news.

1. That we are to go to boarding school, and

2. That we are to play in the Border Junior Tennis Tournament.

Both make my stomach turn. I asked my mother why we couldn't stay on the farm and have her teach us the way she always has. She looked at me with soft eyes and said that our father knows best.

Age twelve. I played in and won my first junior tournament. It was in East London, one windy August. The matches began at eight in the morning. I stood clutching my racket, my kneecaps shivering, and jumped when they called my name.

"G. Forbes versus P. Whitfield."

"Oh God!" I remember thinking—"How good is Whitfield?"

I didn't know then that thereafter there were to be hundreds of Whitfields. Hundreds of shivering kneecaps. Hundreds of those extraordinary little lurches of the heart when they called out my name.

Jack played in the under sixteens, and reached the final, losing to Owen Williams; and Jean, who was then about five, spent the whole week hitting a ball against absolutely any vertical surface that she could find. In those days she went about with an old tennis ball in one hand, and a sawn-off racket in the other as permanent fixtures. Any object that looked even remotely as though it might offer a rebound had a few shots hit against it. "Okay," she would murmur to herself, "now I'm Bobby Riggs." Riggs had been her favourite player since we had travelled to Queenstown to watch the first ever Pro. tour of South Africa by Riggs, Donald Budge, Carl Earn and Welby van Horn.

Jean wore our hand-me-down shorts and shirts and looked like a little freckled urchin. By the time she was eight she was winning the under fourteens and regularly played exhibition matches before the senior finals.

The diehards looked on and muttered about another Alice Marble, and my father watched her with an incandescent gleam in his eye.

In spite of my first victory, I was a bad junior. I disliked the tenseness of the competitions and for a while played cricket and hockey as an escape. But tennis kept cropping up; was always there; waiting.

Without knowing it, we became addicted to it; inexorably infected by its very deepest urgings, by the whole wide character of the game: the touch of a new racket, the smell of varnish on gut, the way a sliced backhand could float on heavy air and bite into a surface of damp clay. The way spins drifted and what they did when they bounced. Floppy hats, sunburnt faces, the ache at the end of the day. The lonely matches on outside courts—the hostile eyes of opponents' parents. The last sixteens, the mixed doubles, the number one seeds. The wins, the losses, the post-mortems over tea and cake. We got into all that—endless successions of arrivals, first rounds, victories, defeats, triumphs, tears. And throughout our tennis lives this order of things never changed in nature, but only in stature. In every close match ever played, you always fought two things—your opponent and the fear inside you, and the worse of the two was the fear. That was what made you miss the easy volley at 40–30, or serve the double fault at 5–4 in the final set.

But wait, I'm losing ground! What I am really trying to say is that there is an enormous amount of agony and effort, an eternity of backhands and forehands, of serves and volleys, of matches won, matches lost, of good luck and bad luck, of triumphs and disasters which must be ploughed through before you can stand on the Wimbledon centre court and, in a gesture of mock despair, hand your racket, handle first, to a ballboy to indicate to the crowd that he might be better equipped than you to continue the match!

We survived the rigours of junior tennis. By the time Jean was thirteen, she had won two major South African senior tournaments, and was regarded as a sort of teenage tennis miracle. Jack and I were not regarded as miracles. Our games were good but not spectacular. He loved the farm life. I felt trapped by it, and wanted to move. Tennis offered me an escape. In 1953 I was chosen to play in the Davis Cup trials at Ellis Park in Johannesburg. I was utterly excited. There were twelve players selected and I was the twelfth. I made the journey up to the city by train. The whole family came to our little station to see me off.

Diary Notes: 1952

Three Dunlop Maxplys have arrived for me at the Post Office. Three. The Postmaster has told the whole town. Everybody knows I've been chosen for the Davis Cup Trials.

My father, who normally hates going into town, now goes in every day. And to crown it all, playing in the town cricket team on Saturday I hit three colossal sixes in a row off a farmer from Queenstown, who sold us an expensive stud ram that wouldn't breed. My father was more pleased about that than the tennis. The cricket club is arranging a farewell party at which I must make a speech!

Who can ever re-examine old memories without feeling a little woebegone and miserable? Who can look at old photographs without that odd feeling of sadness—regret, perhaps, for opportunities gone, chances lost, talents wasted. Who can ever be lucky enough to know when good times are at hand, how good they really are?—Stop for a moment and say, "*these* moments are as good as they come, *these* now, not others, elsewhen."

When I first arrived in Johannesburg from our Karroo farm, I was wide-eyed at the size of it. Set back on my heels, as Claude Lister was to say. I had come to play in trial matches for the Davis Cup team, and felt diminished by my lack of worldliness and the unruly state of my game, which I was in the process, then, of getting together. It was, I remember thinking, quite brilliant in certain aspects, but it seemed to possess a will of its own and often went off at alarming tangents—like a squad of soldiers, all good shots, but all firing in different directions.

I stayed alone at a dreary downtown hotel, and at night the strange city used to close in around me, and drive me upstairs to my room. There are few places in the world as dreary as after dark downtown Johannesburg. I was nervous about everything, even things like catching buses to the tennis, even if they were labelled "Ellis Park", because I was sure they would take me somewhere else so that I would get lost and not be in time for my matches.

The other players in the trials were all big names in South African tennis, and struck a certain amount of fear into my heart—Russell Seymour, Owen Williams, Ian Vermaak, Brian Woodroffe, Johan Kupferberger and the original stone wall, John Hurry.

Trevor Fancutt was a firm friend. And as for Abe Segal! I first came across him in the Ellis Park change-room. He saw me in a corner and shouted out:

"Christ, kid, you're like a mouse! Don't people make noises on that farm of yours?"

He was really rough and ready in those days, and used to wear purple T-shirts and sing *The Nearness of You* very loudly, with his mouth full of Chiclets. He, you see, had the advantage of a childhood in which so many things had gone wrong that he knew there was almost nothing he couldn't cope with. His early life had been a permanent episode of *The Untouchables.* Street fighting, fence climbing, and the general doing of hair-raising deeds were second nature to him. And by then, he'd already been on one hectic, do-it-yourself overseas tennis tour—had worked his passage on a freighter, lived on the smell of an oil rag, been mistakenly billeted at a brothel, harvested apples, befriended several surprised millionaires and once alarmed an ancient English umpire at Hurlingham by shaking his seat, referring to him as "Professor", and implying that he was blind. All Abie had to learn was which knife to use for fish, and that you were supposed to wear socks with a dinner suit. I had to learn to cope with a world which was two hundred times the size I had first thought it was, and filled with people whom I wanted to believe, but shouldn't. I was polite to everybody and Abe was polite to no one. He'd flatten people with raucous statements or contemptuous comments without even knowing what he'd done—like once, when a sweet, smelling-of-cologne lady official, with powder on her upper lip, who was filling in Abe's result on a draw sheet, looked up at him and said:

"Have you got a pencil, Abe?" And he replied:

"Baby, have I got a pencil! Oh, baby, what a question. Have I got a pencil!"

I swear I could see a shiver run up and down her spine. She probably had a brief vision, terrifying and delicious, of herself, helpless in his savage embrace, menaced by his terrible pencil. Abe soon became possessed of the remarkable ability to commit enormous *faux pas*, and, by not being aware of them, surviving them as effortlessly as if drawing breath.

In Athens, for instance, at a formal party given by the Ambassador to somewhere, he arrived wearing a borrowed dinner suit, a purple T-shirt with a big white "A" on the front, and tennis shoes and socks. Ravenously hungry, his eyes hunted the elegant old banquet room for signs of food. Chicken was finally handed round. He finished his serving in a flash, then threw the bones across the room into the marble fireplace. The hostess, hurrying to his side, told him not to worry but to leave the bones on his plate, whereupon he cried:

"Don't be crazy, kid, this is for refills!" Whereupon she laughed delightedly, and gave him one.

Abe appears frequently in this book because he was (and is) the greatest living creator of confusion, chaos and laughter.

After he'd sung *The Nearness of You* for about the twentieth time, I told him tentatively that I had a great recording of it by Lester Young. He at once stopped biting his fingernails.

"Lester Young?" he cried, "how in the hell did Lester Young get down to that farm of yours?"

I told him that we had a bit of a band and that I played the clarinet.

"I've got all Goodman's stuff, and Errol Garner and George Shearing on seventy-eights. And, of course, Lester Young and Johnny Hodges, and the guys at the Philharmonic."

"God, kid," he said, "you can't be so dumb after all. I didn't even know they had electricity on farms!"

(They didn't. We had a gramophone that you had to wind up.)

The next day he arrived at Ellis Park with a pile of records, old seventy-eights, and dropped them in my lap.

"Take 'em, kid," he said, "I got one of these new grams that turns real slow."

That week he also gave me several bits of advice about coping with large cities. Some of them were decidedly alarming.

"Okay, Forbsey," he said one day. "So you're walking down this dark street, mindin' your own business, and suddenly you see this guy looking at you kinda peculiar. All you have handy is a newspaper. What do you do?"

I told him cautiously that I wasn't sure.

"You got to get ready real fast," he said, and then showed me how to fold a newspaper into a hard, tight truncheon, so that, "If the guy jumps you, you can lay him clean out." The alarm on my face must have told him that I wasn't accustomed to the idea of "being jumped", or "laying people clean out" with a newspaper, so he added quickly: "But first, you run like hell. Don't ever get in any brawls if you figure you can run faster than the other guys. That way, all you get is out of breath!"

His method of approach to girls was, predictably, unbelievably direct—"Hey, baby! If the rest of you is as good as the part of your legs that's stickin' out of that skirt, I'm available!" He drove about in a panel van marked "Segal's Fashions", belonging to his father's clothing business. The front passenger seat had become loose, so that, on fast getaways, it tipped over backwards, depositing its occupant, with a sort of rolling motion, into the gloomy rear compartment. With this seat, Abie told me, after I had got to know him better, he could get indecisive girls into the back of the van with a minimal loss of time. I never saw the seat used for this exact purpose. It once, however, rolled Trevor Fancutt over backwards just as he raised a pint of milk to his mouth. Drenched, he emerged from the gloom saying, "Damn you, Abie. That's very trying!"

I began accumulating many other friends in the tennis world. One of these was a mild-mannered young player whose nickname was J-J, and whose tastes and sensitivities coincided almost exactly with my own. We viewed Abie's adventures among loose women with a certain amount of envy. At that stage of our lives we would both dearly have loved to do dashing deeds with women, being fully aware of the proximity of the girl competitors. Things happened continually underneath their demure, white tennis outfits, and it drove us crazy not knowing exactly what they were. Sunburnt legs protruded, pleasant smells emerged, and glimpses of powdered pectorals encouraged thoughts of more thorough investigations. We would sit in the stands, with one eye on the tennis and the other on things like bosoms and thighs. J-J would get, in his own words, "decidedly worked up" at certain times and suggest that it was high time that he and I "cracked one through the covers". His mild manner and cricket-playing background had come up with this particular term for describing the great and wondrous act. That was only after he had gone to great pains to discover whether or not I already had. I assured him that my experience with women was limited to innumerable flirtations, some modest achievements, but a general skirting of the main issue. He heaved a sigh of relief then, and admitted that, although he himself had put a fair amount of effort into several attempts, he too had not yet "cracked it". Perhaps, he said, our combined ingenuities might lead to the actual doing of the deed. I was ready enough to join forces. Morals then were far more old-fashioned than they are these days. It was true that at boarding school there had been a redhead called Theresa, who, for half a crown would allow a hand to be slipped into her blouse and a brief squeeze given to the wonders hidden there. For *five* shillings the same brief access would be given to the inside of her knickers. Heady though this area seemed, it meant the sacrifice of a two-week ration of movies and candy; and in any case, those who had laid out the money reported that it was "not all that it was cracked up to be"—an ambiguous summary, but one which dissuaded the meek from taking the plunge.

So J-J and I decided unanimously to broaden our sensitivities and we yearned secretly for mechanical aids such as Abie's collapsible seat. Industriously we dated girls—carting them ceremoniously to movies, milkbars and the odd night spot. But it wasn't going to be that easy, we discovered. The girls of Johannesburg's northern suburbs were highly sophisticated, and for them one needed money and a smooth approach. And the young tennis girls were far too naïve. Flirtations were all very well, but we wanted the real thing.

"We've got to get overseas," said J-J firmly. "They say that there you can crack it with your eyes closed."

And so we worked at our games and dreamed dreams of tennis titles and conquests of hot-blooded women, and of magical evenings in the capitals of Europe, where, "they" said, romance lurked around every corner.

I came second last in those Davis Cup trials, but managed to take a set off Abe Segal. It was, as it turned out, a beginning. A time to move. And the following year, the opportunity arose.

News that Europe in general, and England in particular, possessed successions of tennis tournaments which took place in *their* summer, which was *our* winter, and which could be entered into and played in by quite ordinary people, filtered through to us by way of the dressing-room conversations of our own South African tournaments. Because of limited funds in those days, the S.A.L.T.U.* could send official teams to compete in the European Zone of the Davis Cup only every second year.

*South African Lawn Tennis Union.

These teams consisted of recognised South African stars such as Norman Farquharson, Eustace Fannin, Sydney Levy, and that greatest of South African players, Eric Sturgess. They were the élite in our eyes, and we viewed them with some awe, listened wide-eyed to their conversations about Wimbledon, Roland Garros, the way the Italians lobbed and cheated and how Frank Sedgman volleyed.

But more impressive to us were the few intrepid individuals who had actually made their *own* way to Europe, entered themselves into the tournaments, and succeeded in winning a few matches. *They* were the ones who riveted us with their stories.

London, according to "Rookie" Rooke, the big Rhodesian, was a tennis player's giant oyster, filled with pearls of every conceivable kind. And, for starters, alive with women, who were, as he put it, "left over from the war". "And love-starved," he used to say, the words whistling through his front teeth. "Craving men, do you follow me? Absolutely dying for men!" Whereupon J-J and I used to prick up our ears even higher, totally unable to imagine why women's lives should be sacrificed for such a reason.

David Lurie returned from England as a semi-celebrity, having taken Tony Mottram, the durable British Champion, to five sets in the semi-final of the somewhere-or-other.

But it was Owen Williams* who really widened our eyes. Determined to get overseas, he had, in 1952, taken a job as a liquor store attendant at a dockside establishment in Port Elizabeth. From there he had become acquainted with the officers of the Union Castle liners, and had begun hounding them for a job. At last, after nine months of persevering, he was appointed third assistant to the vegetable chef on the *Pretoria Castle*. "There were meat chefs," he told me later, "and sea-food chefs, and pastry chefs and dessert chefs and God knows how many other chefs, and they all had assistants who specialised in something or other. I specialised in potatoes."

Owen was put in sole charge of the ship's potatoes. These, being lowly items, were stored in the very bottom of the galley stowage. "In the bowels of the ship," said Owen, "down about twenty ladders, in the pitch dark, right next to the keel, and I suffer from claustrophobia. Once they closed the hatches by mistake and left me alone with the potatoes.

*Now one of the world's best-known tournament promoters.

Trapped! Me and a million tubers, separated from the depths of the sea by a mere inch of creaking steel plate!"

He'd had nightmares about *that*, and had finally arrived in England more of a potato specialist than a tennis player. News of his voyage had, however, been flashed across to England by South African sports writers, and the headline, "Potato Peeler for Wimbledon", had appeared on every London sports page, and had assured him his entry into all the small English tournaments. Human-interest stories are especially dear to the hearts of the British!

A tennis-loving lady called Doreen Malcolm solved my particular travelling problem. She arranged a tour of the English Summer Tournaments for Gordon Talbot, the South African Junior Champion, and me, and presented it to us as a *fait accompli*. There was enough money in my savings account to buy a boat fare and travellers' cheques worth fifty pounds.

With a great lift of my heart, I informed the family, and together we made our way to the Cape Town docks.

2

Diary Notes: 1954

By the time we arrived at the All England Club, it was mid-afternoon; an ordinary middle-of-the-week afternoon, in April. We'd taken the tube at Earl's Court, changed at Putney, got off at Southfields and walked from there. There are shops near the station, then the rows of English houses, and then the road curves away, down and to the right, with the common on the left.

England in early spring! New green and blossom bursting everywhere. I was deeply excited and slowed the walk to make the excitement last. Impossible to write down the feelings you have when you are about to arrive somewhere you've always wanted to get to. We arrived at last, and stopped at the gate. There was no one about, only a few old men tending the lawns. The stadium was low and green; old and comfortable-looking and lower than we'd thought it would be.

In March 1954, the *Winchester Castle* sailed out of Table Bay carrying on board Gordon Talbot and me.

There is no departure as thrilling as that of an ocean liner. We stood at the rails, watching the streamers part, while the tugs nudged us away from the quay and out into the harbour. Behind us, the mountain caught the dusk light, with the misty clouds pouring down her face. Ahead, the brooding horizon, dull red where the sun set, turning to gunmetal and purple. The air that swept off the sea carried upon it the bite of an antarctic spring, and the smell of distance and adventure—acute and agonising in the heart of an eighteen-year-old.

I remember almost every detail of that six-month journey, and could fill a book with it—one of those mild, comfortable books that one reads after taking a sedative in preparation for an early night. But I'll distil it, squeeze it up into a concentrate, a sharp succession of flash-backs like a roll of photographic slides: the hour-long gym sessions which Gordon and I faithfully conducted each morning at six-thirty on the windy decks, smelling the salt, paint and diesel fuel on the wind. The wild and woolly South African air force pilot who shared our cabin and who, in a flash, had fascinated all the ladies on board. Perhaps, because I had never had a lady, he understood the wistful look in my eyes after one of his many requests that I vacate the cabin for a while. When I finally returned, there, on my bunk, was one of his naked ladies. She had soft eyes and round breasts and she smiled up at me and beckoned with a forefinger, thus causing in this order:

1. My first close brush with coronary thrombosis;
2. A flood of apologetic words which spilled from my mouth;
3. A hasty retreat into the edge of the door.

"Are you afraid of me?" she asked. "I don't bite, you know—at least not in anger. Hey, come closer. You're kind of cute."

"Am I?" I asked huskily, rubbing the part of my head that had come in contact with the door.

"Kind of," she said.

The conversation was not of the kind upon which destinies hang, but I finally composed myself and was rewarded with a fleeting touch or two and several warm kisses. That was my first full view of a naked lady and is still one of my clearest mental pictures.

We basked in the equatorial sun and held kissing sessions on tropical nights, watching the turbulent phosphorescence of the wake disappear into the darkness. Had a Neptune ceremony on the Equator, tasted the wines at Madeira and battered the swells of the Bay of Biscay.

At last, one morning, a foggy Southampton emerged from a sunrise full of promise, and, in a daze of images and impressions we docked and boarded the boat train for London. Waterloo. The Cromwell Road. Earl's Court. The King Charles Hotel. A little bedroom with iron beds and eiderdowns. The London Underground—the tube, with its rushing winds and warm smells. Piccadilly Circus, flashing rich and half used-up. Red old doorways. The great signs. Regent Street, Leicester Square, The Odeon, The Prince of Wales, Great Windmill Street, Boots, Dolcis,

Simpsons, Lillywhites, Trafalgar Square. How absolutely wide-eyed we were!

Our first tournament was at Sutton, Surrey—cold, damp, old and utterly English. Billy Knight, Tony Pickard, Bobby Wilson, Bob Howe, veal and ham pie, lettuce and watercress, fragile cucumber sandwiches. Also, Teddy Tinling. A tall man in tennis clothes, who seemed at first glance to be all legs and piercing eyes, approached me and said:

"My dear chap, those shorts you're wearing are appalling!"

They were special shorts, carefully bought in the little general store close to our farm. White ducks with turn-ups and fly-buttons. Teddy looked me up and down:

"Simply appalling. You have no knees," he sniffed, and added: "and the shirt is not really much better." (It was a Perry shirt!) "Come along with me. We shall have to rig you out."

And so I received some Tinling shorts and shirts and, best of all, began a long friendship with Teddy himself. He has a mind and wit as sharp as a razor, and, in those days, his verbal probes used to diminish me, so that I could usually provide suitable rejoinders only after he had left.

They were so simple, those little English tournaments, so utterly artless. Home-made, if you like. Red clay courts, damp and heavy, club-houses of old brick, and inside all the woodwork nearly worn out. Floors, tables, bashed-up little bars. In the change-rooms, wooden lockers, wet floors, and nice old smells, musty as the Devil. They were funny things, those tournaments, but they were open-hearted, and they allowed ordinary people to play them. Everything was absolutely fair and square—and the "conditions" that the players were offered, though infinitesimal, were conditions, nonetheless.

In Sutton, for instance, Gordon and I each received a return rail fare from London (about 6/6d.), cold lunches each day, private accommodation with warm-hearted local families, and 50/– for "expenses". If you won the tournament, you received prize vouchers. £5 for the singles, £2.10.0. each for the doubles, and these stated that you could spend them only on "white apparel". Usually at Simpsons, where white lambswool sweaters cost 50/–.

Each little tournament tried to include in its line-up at least one *star*. Sutton that year had Kurt Nielsen of Denmark, whose deal was similar in structure to ours, except that it probably had a 1st Class rail fare, hotel accommodation at the local pub, and £25 "expenses".

It was, in fact, these "expenses" which finally led to the collapse of the true amateur system, as it became very difficult to define exactly what the term "expenses" covered. Later on, therefore, when the tournaments began to compete for the participation of the big stars, "expenses" became very pliable, and easy to bend.

Who knew, it was righteously argued, how much a tennis star could actually spend in a week if he really set his mind to it?

But at that time, in 1954, tennis in England was about as close to being truly amateur as was feasible. We accepted it thus, played it, and adored it.

Diary Notes: 1954

We told the old man who opened the gate for us that we'd come from South Africa to play tennis. That we wanted to see Wimbledon.

"Club's closed," he said. "'cepting only for members."

"We only want to see the centre court," Gordon Talbot said. "We've come all the way from Johannesburg."

The old man whistled through his teeth and looked over our heads into the distance.

"No harm in that, I suppose," he said at last, and turned away up the drive, beckoning us to follow. He stood with us at the huge deserted arena while we stared down at the patch of lawn. There were no lines, I remember. Just the new green grass and the darker surrounds; an empty scoreboard, and all those empty, comfortable-looking seats.

"There then," said the old man gruffly. "There it is then. That there's Wimbledon. You boys happy now?"

We thanked him and told him that we were.

Bournemouth, Hurlingham, Paddington, Newcastle, Manchester, Surbiton, Beckenham, Roehampton. The little English tournaments unfolded with a mildness matched by that extraordinarily temperate summer. Gordon and I received fifty shillings per week, 2nd Class rail fares, and books of lunch tickets which enabled us to eat egg and ham pie and lettuce in dampish tents. Blissfully happy, we played for our lives, practised at every conceivable opportunity, had mild little sessions with some of the English girls in trains, and won the doubles at Hurlingham, a victory which ensured our doubles entry into Wimbledon and gained us some more Tinling and Perry tennis clothes.

At Beckenham I encountered my first classic Tinling witticism. The tournament was refereed by a pompous ex-army major or lieutenant colonel, as all referees in those days seemed to be. No matter how modest the tournaments were, they always managed to come up with a very British referee, who had a very British moustache, and who used to lay down the law in a very British way.

The one at Beckenham, whose name I forget, was particularly overpowering. The week turned out the wettest in years, so that by Friday, with the courts virtually under water, only the quarter finals had been reached. On Saturday a further deluge made play impossible, and Teddy, making for the tea tent, encountered the referee, chin on chest, staring sulkily at an inundated centre court.

"Good morning, dear Major," said Teddy with infinite cheer. He himself was out of the tournament by then.

"Filthy weather," said the Major. "Dashed bad luck. Damned bad show, not finishing. Could have pushed a bit that first day. Might have finished a few more matches. One never really knows, does one? Too late now, of course. Never finish. Just one of those things."

"Never mind, Major," said Teddy, still cheerful. "Buck up, old lad. You've created a new record, you know?"

"Have I?" asked the Major, brightening considerably. "What have I done?"

"You've become the wettest referee in England," said Teddy, crushingly.

Later, over a cup of tea, Teddy explained to me the rivalry which existed amongst the old breed of referees, and the stigma cast over those who were not able, in spite of the English weather, to complete their tournaments.

"They brood, dear chap," said Teddy, "they brood if they don't finish, and there's nothing as bad as a broody referee."

Diary Notes: Spring 1954

Some of the English county players have extraordinary games—all improvised and home-made. Terribly crafty, though. One of them has devised a remarkable doubles system which almost dispenses entirely with the backhand. He and his partner stand in tandem, holding forehand grips, and completely covering the backhand side. When the odd backhand does present

itself, they throw up a high lob, and then regroup. Of course, they can't live with the really good teams, but they love the game so much and it's heart-rending to see them make their little plans and wiles, which work in county tennis, but which get torn apart by the big teams. They take their defeats stoically, in a very British way, and back in the dressing-rooms their cronies say:

"Had a double, old man?" "Any luck?" And they shake their heads and say:

"Not a hope. We got a two and a love. Not enough guns, d'you see. Much too good."

And they sit down gravely and start taking off all the pairs of socks they wear, and then shower very carefully and then pack all their gear away into old leather tennis bags, then comb their hair and go off to the pub for a pint of draught or bitter. Nearly all of them wear striped shirts with white collars.

Teddy Tinling was possessed of a fearful forehand, a safe backhand and an extraordinary turn-of-the-century type service which necessitated a very high throw-up. While the ball was thus aloft, Teddy was able to accomplish the various manoeuvres which he felt belonged to and were an essential part of his swing. When things went well and the racket and ball rendezvoused satisfactorily, an unlikely cannon ball was produced. Windy days caused Teddy's service to be fraught with tension and often forced him to re-position himself to ensure being present when the ball returned to earth after toss-up. Scarborough, that windiest of windy places, has spawned some remarkable Tinling rhetoric. One tense morning match, for example, he had to contend not only with a gale force wind, but the sun directly in his eyes.

"The whole match got completely out of hand," he recounted, "and would have been laughable if it hadn't been so serious. In the second set, at set point for me, I threw the ball up to serve, and never saw it again! I waited tensely for some time before I realised that it wasn't going to come down, ever again!"

"What did you do?" I asked him.

"My dear chap, what *was* there to do? I simply threw up the second ball, hoping that whatever it was up there that was taking away my tennis balls, wouldn't do it again. I was so relieved when the second one came down after all, that I served a double. It's bad enough to have to serve a second ball on set point when you *know* it's coming down, but the first one *hadn't*, you see, and I wasn't sure!"

What had happened, in fact, was that Teddy had thrown the ball high into the sun and a terrific gust of wind had blown it into the hedge behind him. The match wended its way to the close, and finally Teddy was down at set point against him.

"It was his service," he said, "and when he missed his first ball, I knew I had him because he was serving into the wind. His second ball came straight towards me, and as I was getting ready to hit it, it suddenly turned off at right angles, fell on the line and went into the water jug under the umpire's chair."

"What did you do?" I asked. I was prepared to ask the most inane questions just to make him continue.

"I questioned the umpire," he said, "and made him consult the rule book. There are so many, you see—rules, I mean, and one never knows whether rule two of paragraph three might read: 'a second service on match point which finishes in a water jug may be declared a let'. But there was nothing so I had to concede."

Match points used to give Teddy tremendous problems.

"They rarely come my way," he said, "but when they do, I prepare for the worst. On grass my opponents invariably serve into a weed!"

At Eastbourne, at the end of that first season, Gordon and I found ourselves playing doubles against Teddy and Howard Walton. They both had immense forehands and positioned themselves so that it was almost impossible to hit on their backhands. We were thus confronted by streams of these forehands which we had to volley back, and having at that time limited experience, we made heavy weather of the match. We reached match point at last, and Gordon was given a short lob which he killed with terrific force. It had been raining heavily all week, and where the smash bounced, a small jet of water arose from the grass to the height of about eighteen inches.

"Great Scott!" cried Teddy, "he's opened up a spring! That's all I need—a match point against me where my opponent's smash opens a spring!"

The incident added another story to Teddy's repertoire, already colourful. And often on other occasions I heard Teddy's voice from the corner of the change-room or tea-lounge:

"—At match point with a smash so powerful it opened up a spring!"

By the time Wimbledon came along, I had scored some reasonable singles victories and Gordon and I had won the Hurlingham doubles title. We were accepted for the Wimbledon doubles, but were condemned to the agonies of Roehampton in order to qualify for the singles and mixed. We survived, and again found ourselves living dreams.

In my diary I find a page headed "Wimbledon". How simple, then, were the needs of a tennis player!

Diary Notes: Wimbledon 1954

The big black cars drive right through the iron gates and into the club. People line the road and wave, and it's all sunlight and lawns. At the dressing-room entrance you step out, carrying a stack of rackets, and listen to the people whispering. Wherever you go, they whisper. For Hoad and Rosewall they murmur and chatter away. The dressing-rooms are stocked with Robinson's fruit juices, and the showers deliver steaming torrents. Up in the restaurant there are hot meals, and in the little lounge, desks with All England Club writing paper. Very upstage is Wimbledon. Six new balls every nine games! And the people at the referees' office are kind and respectful. The members stand about in large hats and eat strawberries. Everybody seems to be patient; just standing there, and pleased to be around.

And so, on Monday afternoon at twelve, a large black car with a blue and green pennant on its bonnet stopped before our Earl's Court hotel, and carried us in state to participate in an event which had, for me, hitherto been an impossible dream.

I was moved to tears, I remember, as I took the court for my match against Canadian Bob Bedard, so that I dropped my first service game due to burning eyes, and finally lost the match. But the badge marked "Competitor" lasted for the full two weeks and awarded me all the privileges of the winner.

I watched Jaroslav Drobny win Wimbledon that year. From the competitors' stand, saw him out-think Ken Rosewall. Marvellously deft tennis, all poise and balance, and the colossal forehand lying in wait.

At matchpoint a deafening silence fell. Then Rosewell's backhand return snapped up against the tape of the net and the Wimbledon people leapt to their feet. They had grown to love "Old Drob", as they called him, and wanted him to win, and as he stood there, all smiles, I envied him.

Diary Notes: London

My friend J-J has been behaving in a slightly superior way all through Wimbledon. He left the safety of England for a few weeks to play the French championships in Paris. Upon his return he immediately informed me that he had finally and definitely "cracked it" in Paris. Goaded, apparently by desperation, and egged on by the evil Owen Williams, he had at last found a "marvellous creature with bright red hair" on the Champs Elysées, who, to his utmost surprise, responded to his gauche advances. The reason for the ease with which he persuaded her, over coffee, to accompany him to his room only became apparent after the deed had been done, and she asked him for two thousand francs. He was appalled, but a certain saving of face and money was achieved when she'd finally settled for one thousand. Also by the fact that Owen, who is an expert in these matters, declared that she must have been an "enthusiastic amateur". Professional ladies, he says, always settle the price before and not after. Owen is an expert, because he claims to be the only man he knows who has managed to persuade a "working girl" to let him have the "wicked thrust" on a credit basis. This happened in Barcelona, and thereafter he paid her off on a sort of hire purchase agreement over the week of the tournament.

Whatever the ramifications, J-J has "cracked it", verified by Owen. To me the thing is not quite fair, but I am remaining silent as I myself may yet have to resort to financial help in order to achieve this elusive ecstasy. J-J has offered, in a patronising way, to assist with negotiations—he too has become an expert. However—

During Wimbledon the little hotel where we lived in Earl's Court also housed Hugh Stewart, a big, good-humoured American who taught me how to appreciate lambswool sweaters, and who raised English eyebrows in the morning by eating huge breakfasts, and finally rinsing his mouth with his last gulp of coffee. He was amused and intrigued by British habits, often stopping strangers in the street to ask them where the "Toob" was (he couldn't say "Tube", the British way), and then reminding them not to allow their dogs to "foul the footpaths". Some people hurried away at that warning, others told him they didn't own dogs—"In case you should ever get one", Hugh used to say, very warmly. He taught me all the American songs and introduced me to famous Americans like Budge Patty, Victor Seixas, Tony Trabert, Art Larsen and Malcolm Fox, who sang superbly and later became very rich by doing clever things in Hong Kong.

At Frinton-on-Sea, directly after Wimbledon, Hugh and I found ourselves the guests of one of those unbelievably high-class, commuting, artistocratic English families, who dressed for dinner and who "walked their shoot", every now and again, flushing pheasant and pam-pamming them with shooting sticks in the closed season. Their house was large and echoing, and disarmed us with its silences and the foreboding that things might suddenly and for no reason fall over with a crash, and make people think it was us. The floors creaked loudly at dead of night so that visits to the toilet were matters for grave consideration. The toilets themselves had long chains and used to flush like tidal waves, before dying to throaty gurgles and other internal rumblings, so that one finally returned to bed shaken and guilt-stricken after a perfectly ordinary widdle.

Evening meals were particularly nerve-wracking. We sat, the four of us, at a long table, with the host and hostess at either end and Hugh and I eyeing one another across the middle. Hugh put me out badly the very first night by pulling a series of British faces into his soup, and mouthing British phrases like, "How absolutely too spiffing!" The table surface was polished to the texture of glass, the crockery was fine and shining white, and here the silences *really* gathered. Never was an atmosphere so fraught with the probabilities of disaster. We suffered for a night or two, before Hugh's incorrigible nature got the better of him. Seated in the silence that evening, he allowed the echoes of the murmured grace to wander away, then suddenly cleared his throat with a roar that shook the house, picked up a slice of the diabolically crisp toast (which had defied us to eat it for two nights), put it in his mouth and chewed deafeningly. He stopped chewing, cocked an ear and said:

"Did you hear anything?"

"Can't say that I did," said our host.

Hugh chewed vigorously again, stopped, listened and said:

"There it is again!"

This at last evoked a short, hearty British laugh, and for a while drove away the devils of silence. But there was more to come.

On our last evening, it was suggested that we dress formally for dinner, so Hugh and I produced jackets and ties and duly repaired to the dining room. The table was superb, glittering with crystal and slippery as ice. There we found our host, immaculate in black, and his wife, regal in a gown which displayed her creamy shoulders and bosom, falling away to a cleavage which, under less stringent circumstances, would have been strongly alluring.

We took our places gingerly, sharply aware that things seemed ready to slide about at the slightest provocation. The table knives, too, were of a peculiarly whippy design so that when the roast lamb and gravy were served, I was in a nervous state, and set about it with fiercely controlled concentration. Things went so well, however, that by the time I had reached the last mouthful or two, I became over-confident. Cutting at a piece of rind, the end of my knife bent, then slipped, sending a single gravy-soaked pea downrange with the speed of a bullet. It struck our hostess above the heart, clung for a moment then quickly and silently slid down the skin of her cleavage and disappeared into her creamy cleft, leaving a faint gravy trail.

Three pairs of popping eyes followed its course, watched her give a little start of surprise, then press a red-nailed hand to her bosom, covering the gravy.

"How most extraordinary," said our host, blinking his eyes.

"How silly," said our hostess lightly.

"How puzzling," intoned Hugh, with a straight face, and in a British way.

I said nothing, was speechless, and wondered distractedly where the pea would finish up. Lodged in her navel perhaps. At dead of night, if the mood took him, which I doubted, our host would be able to follow the gravy trail downward with the tip of his tongue, and, finally, come upon the pea, nestling in who knows what exquisite cranny. He could eat it. Have a snack en route. But we never did find out where the pea had gone. As far as we were concerned, it had simply moved in a most mysterious way.

The first tour wended its way through the late European summer—Deauville, Frinton, Hythe, Worthing, Ostende, le Zoute, Spa and back to England—Budleigh Salterton, Torquay and Eastbourne, where Gordon Talbot opened up the memorable spring for Teddy Tinling. At Spa, in Belgium, I had my first tournament win, beating Phillipe Washer in the finals. Phillipe was a nobleman, handsome and aloof, who used to own three sports cars which he drove about Europe at speed, with a scarf around his neck and beautiful women at his side.

In Deauville, we were housed at the Grand Hotel, with flags outside and magnificent doormen, and shrimps in white porcelain bowls for breakfast. There I had a strange, heart-rending little romance with a Canadian girl whom I'd seen watching me play against Rex Hartwig of Australia. She had grave, grey eyes and long fingers, and was waiting at the gate when I left the court, and again in the little bar in a corner of the clubhouse.

But first, Rex Hartwig. He was a semi-Hopman man, a renegade really, with a soaring talent that could have turned itself into one of the great tennis games of all time. But it was not quite controllable. His game ran around him like a covey of quail escaped from a basket—darting and beautiful, but almost impossible to get together. On court, everything he did seemed to take place in fits and starts. He whipped brilliant shots out of anywhere at all with the utmost lack of fuss, and sometimes, with equal nonchalance, whipped out a cock-up or two, these causing his mouth to rattle off a few curses, as though it had received an impersonal instruction from his brain.

Playing him that July in Deauville was important for me because it was the first time that I had concentrated well for an entire match, and had nearly succeeded in beating a world-ranked player.

But the romance. The Girl with the Grey Eyes.

Karen.

Good God!

We walked along the moonlit esplanade and played miniature golf. Watched the extraordinarily rich people leave their cars for the casino, bought ices on the beach in the blinding midday sun and talked endlessly. And late at night she would suddenly get a sad and frowning look in her eyes and cover me with kisses which she had warded off all day. Very tender kisses that smelt faintly of Arpège and garlic. But when I asked her to accompany me to my sumptuous room (which I was dying to show to someone), she would break away and hurry off at a fast walk to the *pension* where she rented a little attic room—to which, I must add, I had never been given access. It was very bewildering for a farm boy. I began to think that Canadians must have methods incomprehensible. But each day that week she came back to the tennis and each day we spent together in irresistible companionship. Saturday night came at last, and I was leaving for London on an early Sunday flight. We were sad that day, both admitting as much, and when my ration of kisses came up, being the eternal optimist, I began again.

"Karen! Come up to my room. Just this once. We'll have coffee. They bring it up on great white trays!"

She looked at me thoughtfully and nodded. I was so excited I could hardly speak and for a while couldn't get my room key to open the door. Inside, we sat on the great white bed, hand in hand, waiting for the coffee. It came at last and got poured.

Again the kisses.

Suddenly she broke away and gave me a sharp look.

"You must wonder about me," she said shortly. "Of course I've wanted to come here with you. But I'm not like other girls. You didn't know that, did you?"

I shook my head.

"Well, I'm not. And I didn't want you to know, because I wanted to see you each day. Now you're going away, so it doesn't really matter."

She wanted me to say that it did, but I only realised this later.

"Karen!" I said, "what on earth are you on about?"

I couldn't help feeling that I was in one of the old movies that used to come to our little town hall where the heroine has tragic eyes and the hero knows she has a strange past, but is too noble to care. She watched me watching her and her grey eyes got huge and defiant.

Then, all at once, she got to her feet, and keeping her eyes fixed on mine, she began to undress. I sat there, dumbfounded, transfixed, with my mouth open and a massed choir starting up somewhere inside my head.

So. The shoes first, the stockings, then the belted skirt, all methodically removed. Nothing wrong with her legs. Absolutely nothing. They were in fact long and well shaped and there were two of them. The scarf next, and then the cotton blouse, button by button. By the time she'd got them all undone and had slipped the thing off her shoulders, a creeping paralysis was taking hold of me. Napoleon could have walked out of the bedroom cupboard with his arm in his jacket and a muzzle loader pointed at my head, and all I would have done was to motion him to go back inside.

She didn't pause, but as she reached behind her to undo her bra, she said simply:

"I have no breasts, you see. They absolutely wouldn't grow," and bit her lower lip.

She was almost right. I had always carried in my head an image of breasts which spilled out of bras when they were undone, like Howard Spring's heroines. Hers certainly didn't "spill out". In fact, they even seemed to shrink a bit when the fresh air got at them. They *had* hardly grown at all, and the bra was mostly padding—one of those stiff little 1954 models that could stand up on its own in the corner. But the lithe, boyish body which emerged when she slipped out of her knickers and stood there, her eyes full of tears, was definitely that of a girl.

In other rooms in that grand old hotel, I suppose expert lovers were at that moment busy drumming up their sophisticated ecstasies. We made heavy weather of ours. She lay down on the great white bed and asked me to make love to her. My mind, meanwhile, was busy trying to cope with about forty-six different emotions which were all jockeying for positions in the front row of my head. Here at last, alone in my room, naked, acquiescent, stretched out upon my bed, was my first golden opportunity finally, in the words of Williams and J-J, "to crack it". And scotfree to boot. A cryptically worded cable flashed haphazardly through my mind—CRACKED IT WITH FLAT CHESTED CANADIAN STOP GIRL STOP NO MONEY INVOLVED STOP.

Except, of course, that it didn't work. My body, taken by surprise, absolutely refused to see things my way. It was like getting a complete sitter at match point in the fifth set, and then finding that you'd dropped your racket on the way in to kill it. I sat down beside her in an agony of embarrassment and told her that she was very beautiful. And it was only by a miracle of diplomacy that in the dawn hours of that far-off Sunday morning, when I finally walked her back to her room, we still believed in one another, and in the fact that, although not lovers, we were very satisfactorily in love.

We finished the tour at Eastbourne, and after a few days in London, it was the boat train again and the mail ship at Southampton. This time, the gods who provide cabin companions on boats had provided me with two just as extraordinary as the mad pilot on the outward journey. One of them was the ballroom dancing champion of the world, who taught me the London jive, and the other was a huge, weather-beaten game ranger whose sole belongings consisted of a khaki safari suit, canvas haversack and a leather case containing a double barrel Westley Richards 500 Nitro Express, which he took out each day to assemble, polish and oil with loving care. Thank God for the game ranger. He took it upon himself to convert me into an extrovert and used to fill me up with beer, then lie on his back on the lower bunk and give me instructions on the coarser, and more daring side of life.

Somewhere in his past he must have had a disastrous love affair, for his musings about women were dark and sombre. Women, he held forth, had no sense, were fickle, wily, shrewd, possessive, faithless, and talked too much. They made a man's life a misery and, in short, were good for only one thing. Marriage was insane.

"No, Forbes, my boykie," he exploded several times, "you don't marry women, you *poke* them!"

In his drunken moments his diatribes sometimes became so gloomy that he would haul out his guncase. Opening it he would take out the black and shiny rifle.

"This you can trust, Boykie. This, not bloody women!"

And, on one particularly maudlin occasion, he said with owlish affection:

"If they made rifles with fannys, Boykie, there'd be no need for women at all!"

I would be on the top bunk, neither agreeing nor disagreeing, but he apparently read agreement into my silences.

When we put in at the Portuguese island of Las Palmas, the ranger had a complete schedule worked out. First, wine-tasting, followed by a good meal, and then, as he clearly put it, "a good long *poke*". Although my body began to play up immediately, there was no way I could back out, particularly after all the effort he had put into my education. Where, I enquired, was this activity to take place?

"At Nellie's," he said; the best girls on the island, and he knew them all. All from good families, busy rebelling against disciplinarian parents. "Wait and see, Boykie," he said, "and leave it to your Uncle."

Nellie's was an old white double storey with steps, columns, arches and a little palm court. We made it up the steps and he pressed the doorbell with one hand and pounded on the door with the other. It opened. Yes, they were open. Yes, always plenty of girls. No, Ramona had gone back to Lisbon, and Philomena was on holiday, but there were other Ramonas. Yes, many. The air inside was soft and warm as honey, mildly impregnated with perfume, incense and talcum. Red carpets; curtains and carved wood. The trappings of lavish sin, slightly second-hand, but in good repair. Sweet wine in rose-coloured glasses, and then shuffling and laughter as the girls filed in. The ranger gave a roar like a bull.

"Hey! Hey! You little beauties! Forbes, my Boykie, look at 'em. My God, I wish there were ten of me instead of one."

He kept this patter up as he walked the half circle they made, and lifted up their chins. Fifteen shillings, I heard him say. But the paralysis was creeping in again—Oh God! The ignominy of failure in this love-swathed place. An agonising image of the game ranger, standing at the ship's bar with his tankard aloft, shouting: "Forbes cocked it up!" flashed through my mind and I turned to go. But a soft hand took mine, and I got led off away down passages and up stairs. A key was turned and curtains drawn across a window which gave onto the palm court.

For fifteen shillings, that tropical afternoon, I was handed one of the great favours of my life—a guided tour through the miracles of love-making by a young, warmhearted expert. A tour during which the question of failure never even cropped up. A masterpiece. A godsend.

It was only hours later, when in a happy daze I climbed the ship's gangway behind a still boisterous ranger, that it occurred to me I could safely cable J-J and inform him jubilantly that I had finally and definitely "CRACKED IT!"

3

One must be sure to get on the right side of the Crossroad gods. The ones who set up the forks in the paths of people's lives. Sketchily signposted, mostly. They crop up all the time. Some are simply detours, others lead away from one another and never meet again. The one I came to when I returned home after that first tennis excursion said, on the one hand: "farm and country", and on the other; "tennis sector". I took the tennis side. It led me away from the quiet life which I had lived and infused into my blood the urge to move. Taught me to know cobbled streets, airport bars, langoustines and black olives, and laced my life with a fine bubbling excitement.

I returned to South Africa and discovered, to my surprise, that I had become a reasonable tennis player. Moreover, I firmly believed then that I would become much better—the best player in the world, perhaps. I did become better, but never the best in the world, nor Wimbledon champion and now, looking back, the reasons seem quite plain.

I did not at any stage ever commit myself strongly enough to the business of becoming Wimbledon champion; and I hopelessly underestimated the dedication and patience required to achieve perfection; didn't think it was special enough; fondly believed that some preposterously benign tennis gods would help me out with let cords or flukey shots when I was in dire need of them. They didn't, of course. They very seldom do. The only people upon whom they bestow flukey shots at very critical moments are either those who have irrevocably dedicated their hearts to those moments, or else, and on rare occasions only, to those who have approached the moment with such honest courage and daring and valour, that, in reluctant admiration, they have awarded them the benefit of the doubt.

Of course, there were several times in my career when a few strokes of really good fortune (sheer arse, the Australians would have you call it) would have led me to thrilling tennis achievements. As it was, there were some fine ones, but the really big ones always got away.

Am I raving on? I doubt it. There it all is, right there. For those of us who are too conservative to risk too much, the only path to the very top is patience, commitment, dedication and hour after hour of concentrated effort. But, above all, the deep, utterly inexorable desire to achieve the goal.

I found it all out too late; and by the time I had, the doubts had crept in; and with the doubts came the flaws in that greatest of all natural attributes; the marvellous, dauntless, heraldic, unquestioning confidence of the very young.

That is all in retrospect. Right after that first tour, I was full of confidence about my tennis future. Over-confident, in fact. Had I not, I asked myself, improved immeasurably in a short spell of six months' exposure to the rigours of world-class tennis? I thought then that I "had it made", and assumed the slightly bored haughty air which hangs about young players before they get wise and realise how many things can go wrong.

That year I approached the Davis Cup trials with far more confidence than ever before. I was, I knew, much better equipped; not only to go through the motions of playing tennis, but actually to win matches. When you consider becoming a world-ranking tennis player, you need to decide *above all else* just how you are going to go about the business of *winning matches*. A section of your game has got to be *lethal*; able to destroy your opponent. You need at least one really great shot or attribute around which to anchor your game. My anchor was a good service and volley, a style of play very much in fashion at that time, and best suited for fast courts. Ted Schroeder, Vic Seixas, Mervyn Rose, Frank Sedgman, Budge Patty were all essentially serve-and-volley players. Even the great Gonzales used the technique almost all the time. I introduced serve and volley into that year's Davis Cup trials, and finished second to Russell Seymour, beating everyone else and surprising the entire South African tennis world.

During the trials that year I stayed in an apartment overlooking the Wanderers Club. It belonged to a chiropractor called Doc Andy. Owen Williams and Trevor Fancutt already lived there, also Leon Norgarb, when he came to town, and Malcolm Fox when he visited South Africa to play the summer tournaments. It didn't really matter how many players moved in, as the flat had a large number of rooms, and each room had manipulating tables or machines for bending or stretching people, which could be adjusted and used for sleeping on. One of these machines was particularly extraordinary. When switched on, it would make a purring noise and begin a pitch and roll motion which was supposed to ease tension of the spine. While it probably achieved this function efficiently, it also provided, as a sort of by-product, remarkably suggestive hip actions to the would-be patient. By adjusting a knob on a rheostat, the motion would become more and more violent until one could virtually use it to practise for breaking horses, or training for a rodeo.

The machine fascinated Owen, who, even at that time, kept an incessant eye open for labour-saving devices. He would switch it on and listen to it purr, then watch with satisfaction when, as he speeded it up, it heaved away like a demented charger.

"You know, Forbsey," he said to me one day, "if one could get a woman on that thing, one would virtually be able to free-wheel!"

It was about then that he began courting Jenny, in a typical devil-may-care way, not realising that his bachelor career was forever doomed. Jenny was and still is a marvellous lady, full of fire and fun, with a full gleam in her eyes. *Her* breasts, as I discovered one afternoon when she and Owen, busy scrubbing one another's backs in the bath, insisted that I serve them tea, were definitely capable of spilling out of bras.

One night, while Leon and I were asleep in the players' dormitory, Owen apparently (he never *actually* admitted it) persuaded Jenny to try the spine relaxer. Together they must have mounted the machine and taken up their positions. A switch was thrown and tremendous purring ensued. Not content, the intrepid Owen reached for the speeding-up lever and accidentally moved it to full speed. Immediately the cavalry arrived, hell-for-leather in the grandest fashion. Leon and I were awoken by shouts of alarm and ecstasy, rising to a crescendo before ending in a solid thump. Sounds of re-arrangement took place, giving way to gales of secret laughter and finally more purring. We eyed each other across the room (Leon and I, that is) and winked knowingly. The prospect of mechanical aids had secretly intrigued us as much as it had Owen, but the very concept of persuading a lady to accept them was completely beyond us. Looking forward, thus as we were, to a graphic account the following morning, we were doomed to disappointment. Owen looked puzzled when we questioned him and said that we must have dreamt it. Jenny was equally enigmatic, giving us only a Mona Lisa-type smile, but years later, when after a glass or two of wine, I re-questioned her, she laughed and said, with a superior air, that it was the first time that she's ever managed to unseat him.

The months spent at Doc Andy's were amongst the happiest of my life. He was a marvellous man, a healer of people, a body craftsman, a repairer of minds. And the worst thing of all was that, at the time, we never really realised what a remarkable man he was. He gave us water to drink which he had set out in the morning sunshine in a jug, and fresh vegetable juices. And played music during breakfasts.

Apart from practising tennis, I worked for a while behind the counter of a sports goods store, advising people about rackets. Even this mild exposure to people apparently preyed on my mind and affected my subconscious. One evening, sharing a room with Trevor Fancutt, I sat up with a start and called out urgently:

"Trevor! Trevor! There is a customer in the shop," then collapsed back upon the pillow. Trevor, who also worked in a sports store, got out of bed with a sigh, all bedraggled in his pyjamas, and began serving "the customer":

"Good afternoon, sir," he said. "Can I be of help?"

This woke me up, and I sat up in bed again and said:

"What on earth are you doing?"

"Serving this gentleman," said Trevor.

"Which gentleman?" I asked.

"The customer you said was in the shop," he replied.

I laughed uneasily, suspecting what had happened, but for once keeping my head.

"You're dreaming," I said, "we're at home. This isn't a shop."

"That's what I thought," he said, climbing back into bed with a puzzled look. And the next morning, upon consideration, he mused:

"I was about to sell him one of my new rackets at a give-away price!"

Each morning at eight, Trevor and I would put on ties and sports jackets and drive my little Morris Minor into Johannesburg to take our place behind sports counters. It was here that I learned to work cash registers and how to persuade people to buy things. Apart from selling sporting impedimenta, our store was also the agent for Reg Park weight lifting equipment. Reg had won the Mr Universe competition about twenty times, and each month he used to spend a morning in the store to promote his gear, doing one-arm curls with two-hundred-pound barbells, and pulling open chest expanders which I couldn't budge an inch.

I used to watch him wistfully and dream about how firm my wrist would be on the backhand volley if it was as big as his wrist.

"Imagine, Reg," I said to him one day, "if we could attach your legs to my body how fast we'd be! Like one of those light sports cars with a huge motor!"

But the idea didn't seem to appeal to him (perhaps because he suddenly had the alarming vision of being left with *his* body and *my* legs!).

To cope with Christmas rush, Mr Duckworth, the owner of the store, employed a young girl. She was about eighteen, a fairly good junior tennis player, with a pretty face and superb legs, which used to distract Tony Barnes, the other permanent assistant, and me to the extent that we would sometimes start out selling, for instance, a tennis racket, then in the middle of the negotiations, forget what we were talking about and end up quoting the price of a Len Hutton cricket bat.

Mr Duckworth told us to utilise our spare time in going through the various items of stock with Winsome, the girl, and explain to her how they were to be used and sold. This we both did with great gusto—rifling drawers of golf pegs, cricket balls, racket grips, sports shoes, in fact all the artefacts craved by would-be sportsmen at Christmas. Pursuing this pastime with Winsome one day, I suddenly came upon the drawer containing cricket boxes. For people unfamiliar with cricket, these objects are used to strap onto the batsman's crutch in such a position that if the ball, hard, red and shiny, despatched by a fast bowler, eludes the bat and slips through unexpectedly, it prevents the batsman from being permanently and forever done in. On the spur of the moment and partly as a joke, I told Winsome that the "box" was a knee-guard for hockey players, and jokingly strapped the contraption to my knee to demonstrate. At that moment a spate of customers entered and I quickly undid my knots, returned the box to the drawer and forgot the incident.

The Christmas rush duly descended upon us, and merchandise was despatched with the frenzy evoked only by the madness of such times. One afternoon a hush suddenly fell over the crowded shop. I looked up from the two-hundred-pound set of barbells I was busy trying to demonstrate to see Winsome, with one marvellous leg raised, her foot resting on a chair. Before the admiring and astonished gaze of two burly hockey players and a host of other customers, she was carefully strapping the cricket box to her knee. Completing her handiwork, she gave the box a pat, looked up and said brightly:

"And that's how it goes on."

"And what does it do?" asked one of the hockey players with a straight face.

"It stops the balls hitting the knee," said Winsome.

"I see," said the hockey player. "I thought that it was supposed to stop the knee from hitting the balls!"

"Well, that too," said Winsome, still unsuspecting.

It was Tony Barnes who finally broke the silence with a sound like a large animal belching after a meal of greenstuff. Pandemonium reigned and explanations were made. Although taken aback, Winsome, being resilient, was not really fazed.

"How should I know what you men have got to protect?" she enquired artlessly, and caused Tony and me to lose track of things again, just briefly.

The Davis Cup trials led immediately to South Africa's little summer circuit of coastal tournaments. We would pack our bags and drive south with not a care in the world. My diary covers one circuit very briefly—probably because the days were filled with tennis and the evenings with the business of chatting up the brown-legged seaside girls.

Diary Notes: East London, Port Elizabeth, Cape Town—Summer 1955

The coastal tournaments again. South African summer. We drive down from Johannesburg, stop over on the old farm, then plunge off the plateaux into the low country. Soft, temperate, coastal breezes and the smell of mimosa.

East London. Laughable little port, washed by sunlight and salty air. The locals don black tie for the only night club, and behave in a very worldly way. But here, in this outpost, they are still settlers at heart, and drink whisky and Coca-Cola to make merry.

Port Elizabeth with its winds. Heavy and incessant. The cluster of courts, on the little promontory. Here the winds really blow, damp, heavy, laden with salt and things marine. One feels as though one is playing underwater, and considers frog-feet instead of tennis shoes and a mask and snorkel, even. Today, a full-blooded hurricane. Force ten or eleven. On court fifteen, I fight and fight against the wind and a nuggety little four-foot opponent who seems able to play below the weather. Finally, in a fit of temper, I hurl my racket into the teeth of the gale. The wind catches it, whirls it over the car park, around the top of a palm tree, past the head of the umpire and back to me. It is the first time a hurled racket has ever returned to the hand of the thrower.

"Things have reached a pretty pass," I say to myself testily, "when one can't even throw one's racket away successfully!"

Cape Town next, with its huge, grey mountain. Here is a sublime place, blown clean by the sea winds, saturated in tradition. The tennis courts cling to the mountain side, set about by giant oaks, while up above, the mists whirl around the grave, rock walls. Inscrutable fastnesses. Marvellous distances, air like crystal. Take the little road which leads to the Rhodes Memorial—a grave, stone structure with the great bronze man, pointing northwards. Below the inscription:

The immense and brooding spirit
Still shall quicken and control
Living, he was the land,
And dead
His soul shall be her soul.

I read it, over and over, and think the words very moving and beautiful.

4

In 1955, I was the junior in the Davis Cup team, the seniors being Russell Seymour, Ian Vermaak and Abe Segal. Russell and Ian were conventional types—who played, most of the time, the mild conventional tennis that seemed the norm for South Africa. Abie was anything but conventional. His childhood in a tough Johannesburg suburb had left him with a sketchy education, a brusque manner, a marvellous defence system and a forthrightness in his approach to life which often verged on the methods used by bulls in their dealing with gates. From the intricacies of an obscure family tree he had inherited a large heart and strong determination. From a succession of gangster films he had picked up a latent sneer, a bogus American accent, and still more methods of dealing with people who caused him trouble. He admired Frank Sinatra, Bogart, Mitchum, Kirk Douglas, Ustinov and any other people whom he considered not to be "full of crap", and disliked, almost viciously, anything that suggested fastidiousness, meanness and small-mindedness of any kind.

His odd upbringing enabled him to go through his whole international life in a worldly, Bogartish sort of way, while constantly peppering it with marvellous social gaffes and such verbal utterances as:

"Athens! Sure I played Athens. Except when I played Athens it was called Constantinople!"

Or:

"Rome's great! That's where they got slow courts and that guy Horatio who kept a bridge."

He was highly suspicious of art and literature, drawing most of his facts from magazines like *Time* and *Argosy* and sometimes even *True* and *Climax*.

"Let's face it, Forbsey—those guys like Joyce, and Conrad and Lawrence Durrell, even that guy T. S. someone—they're great writers, but basically they write a lot of crap. I mean when you really *read* one of their books, and don't just carry it around. I mean, I once read the whole start to one of those books and finally I said to myself: 'Nothing's happening, for God's sake, and nothing was.' And as for those Russian guys. They've got so many names going for them that even *they* can't work it out!"

Without doubt, Abe was an action man. In his life things were required to keep moving, and if they didn't, he helped them along.

It is essential that I write more about Abie. There was a bond between us from the beginning—a friendship between opposites—it was Abie who coined the name "Forbsey", because he couldn't remember my first name, and because it was the fashion then amongst the young Australian players to use shortened surnames. Hoadie, Rosie (Mervyn Rose), Sedge (Frank Sedgman), Macker (Ken McGregor), Fraze (Neale Frazer), Coop (Ashley Cooper), etc. It was true to say that Abie profoundly affected my life. He dented my introspection, made me shout a bit, and do the few daring things which, from time to time, I have managed to do. People should always force themselves to do daring things.

How often have I arrived at his Bryanston house; knocked; received no answer and wandered in. Golden girl Heather on the patio, asleep, facing the sun; Abie's wife from Bermuda. She wears small swimming-suits and has legs a mile and a half long, and a permanent coppery tan. All her life she has been, for me, the true island girl—bluer than blue eyes, blown hair, and the extraordinary tawny skin. Thrombosis material for susceptible males!

Abie is in the bathroom, more often than not—either on the throne or examining his feet—sometimes asleep in the bath. He opens an eye as I enter, lifts a foot out of the water and puts it on the edge of the bath.

"Look at that, Forbsey," he says. "Did you ever see a foot like *that* before? Anywhere in the world, I mean?"

Abie's feet are extraordinary. Size twelve for a start and arches which arch the wrong way. All the toes the same length and overlapping each other; plaited, almost. Random knobs and lumps crop up, with two very large ones on either side. I have an irresistible urge to get to work on them with a pair of pruning shears, and prune them, literally, like odd-shaped trees.

"They've gone worse," Abie is saying gloomily, "so this afternoon I take 'em to the clinic. There's nobody around except for this one guy in a white coat, sitting at a desk. I sit down on the other side of the desk and take off my shoes. He jumps up when I show him my feet, then suddenly gets real interested.

"'How extraordinary,' he says.

"'What's so extraordinary?' I ask him.

"'Your feet', he says. 'There aren't too many feet like that about. You have very rare feet!'

"'Oh!' I says, 'Now suddenly my feet are rare!'

"'Yes,' he says, 'very rare. It's a pity that you weren't here this morning.'"

"'Why?' I ask.

"'Because my kids were here,' he said. 'I could have shown them your feet and told them that's what would happen to *their* feet if they didn't look after them.'

"'Oh, really?' I says.

"'Medically,' he says, 'you can't walk at all. There's no way you can stand up.'

"'Listen,' I says to him, 'I don't need a doctor to tell me I got bad feet. I *know* I have bad feet. What I need a doctor for is to tell me *not* to worry about my frigging feet; that they're improvin'.'

"'Okay,' he says, 'they're improving.'

"'Like hell they are!' I say to him, 'They're getting worse!'

"'Look,' he said, 'they're either getting worse or they're improving. You tell me what to tell you and I'll tell you.'

"'You mean *you* want *me* to tell *you* what to tell *me* about my feet,' I says; 'what kind of a doctor are you, anyway?'

"'A gynaecologist,' he says."

Abie gives a snort of laughter.

"Would you believe it, Forbsey?" he says, "there I am, showing me feet to a gynaecologist! Mind you," he adds, "they're abortions at that. So maybe he *was* the right guy!"

A sample of the unique Segal dialogue. All Abie's methods are unique. He has the broad picture of life perfectly in focus. But the details bore him to tears. Formalities drive him crazy. With Abie, unbelievably enticing things have to be happening continuously, otherwise his attention wanders.

With him on the team that summer, I knew that things might move faster than usual. And I wasn't far wrong.

Diary Notes: Oslo 1955

My sleepwalking afflictions have been playing up again, lately. Perhaps because of Davis Cup nerves, or the rich Danish pastries which Abe buys, then eats half of, then becomes conscience-stricken about his weight and gives the rest to me. We've been sharing a room this week, and on a few occasions I've scared him badly. Last night, after I'd taken a shower and was putting on my tie, I felt his eyes boring into my back.

"And what," he asked explosively, "are you thinking of doing tonight?"

I struggled to meet his eyes and keep my reply nonchalant.

"Nothing special," I said. "Have a meal, see a movie, perhaps. There's the Magnificent Seven on down town. In Danish. You've seen it seven times, but never in Danish. How about that?"

He was not to be sidetracked.

"I mean, Forbsey," he said grimly, "tonight. After you've gone to sleep. Are you going to take it easy, or are we gonna have one of your midnight surprise shows. A raid, or something."

"Come on, Abe," I said, "it's not that bad. You exaggerate the situation tremendously."

"Exaggerate," said Abe, lapsing into his habit of discussing really impossible situations with himself. "I exaggerate, Forbsey says. I'm the one with the nervous tic and the bags under my eyes, but I exaggerate."

His private discussion complete, he looked back at me.

"You're unreal," he said. "To handle you, I have to bring along my own psychiatrist to tell me three times a day I'm still sane. What did they do to you on that farm of yours when you were a kid? I thought farms're supposed to relax you, with all those cows and things. Aren't cows supposed to be relaxed while they chew that thing of theirs? What's that thing they chew while they're busy makin' milk?" (Abe's knowledge of things pastoral is very sketchy.)

"The cud," I said, distractedly. I couldn't get my tie straight.

"That's right, the cud," he said. "Why don't you try chewin' the cud for a while before you go to sleep? Maybe that'll cure you. A nice relaxin' cud-chew."

"People don't have cuds," I said.

"Maybe we could buy you a cud," Abe went on. "I wouldn' mind chippin' in. Anything to relax you while you sleep."

"Abe," I said firmly, "I am perfectly relaxed."

"Relaxed," he said. "Yes. He's relaxed okay—until midnight, when I suddenly find myself walkin' the plank." He turned to me again. "Maybe you

should go get yourself examined," he said. "If they can't prevent it, maybe they can at least find out a way so you know what you're going to do in advance. That way you could say to me, 'Look, buddy, tonight you're going to be machine-gunned at about one in the mornin'.' Then at least when the bullets start comin' I know what to expect!"

In spite of my heated denials and refutations, I have to admit that Abe has a point. I have, on occasions, done very odd things in the night. Most people, I suppose, have dreams, and a few even go for the odd stroll, usually quite harmless and uneventful. My activities are far more complex, and are almost limitless in range and variety. I first became aware of this affliction while at boarding school, when having gone to sleep in my dormitory, as usual, I awoke sitting at my desk doing maths. Our classrooms were a separate block of buildings, at least three hundred metres from the dormitory and linked by an unlighted gravel pathway. Perhaps the shock of that excursion and the subsequent cold, dark return to my bed triggered off a chain of strange events which have persisted at erratic intervals throughout my life. On another occasion at school, I awoke in the act of practising place kicks in the dark, empty rugby field. Lesser events were commonplace. I might leap up suddenly and close all the windows, imagining a thunderstorm, actually *hearing* and *seeing* the lightning. Or stand on top of my locker, to avoid a sudden flood, or shout commands or warnings, or dive under my bed to escape avalanches. The bouts come and go—usually triggered off by tense activity during the day. For weeks I may sleep like a child, then suddenly be set upon by nights of hectic activity.

Tense tennis tournaments or Davis Cup matches are, of course, ideal breeding grounds for nightmares. On several occasions while rooming with Abe I have stealthily left my bed, then crept up on him and pounced on top of him,. shouting, "Knock off the easy ones, idiot!" Abe has been very nice about these things, but recently, I suppose, he feels that enough is enough. I agree with him completely, but am powerless. Sleeping pills, maybe? Abe says I need "to have my head shrunk". He's probably right, at that.

Our return to England was marvellously warm. We played at Connaught, and stayed in a little hotel in Epping Forest where two soft, pink English girls brought our breakfast to us and sometimes came back at dead of night to sip gins with us. How extraordinary English girls are, in the spring time. Little layers of puppy fat around the waists, hair which smells of yesterday's talcum, and skin as pale and soft as skim milk.

Warm, capable girls with clear eyes and hardly any wiles; bubbling with chuckles. Abe, rough as gravel, recognised their honesty instantly and never did them down, even the ugly ones. Always left presents in the room when we left.

Bournemouth thereafter was Bournemouth, and will probably always remain Bournemouth, and from there we broke new ground, travelling to Oslo to play Davis Cup against a Norwegian team who had, it seemed, from a tennis point of view, certainly, been hibernating all winter and just woken up—being white as snow and blinking when the sun came out (which it did, one afternoon, quite suddenly). Oslo was memorable because it was there that it snowed on the day before the dreaded night demons got me.

Abe and I, ensconced in the splendour of a suite at the Grand Hotel, Oslo, were rooming together for the first time. I had always been a bit nervous of Abe and had delayed thinking about the possibility of sharing a room with him for as long as possible. But, in Oslo, it was unavoidable. Firmly he picked up my bags, calling over his shoulder, "Get your ass along here, Forbsey. Seymour's psycho and Vermaak snores." The die was cast. I gave a nervous start. Here was Abe, fondly thinking that I was a farm boy who slept without stirring. It was only after dinner, and when we were at last inevitably going to bed that I decided to give him some kind of warning. Even then I waited until I was brushing my teeth before I spoke, half to sound casual, and half hoping he wouldn't hear.

"Abe," I said, my mouth full of toothpaste, "Listen. I, er, sometimes do things in the night."

"Oh," he said. "You do things in the night." He looked at his reflection in the mirror and said to it: "He does things in the night. That can't be a problem. I mean, what can a man *really* do in the night that could be that bad?" He looked at me in a kindly way. "Don't worry about it, pal. Listen, we all do things in the night. Sometimes. Just be bloody careful what you do, that's all, and keep your hands to yourself." He looked at me sharply. "Like what, for instance?"

"I might leap," I said sheepishly, "or shout out." I felt a bit of a fool. "Sometimes I walk about quietly for a while, or unpack my case. I never know until I've done it."

"Bullshit," said Abe. "You're puttin' me on. Don't give me that kind of crap just when I've got rid of Vermaak and Seymour. I can't be the only guy in this team who's normal!"

I left it at that. After all, I told myself, I didn't do things every night, and I *had* warned him. And so it was. For three nights I slept like a child.

Abe had obviously forgotten my warnings and I began to hope that the mere magnitude of his presence had flushed the evil spirits from out of my nocturnal id. On the Wednesday of that week, the cold snap came, coinciding as these things often do, with the collapse of the hotel's central heating system. Snow fell, and things became generally below zero. Simultaneously, I was told that I might have to play the singles, if Seymour's 'flu persisted. My nervous juices, I suppose, began to act up. That night we went to bed shivering in an icy room, creeping under the huge feather quilts with a sigh of relief.

Disaster struck at about midnight. I awoke, I was cold, and convinced that Abe had taken my quilt. "The bastard," I thought, with subconscious courage, and proceeded to remove his feather quilt, carefully laying it on my own bed, and going back to sleep. Five minutes later, inevitably, Abe awoke, frozen to a palish blue. Rapidly he searched around, under, over, behind his bed. The quilt had gone. To all intent and purpose, vanished literally into thin air.

"I couldn't figure it out," said Abe in one of his many explosive subsequent musings. "Holy shit, I says to myself, I have got to be losin' my mind. Maybe I dreamt that it was a huge marshmallow and ate it! So, I start gettin' nervous and feel my stomach. By now I'm startin' to get stiff. I figure I've got about ten more minutes before I get that stuff called Rigor Mortis."

I, meanwhile, perfectly comfortable beneath my double layer of feathers, was oblivious to Abe's torment until I was awoken by the light being put on and Abe's voice.

"Forbsey! God all bloody mighty. Singles or no singles, this is beyond a joke. Look at me. It'll take me a week in the sauna to get my blood movin'. They're gonna need a blow torch to get me out of bed!"

It was a heavy week for me. Although I was spared the opening singles match, the mere thought of it must have set my nerves on edge. The following night I saw a desperate-looking man put his head around our door, produce a hand grenade, pull the pin out with his teeth, count slowly, then roll the smoking thing under Abe's bed. In a flash I'd leapt out of bed and sped to the bathroom where I crouched, holding my ears. Suddenly I remembered that Abe was still in deadly peril. Dashing back into the bedroom I grabbed him by the arm and heaved him out of bed. One is extraordinarily strong at these times.

"Get to the bathroom," I shouted, "there's a grenade under your bed!"

In a moment we were both in the bathroom, crouched down, holding our ears and waiting for the holocaust. Nothing happened. Presently Abe looked at me in a strange sort of way.

"Forbsey," he said releasing his ears, "what's happening?"

"There was definitely a grenade." I said, beginning to feel the first stirrings of doubt. "Under your bed. Absolutely definitely."

Abe's position of refuge was low down beside the bath, next to the full length mirror. He turned and regarded his tousled reflection.

"It's me all right," he mused. "Definitely me, lyin' next to the bath, holding my ears, waitin' for a grenade to go off." He turned to me and asked in a kindly voice. "What kind of grenade?"

"Just an ordinary one," I muttered, feeling a fool, furious with myself, but still under the influence of the nightmare.

"Just an ordinary grenade," said Abe. "Not an unusual one." He gave a shaky snort of laughter. "Just a run of the mill kind of hand grenade."

Getting up, he peered round the edge of the door, entered the bedroom and looked under his bed:

"Jesus, Forbsey!" he said, "I mean, Jesus!" His voice carried a finality beyond exasperation. "You're not for real. With you, every night's like bein' in a movie. First I think I'm Titus Oates, or that Scott guy, then I'm at Omaha beach in a shell hole. If this goes on, in a week I'll be the world's only double VC, and clean off my head."

It was to go on for some time. The third night of that memorable week I awoke, and, frozen with horror, saw the wall above Abe's bed collapsing on top of him with deadly acceleration. Again I acted with incredible speed and bravery, leaping out of my bed to stand astride his pillow and support the wall. Abe's eyes shot open to their widest in an instant, but only a small section of his hair stood on end.

"The wall's falling. Help me hold the goddam thing up," I ordered through clenched teeth.

"Oh, the wall's falling," said Abe wearily. "That shouldn't be a problem. Why don't you just let it fall and go back to bed."

"You bastard—!"

I invariably felt a great mixture of anger and foolishness after these incidents and behaved as though they had nothing to do with me and were not my fault. Abe eventually grew used to them, and became very protective, telling his friends that he had better go and "make sure Forbsey doesn't check out of the hotel in the middle of the night with my gear", or some such remark. The possibilities of this particular situation intrigued him for a moment, and he pursued it enthusiastically.

"Imagine," he said, "what would happen if one night you dreamt you were urgently needed for a match in Hong Kong. That wouldn't be a problem for you. You'd pack, take a cab to the airport, tell the driver to contact me about the fare, and get on a plane. Then you'd probably wake up when they started serving breakfast on the plane an' ask the stewardess why the hotel was movin'.

"'We're going to Hong Kong,' she'd say.

"'We can't be,' you'd say. 'I've got a doubles with Segal at Queens Club.'

"'Never mind,' she'd say, 'maybe they got a Queens Club in Hong Kong.'

"'Then you'd start to panic and tell her that it's the wrong Queens Club!'"

Abie's madness!

Diary Notes: Copenhagen 1955

Now there's this thing about chatting up girls. New sort of art form. Abie's the best at it. The top seed and also impatient as hell. Things have to happen immediately. If it suddenly comes to him that girls are needed, you have to galvanise yourself into action. Broads. If I ask him where to find them he gets scornful.

"Jesus, Forbsey, go out an' make the right noises, buddy, an' they come out of holes in the ground! Listen! You think they don't want a bit of action?" he gives a snort of laughter. "The world's full of broads, buddy, an' the only time they're not lookin' for a bit of action is after they're dead!" And if I still look dubious he goes off and hunts for both of us. Once he even unearthed girls for the whole team, like a bird dog.

Meanwhile, in his rough way, he's an expert at it. Like in the queue at the airport, waiting to get on the plane. I'm right behind him, and in front of him is this girl—great, with all kinds of eyes and legs. Abie takes one look at her and goes into action. He starts to sniff and sniff, turning his head this way and that. "God damn," he says. "Somebody around here smells like Christmas!" The girl immediately turns, and he pounces. "Oh, it's you," he says, "that figures. I knew it couldn't be the idiot behind me!" And she starts to shake with laughter.

Now if I'd done that, she wouldn't have turned round. I'd have had to keep on sniffing and saying, "God damn, somebody around here smells like Christmas," about five times until the security people came and took me away.

Last night, after our meal, we walked in the Town Gardens. They have an amazing stall there, full of white china crockery. You pay a bit of money and get six wooden balls to let fly with. I never missed—an orgy of shattering. I picked off all the teapots with the first six throws. Because of all the practice I'd had throwing stones at things in the Karroo. As I turned to buy more balls, Abie, who was watching, said: "God Almighty, Forbsey! You just stay here an' keep on crackin' their teapots an' I'll go and nab us a couple of broads." He was back in a few minutes with Ushi, and I was told to, "keep her while I go find another". Ushi. Absolutely Scandinavian. She knew about twenty English words to my Danish "Tak", and although she had a bit of a hook in her nose, she was not bad for a three minute foray.

We smiled at each other, and six teapots later, Abie reappeared with Heike. Dark-haired, this one. Definitely an older woman. Black sweater, bulging with sharp pointed equipment. "She's a dancer," said Abie, explaining everything. "Great legs, Forbsey. With legs like hers, you don't need arms!"

He was carried away by his success and was raving on a bit.

The Danes were much tougher than the Norwegians, having in their team Kurt Nielsen and the Ulrich brothers, Torben and Jorgen. Nielsen was a mighty player, a first-tenner, in tennis language, and even at that time there was sufficient mystery about Torben to give each of us a private set of jitters. Abie hid his by claiming that there was "No way a guy could keep all that load of religious crap in his head and still play tennis." It was no use telling Abie that just because he "moved in a mysterious way" Torben was not necessarily religious. At that time, all things that seemed to Abie to be in any way mystical or occult got lumped together and labelled "religion". In Torben's case, considerable weight was added by his Christ-like image—long hair and bearded face, out of which shone eyes bright with sensitivity and things incomprehensible.

As it was, we ended up by narrowly losing the match, but as I was still the junior of the team and not involved in any of the critical matches, the loss did not personally affect me. I was more interested in the fact that Torben Ulrich played the clarinet in one of Copenhagen's best jazz bands, and that he'd agreed to have us visit his club. That was where we'd taken the two girls that Abe had found while I was cracking teapots. It was a barish club, I remember, full of wooden tables, where you sat on hard chairs and listened. Torben welcomed us in his usual way, reserved and confiding, and sat beside us, licking at the reed of his clarinet while we drank beers. The band hammered out several songs, and I kept expecting Torben to get up to join them, but he just sat there, intent and listening.

"Play, Torben," I urged him.

"I must wait," he said, "until something happens inside me. So far nothing very much has happened."

For some considerable time, apparently, nothing very much continued to happen, and then, just as I was beginning to give up all hope, Torben suddenly got to his feet and walked to the bandstand. He nodded to his colleagues, counted in a rhythm, and then, on cue, he put the clarinet to his lips, took a breath, closed his eyes—and did nothing else at all. Nothing. Didn't blow a note. After several minutes of agonising suspense he returned to the table and sat down again, sheathing his clarinet.

"Do you know, Gordon," he said seriously, "I could not think of a single note to play!"

"*Shit*, Torben," exclaimed Abie, unimpressed. "There had to be *something*. You could have just blown into that thing. You never know. You may just have 'fluked a few notes'!"

"Sometimes," said Torben, "just blowing is not enough. Music is, well, you know, more, I think than just simply blowing."

It was my first experience of the Ulrich intricacies. There were to be many more.

Slightly chastened by our loss, we recovered our spirits and began preparing for the next tournament. Rome. Where all the Italians played.

Diary Notes: Rome, Summer 1955

Today, Abie forgot to pack his tennis socks and jock-strap, for about the twentieth time this month, and borrowed mine. As usual, I received them back in a very dodgy condition—stretched to twice their size, for a start. In the dressing-room, after his match, he dumped them in my lap, and while I was contemplating them, Roy Emerson began singing in the shower. Emerson has a singular showering technique. Thus:

1. *Remove all clothing excepting tennis shorts.*
2. *Enter shower. Adjust temperature.*
3. *Cover body in soap suds from head to foot.*
4. *Scrub body.*
5. *Scrub tennis shorts.*
6. *Commence song of the week.*

His delivery is enthusiastic, but inclined to drift off key. This week the song is one of the current hits:

"Many a tear has to fallllll
But it's allllll
In the game.
All in that wonderful game
That is know—"

"Shad up. Shad up. Shad up, bloody Emerson!"

It was Drobny. He had entered the dressing-room, covered in the marks of a titanic struggle. Red dust, sweat, dirty shoes, fogged-up spectacles, tousled hair, generally unkempt. The singing stopped. Emerson's eyes appeared around the edge of the cubicle, then disappeared. Drobny dropped his rackets into the silence.

"That is known," came from the shower, "as LOVVVVE."

"Bloody Australians," said Drobny.

Another silence humming with prospects.

"Once in a while she may call-l-l-l,"
(came from the shower)
"But it's all-l-l-l-
In the game
All in that mad, crazy game—"

"Emerson!" shouted Drobny. "Shad up singing or I'll get really mad."

Emerson's head reappeared from the shower. "What's up, Drob?" he asked, infinitely cheerful. "What's up? Did you play like a cunt, or what?"

Emerson is one of tennis's all-timers. An unbelievable disposition—perhaps the perfect combination of kindness, humour, determination and ruefulness. Tremendous lust for life—Emerson.

The tennis stadium in Rome, called Foro Italico, is a heavy marble affair, with sunken courts, red, wet surfaces, slow and soft as Mozzarella cheese. Tennis in slow motion, under a Mediterranean sun, watched by statues and cypresses. Here the net-rushers curse and toil, and the groundstrokers adjust their grips, lick their lips and pound away at their top-spins, with all the time in the world. The club house, also marble, smells of capucino and overlooks the outside courts. Arriving at Foro Italico on the opening day of the Italian championships, one is struck dumb by hundreds of groundstrokes. Every young Italian player of any consequence sports immaculate forehands and backhands. Stand at the railings of the little cafeteria and look down over the sunken courts, and all you will see are the thousands of them, deep and heavy. Balls moving back and forth, carrying the marks of the wet, red clay. These were the hunting grounds of the great Italians—Cucelli, Del Bello, Gardini, Merlo, Pietrangeli, Sirola, Panatta.

Not Forbes and Segal.

In Rome, net-rushers were cannon fodder. On the way to net, one automatically had visions of the valley of death; the six hundred; the whistle of ball and shot, and danger to life and limb. Inevitably, we lost early on (though I once took Larsen to five sets) and so there was plenty of time for practice and sightseeing. The Colosseum, St Peter's, the Catacombs, all the old places. In the Sistine Chapel Abie gazed upwards and said:

"Forbsey, would you believe that this whole roof was painted by a guy called Angelo. Old Michael. God damn, I bet he ended up with a chiropractor havin' to do one hell of a neck job to him!"

Diary Notes: Rome 1955

Giuseppe Merlo is small and handsome and drives everyone completely demented by the way he plays. He has no service whatsoever; just tosses up the ball quite carefully and, with a slightly pained expression, pops it into play. His racket is about half the size of everyone else's, and so loosely strung that you can't hear him hit the ball. On the forehand side, he holds the racket halfway up the handle, and on the backhand side he just adds his other hand, which means that his hands are back to front. His shots sneak past the net-rushers like bullets out of a silenced gun, so quietly that they are never sure when exactly the point has ended.

He's beaten almost everyone on clay. It's unfair, really, because the general opinion amongst the players is that it's impossible to play the way that he does, and that he should lose all the time, and never win.

Until Pietrangeli and Sirola came along, the Italians specialised in the unorthodox. Gardini, one of their greatest players, used to move about the court like a spider running over water, and had a game consisting entirely of forehands and lobs. Matches between him and Merlo used often to be mammoth affairs during which spectators opened picnic lunches and knitted sweaters. Invariably these matches would end in huge Italian dramas, with both players collapsing with cramp and appealing to various gods, umpires, linesmen, spectators and gods again.

Tennis in Italy.

Quaranto Quindici.

A law unto itself.

Having survived the rigours of nocturnal Oslo, and the constipations of the pastas of Rome, we travelled to Paris.

How agonising and unattainable is the appeal of Paris. There it lay, unforgettable in the mild May sunlight, with its avenues and boulevards, fresh new leaves and sly sophisticates, all fashionably got up. That first evening we walked the Champs Elysées—wide and sparkling, and the city touched us, although it was then all too rich—an acquired taste, like old whisky, for people accustomed to lemonade.

At the top of the wide street the American Bar shouted at us and Abie immediately removed his thumbnail from the corner of his mouth and gave me a nudge. "There's the action, Forbsey," he said in a satisfied way. "Too much of this French can soften your mind. At least in there they'll understand about beer and meatballs."

In those days, Abie had a vicious appetite which would often pounce upon him between meals and create immediate and intense culinary demands. Often he would do a quick sidestep into a self-service section of a delicatessen and trim the counter, sometimes arriving at the pay desk with an empty tray, having eaten his whole meal in a series of gulps *en route*. His power of ingestion staggered me.

"You must have a crop," I said to him one day after a particularly intense foray.

"A crop of what?" he asked.

"Not that kind of crop," I replied; "the other kind."

"What other kinds are there?" he asked.

"A bird's crop."

"You mean birds," said Abie, "or birds? Say what you mean, Forbsey."

"Birds with feathers. They don't chew, you know. They eat into crops and whatever they eat just lies there and sort of dissolves." With Abie, one never had to bother about clinical details. "That way they can be sure to get their share of whatever's going."

"A crop, hey," said Abie interested. "That sounds like a good deal. That way I could eat two meals at a time and carry one of them as a spare!"

The idea intrigued him enough to trigger off one of his monologues.

"I'd be out there in the fifth set," he said, "playin' someone like Woodcock. At about nine-all, he'd be gettin' real exhausted, an' I'd just switch over to my spare meal! That would *really* psych everyone out. 'Watch Segal,' they'd say, 'he carries two meals!'"

Diary Notes: Paris 1955

The French foods sometimes confound Abie and me.

At the Racing Club where we practise, they have a fantastic al fresco lunch all laid out. You help yourself.

On the table are these huge artichokes which have fascinated us for some time. We always see the French carrying them about on trays.

"I'm going to give one of those green bastards a go," says Abe, and sticks the biggest one on his tray.

He can't wait. As we sit down he breaks off one of the big outer leaves, sticks it into his mouth and begins chomping. Tremendous milling process inside his head, and then after a minute or two he gets a pained expression, and pushing a finger into his mouth, he pulls out this soggy wad of stuff that looks like jute fibre.

"Christ, Forbsey," he says, "these French must have tough jaws. How the hell do they eat these things?"

Later, Pierre Darmon came over and explained to us how you eat artichokes.

"This is the only thing in the world," said Abie, "that you end up havin' more left than you started out with."

Food for Abie was very important. To begin with, he needed a fair quantity to drive his fairly considerable plant and machinery. But there was more to it than that. More than anyone else I know, Abie loved, absolutely revelled in, the act of alleviating hunger. The hungrier he was, the faster he would eat. And, at such times, speed more than quantity seemed to be the essence. A fair-sized steak, for instance, would last about three gulps, while meatballs went down whole, like oysters in lemon juice. Somewhere in the primaeval mists of Abie's breeding line, there must have been a canine strain. There was only one person whom I ever saw eat faster than Abie, and that was Orlando Sirola eating spaghetti. I mean, *all* Italians eat spaghetti twice as fast as anyone else, but Sirola simply annihilated it. A large bowlful would disappear in a flash. There seemed to be no question of it being chewed. Forkfuls would go into his mouth, like hay being loaded, and effortlessly slip down his throat.

In the Foro Italico restaurant once, we sat at a table beside Pietrangeli and Sirola, and Abie viewed the Sirola spaghetti assault with awe.

Here, at last, he must have decided, was a form of food that could be eaten even faster than steak.

The next day he ordered spaghetti for lunch, as a starter. When it arrived, he seized a fork, inserted it, wound it round until the spaghetti had reached the approximate dimensions of a tennis ball, then stuffed it into his mouth, and with a thoughtful faraway look on his face, he swallowed it. The experiment was apparently successful, for the rest of the plate got dumped in the same way: "Now I've figured out," he said happily, "how these Italians eat spaghetti as an hors d'oeuvre. If you eat it fast enough, you don't know you've eaten it, and then you can go on and have steak and salad!"

Later that afternoon, when I went into the dressing-room to change for our doubles, I found Abie busy with a packet of Eno's Fruit Salts.

"Jesus, Forbsey," he said, "that spaghetti's hard to move. Maybe the steak's just sittin' there, waitin' to get by!" He downed a huge glass of foaming salts, and did up his shoes with a jerk.

Throughout our doubles match he retained an intense, anticipatory sort of look, as though he wasn't quite sure of his immediate future. Once or twice, as he passed me on his way to net after a big serve, I thought that I detected pressure leaks, and these suspicions were verified when we eventually led by two sets to love, 5–3 and my service to come. As I got ready to serve, Abie approached me and muttered with clenched teeth: "Better hold this one, buddy, or we may both never make it off the court. You've heard of being swallowed by an avalanche—well, just bear that in mind!"

With both of us, so to speak, under intense pressures, I held my service. Abie shook hands very briefly and then set off for the locker room at a sort of stiff-legged trot. No sooner had he disappeared inside, than I could swear that I felt a sort of distant rumble: a distinct tremor that would, without doubt, have shown up on the Richter Scale.

Diary Notes: Paris 1955

Roland Garros is tucked into the woods in the Bois de Boulogne. The Renaults and Citroëns arrive at our little hotel near l'Étoile to take us to the courts. The drivers wear berets and smoke Gauloises and grunt at our questions. You wind through the little streets and finally cross the river and plunge into the trees. Soft European woods, with moss and dead leaves underfoot. Sometimes we pass Longchamps and the Racing Club, but there are so many different roads that the tennis courts always take me by surprise when we come upon them.

You can go for quiet training runs through the woods and hardly hear your own footfalls.

The Roland Garros Stadium in Paris was disappointing after the splendour of the city; a gaunt, concrete amphitheatre which held thirteen thousand people, inflicting each with a raw behind and softening only when it was filled up. Paris was memorable for me that year because:

(a) It was the first time I had been there.

(b) Because I won the mixed doubles with a young American girl called Darlene Hard, who was playing her first tournament in Europe and whom, by chance, I met and entered with on the morning they closed the draw.

(c) Because Russell Seymour and I beat Mervyn Rose and George Worthington in a doubles match at 15–13 in the fifth set, having saved eleven match points, and:

(d) Because a lunatic Australian player dragged me into a brothel and made me watch an "Exhibition" pronounced (and performed) the French way, and thus introduced me to my first taste of the tricky side of love.

(e) And because I came within a hair's breadth of defeating Ham Richardson, one of the best players in the world and an *expert* on clay!

The doubles match was one of the most remarkable in which I have ever played. Russell Seymour was considered more of a singles than a doubles player, and as Abe Segal and Ian Vermaak were our recognised doubles pair, Russell and I had to make do with one another's methods.

We ploughed through several rounds of young Frenchmen, then found ourselves facing Rose and Worthington, who were Australian, seeded, and considered to be very tough to beat.

We got into the match from the very start and sneaked the first set before they had woken up. Angrily they retaliated and took the second, and then, amazingly, we found ourselves locked into a tight third set with neither side giving an inch. We began playing points which defy description. Rallies developed which balanced themselves on the very edge of impossibility—cascades of volleys which sometimes left all four of us open-mouthed. French spectators packed themselves tightly around the court to watch us win a long third set, then lose a short sharp fourth.

The fifth set made all that had preceded it look tame. All told, we had eleven match points in our favour and Rose and Worthington had thirteen. Twice Worthington served for match, and in one of these games they led forty–love. Three consecutive match points. Somehow we fought back to 40–30. Worthington gathered the balls to serve to me on the left court, and as he was about to serve, Rose, who was up at net, called out to Worthington over his shoulder:

"Watch the line, Wortho, I'm going across!"

"No, don't," Worthington called back.

"I'm going across!" cried Rose again.

"No. Don't," said Worthington firmly.

"Okay, I'm going," cried Rose.

I listened wide-eyed. I had never heard doubles partners shout tactics to one another across the court. They usually made secret signs. More puzzling still, was the fact that they didn't seem to understand each other. I decided to consult Seymour. "What the devil is Rose going to do?" I asked him urgently.

Russell gave the short bray of a laugh he used when he was really desperate. "You tell me!" he said. "He's either going across or else he isn't!"

"Well," I said, "what should I do?"

"You must either go crosscourt or down the line," said Russell.

Nobody was being very helpful, so I got ready to receive. Worthington served a high kicker to my backhand and moved in behind Rose to "cover the line". Rose, meanwhile, true to his word, set off across the net to cut off my return. One of the cardinal rules of men's doubles is that you *watch the ball* and *not* the net-player. Really good doubles players eventually develop a method of being aware of what opponents are doing while still watching the ball, but it is a tricky business and never fool-proof. I was vaguely aware of a tremendous scissors movement taking place on the far side, but I'd committed myself to the crosscourt return, and so made the best of it. I gave the ball a low slice and knew at once that it was either going to be a very good shot, or else just too low. It was not quite either. It hit the tape of the net with a whack, ran along the top for about two feet, parallel to the moving Rose, then toppled over onto his side of the court. Rose lunged, but couldn't possibly dig it out. The crowd went crazy, and Russell, who was given to understatement, told me that I had hit a "useful return".

We won the set at 15–13, and the match, and in the next round beat the

French team of Robert Haillel and Pierre Pelizza before losing to Pietrangeli and Sirola in the quarters.

The brothel incident was less athletic, but almost as remarkable and was, as I have said, all the work and ingenuity of a lunatic Australian.

Why he chose me, I never understood—we had met only briefly and were not well acquainted. Perhaps like my friends the pilot and the game ranger, he sensed in me a yearning to do some dangerous deeds with women. As it was, I would never have conceived or undertaken the venture single-handed. The painted ladies who lined the little streets at Place Pigalle fascinated me, but I passed them at a near jogtrot, for fear of being "got in the night".

The lunatic Australian was big and raucous, and having finished his meal of vegetable soup and steak with *petits pois*, he pushed back his wooden chair, drained his beer and said, "Come with me", in a way which I couldn't disobey. Off we went (in a taxi, no less. No Metro for him) and were set down at the famous little square.

Of all the seamy places in the cities of the world, Pigalle, I think, has the softest touch. It did then, at any rate. It is sly and seductive, unhygienic and sometimes vulgar, but seldom vicious. In those days, it was almost gentle. The girls in the bars would chat and nibble and smell of sinful scents, and good-naturedly agree to almost anything. My Australian, having answered, "Wait and see mate, you'll be all right", to all my questions, finally stationed himself in the middle of a little cobbled street and brazenly confronted the line of girls on the sidewalk.

"All right, ladies!" he cried. "It's your lucky night. Let's have a look at you!" He turned to me. "You choose one, and I'll choose one," he said, "and then we'll make negotiations."

He was a swift chooser.

"Got mine," he said. "You got yours?"

Hastily I selected a tall one who seemed to have soft eyes. I pointed.

"Right-ho," he said. "Good choice. Bit of length can't do any harm." He beckoned them over with two forefingers, and they approached giggling.

"How much?" he said firmly. "Com bien? For une exhibition? Un très bien exhibition extraordinaire!"

There is no sound more remarkable than an Australian tennis player delving into French.

"Aaah!" they said, laughing and nudging one another. "Une exhibition! Aaah! Monsieur est très romantique! Pour faire une exhibition formidable, six mille francs. Seex thousand francs!"

"Bloody hell," said the Australian. "Seex thousand! Have to be one hell of an exhibition for seex thousand! We'll pay you five. Tu comprends? Cinq. Cinq bloody mille, and not a dollar more!"

"Aaah, monsieur! Cinq mille?" Their mouths turned down at the corners.

"That's right, cinq mille. And we'll throw in another five hundred if you are très, très formidable!"

The bargain was struck, and they set off, beckoning us to follow.

By now I was in the customary state of nervous tension which beset me whenever I felt that something uncontrollable was about to happen. It was true, certainly, that I had successfully cracked it. But the possibility of performing in a group was another matter altogether, producing disturbing visions of calamity in the presence of three people. In a display of what I judged to be nonchalance, I paused at a fruit barrow and bought a bunch of bananas.

"Bananas!" said the lunatic Australian, "hell-of-a-time for bananas. Could come in handy though." He broke one off the bunch and ate it thoughtfully while we turned into a little doorway. "Mind the skins. Don't want to slip on our asses on the way down, do we?"

The room into which the girls led us had a large bed and a smell of Paris and old perfume and other things essentially French. Coyly they began to undress, gradually revealing all the lacy things that fit onto ladies of that kind, collapsing against each other in a gale of giggles at the sight of the bananas and continuing until I began to wish I'd selected some other kind of fruit. They were naked at last, and began caressing one another with soft little mewing sounds, and touching their tongues together—their fingers, thighs, tummies, arms, bridling coyly, with sly words and breathy laughter.

I sat watching, transfixed, while the lunatic Australian muttered, "Bloody hell," to himself occasionally and sometimes also, "Would you bloody credit it?" "Would you ever bloody well have believed that?"

"All right," he said at last. "That's enough of that; now show us the exhibition." And they gravely began a demonstration of the various love-making positions.

I was filled with unease and curiosity and stood in a corner, eating bananas like one possessed. At last it was over.

"Only nineteen," said the lunatic Australian—"I thought there were supposed to be fifty-seven—" He looked across at me.

"You finished your bananas yet, Forbsey?"

More laughter.

With a little skip and a sly smile, the girl I had chosen, whose name I remember was Françoise (inevitably!), took me by the hand and led me off to another room.

Later, when I found the lunatic Australian in the street below, we walked off to take the Metro.

"Make bloody good wives, those kind of French girls," he said laconically. "A man could do worse than take one of them home to tea."

In those championships I played one of my best-ever matches on slow clay. In the third round I found myself drawn against Hamilton Richardson, who was ranked about second or third in the United States and who was one of the players whom, during our farm practice sessions, we used to "become".

We played for hours, I remember, and for me the match was fine, and filled with deft, thrilling shots that I had never believed I could make.

Finally, it was the fifth set, 5–4 for me, 15–40, his serve, match point on the centre court, the Roland Garros Stadium, Paris, France and the kind of hush that falls upon crowded tennis stadiums when seeded players are about to be beaten by unknown juniors. To add to the already tense situation, Richardson missed with his first service and was left with one ball between himself and disaster. There was no doubt about it. If ever I was to play a remarkable shot, this was an opportune time.

Twenty-five separate pieces of other people's advice flashed through my mind . . . and these in addition to the random bits that I was giving myself at the time. Eventually out of the confusion emerged a cryptic instruction that Abe Segal had once given me:

"If ever, Forbsey, you get to a real big point, just forget everything, look at the ball carefully and hit the shit out of it. That way, even if you hit it over the fence, you feel a hell of a lot better than if you just stand there crappin' yourself and bein' careful . . ."

In those days I had a sliced backhand and was unable to "hit the shit out of the ball" if it came on that side, so I decided to "run around my backhand" at all costs and bring my forehand to bear. My decision coincided with one by Richardson to serve to my forehand his second service—a brave move, and one which left me waiting tensely with a forehand grip held ready, about four yards from the passing ball. The failure of my strategy appalled me and I could hear in my mind Abie (who was watching from the stand) saying under his breath: "Jesus, Forbsey, where the hell are you goin'? You got to be in the right area, buddy. Don't leave before the action starts!"

Unnerved and preoccupied by these gloomy thoughts, I did not give the forty–thirty point much thought, deciding at the last minute to "play it safe". The result was a tame backhand into the middle of the net, and the end of a marvellous opportunity, offered and retracted by the sly gods which control such situations. Bloody tennis gods! They could easily have had Richardson miss that second serve!

My performance evoked some dressing-room advice from Tony Trabert (another one of our farm heroes), who said to me: "Listen, kid. When you get to very important points, forget about everything except watching the ball. Then hit it firmly and make your opponent play the shot." His advice was sound and carried me through quite a number of tennis crises. But I still believe that I might have won that match point and a lot more had I gone to the trouble of having one of my rackets *painted black*.

Diary Notes: Summer 1955

Abie has taken up poker. He arranges his face into a slanted smile, narrows his eyes, and sardonically produces a pack of cards to practise his shuffling with. I think he thinks that if he can manage to shuffle extravagantly, the rest is easy. He's mad, of course. The poker school consists of a very tricky bunch of players. Mervyn Rose, Don Candy, Sven Davidson, Herbie Flam, Malcolm Fox, Hugh Stewart and Warren Woodcock. Others occasionally sit in. They're very good, and know every trick and percentage backwards. Malcolm Fox is supposed to have virtually cleaned out an entire troop ship on his way back from Korea. Warren Woodcock has an angelic face, and Mervyn Rose is evil, through and through. Abie, meanwhile, believes that there is nothing to it but shuffling and dealing. He absolutely relishes the way they look across at each other, eye to eye, adjust the stakes and say: "Your hundred, and another hundred." He'd like it even better if they could play in lire and he could say: "Your million, and another million!" He also likes the way they arrange themselves at a corner table surrounded by awe-stricken onlookers, who are riveted by the piles of money. Woodcock and Rose, apparently, have encouraged Abie to play. It's his own fault, of course, because he loves to act the big spender, and have everyone believe that if he is not already a millionaire, he's about to become one at any moment. He's been losing steadily for the last week. Twice I've caught him in the corner of the dressing-room, doling out money.

But this afternoon, catastrophe struck. As usual, they were playing in the players' restaurant at Roland Garros, a dungeon of a place. The table was littered with "sandwich jambon", cokes and ashtrays, with the air decidedly thick.

"Seven card stud", Abie says the game was called. A tremendous round developed and the pot grew and grew. By the time the stragglers had fallen out, at least three hundred dollars in French francs lay on the table, in carelessly crumpled notes, and only Abie and Mervyn Rose remained. A fortune was at stake.

By the time they had finished betting, the pile had grown to a thousand dollars, and then Abie's full house of aces and kings was pipped by Rose's four miserable nines. Gloom and tragedy, and frantic telephone calls to Abie's "shippers". Whatever they are. Whenever Abie runs out of money he phones up these mysterious "shippers". I asked him how one went about getting "shippers", and he told me that "good shippers are one hell-of-a-hard thing to find".

Just at that time tennis was weighed down with literally dozens of the most extraordinary characters. Colourful lunatics, one could almost say. To the extent, almost, that anyone young and unsuspecting coming on the scene might be excused if he thought that in order to reach the top in the game, one needed to be slightly touched.

Of course, Trabert and Seixas were reasonably sane, and so were Harry Hopman's squad of young Australians, Hoad, Rosewall, Hartwig *et al.* But as for the rest, virtually the whole lot were, to a greater or lesser extent, off their heads. Looking back at those tennis years, I find a whole list of names marching through my head. Art Larsen, Warren Woodcock, Herbie Flam, Torben Ulrich, Hugh Stewart, Gardner Mulloy, Mervyn Rose, Andre Hammersley, Fausto Gardini, Beppe Merlo, Pietrangeli and Sirola, George Worthington, Gil Shea, Don Candy, Freddie Huber. Abie Segal, of course. Even Drobny and Patty had their moments. As a newcomer I used to look on, amazed. Don Candy, for example. Now *he* had the charm of a truly funny man. His matches would always develop into critical situations and invariably, at such times, bad calls would occur, usually involving Continental umpires who spoke just enough English to intensify confusion. In any case, umpiring in Italy, Spain and almost all Latin countries was notoriously partisan, and chaos prevailed almost at the drop of a hat. Candy soon became keenly aware of the absurdity of such situations, and adopted a policy of countering chaos with chaos. Often we would watch his matches, eagerly awaiting incidents. Some of his better inventions bordered on lunacy.

During one particular match, for instance, linesmen's chairs were in position, but no linesmen. Drama was in the offing. Inevitably, at a critical deuce point, the bad call turned up and Candy pounced.

He began gesticulating and arguing in furious Spanish gibberish for a full two minutes with the empty chair on the offending line which he felt should contain a linesman. Then he suddenly stopped, walked to the umpire (who had made the call in the first place), pointed to the chair and said:

"I want that man removed!"

"There is-a no one there," said the umpire.

"Well, I want you to get someone," said Candy, "so that I can have him removed."

"But-a if-a you get-a someone, and then you remove-a him, then-a you would have no linesman," said the umpire, mopping his forehead.

"But we already have no linesman," said Candy.

"Then-a why-a you-a want to remove him if-a he comes?" asked the umpire.

"Because he made a bad call," said Candy.

"But-a he wasn't there," said the umpire.

"But if he had been, he would have," said Candy.

"Ah, then, if he had," said the umpire, "then-a you could remove him."

"But I couldn't," said Candy, "because there's no one there!"

"THAT-A- WHAT I SAY!" shouted the umpire. "There's no-a one there!"

"Instead," said Candy, "we play a let. If you play a let, I will not insist on removing that man," and he pointed again to the empty chair.

"All-a right!" said the umpire wearily. "We play a let. Mamma Mia, a let, a let-a."

On another occasion, faced with an appalling decision by an Italian umpire who could speak no English at all, Candy approached the man, pulling faces, moving his lips, shaking his racket, tearing at his hair and generally going through all the motions of a furious diatribe, but silently, without uttering a sound. The umpire watched him with growing alarm. He put his finger in his ear and shook it, then clapped both hands to his ears and released them. This he repeated several times. Suddenly he descended from the chair and with a worried look on his face, he hurried off the court, probably to see a specialist. Candy watched him go then climbed into his chair and in a loud voice reversed the decision, immediately causing his Italian opponent, who had been watching the proceedings in a smug sort of way, to go into apoplexy.

Candy's methods were never vicious. Sometimes he would approach errant linesmen and whisper something to them in a very confidential way. This caused volatile opponents to rave about it being unfair to influence linesmen, to which Candy would reply:

"Relax. I was agreeing with him. There is no rule which says you can't agree with a linesman!"

He was what could be called an industrious player. No fabulous flights for him. he gave workmanlike performances, running round the backhands and hitting conservative topspin forehands from close to his ribs. His service was utilitarian, his backhand safely steered and his volleys sound. But he had a huge heart and a great deal of Australian cunning and resource and although he didn't win many big tournaments, he badly scared nearly all the top players a number of times.

Then there was always the possibility of overhearing snippets of conversations between Candy and Torben Ulrich, who at the time was busy inventing his remarkable world of meditation, profundity and dreams. Whenever Candy came upon Torben Ulrich in one of his profound moods, it seemed to trigger off within him an opposite reaction and he used to put on an air of excessive heartiness and good fellowship.

"Good morning, Torben!" he might say lustily, to which Torben would often reply, slowly and deliberately:

"Explain to me, Donald. What exactly is a 'Good Morning'?"

"Sunny!" Candy would say. "No rain!"

"Aha, then," Torben would reply, "perhaps it would be more accurate to say, 'Sunny morning, Torben', because you see, for me, a sunny morning need not necessarily be a good morning."

"All right then. Sunny morning, Torben!"

"Yes, Donald. You are right. The sun is certainly shining."

Such exchanges took place in dozens of variations, always with a bland display of off-handedness, each treating the other with suitable indulgence of the kind with which fathers treat small children. Once in the midday heat of July in Athens, Candy came upon Torben sitting reflectively on a bench at the tennis club, with a wet towel on his head. Don sank down beside him.

"Hot," he said in a precise, firm voice.

"Yes," said Torben. "You could say that it is hot."

"Too hot to practise tennis," pursued Candy.

"I am not going to practise tennis," said Torben.

"I thought you were about to say to me, 'Let's practise tennis'," said Candy.

"Even if it were cool," said Torben, "I would practically never say that to you. It would be much more likely that I would say to you: Donald, I think that it would be better for both of us if we *did not* practise tennis!"

"Then that's settled," said Candy firmly. "We are not going to practise tennis today."

"Yes," said Torben. "That's settled." Then he added: "In a way, you know, it was never really *not* settled."

On still another occasion (one of the rare ones when Candy and Ulrich *did* get to practise) they had been playing for some time when some eager club members approached the court. As usual during tournaments, practice courts were at a premium, and the members waited impatiently. At last one of them spoke to Ulrich.

"Have you been playing long?" he said.

"As long as I can remember," said Torben.

"How much longer will you play?" asked the member.

"We may go on for many years," said Torben. The member looked disgruntled. "You see," said Torben in a soothing way, "we hardly ever feel like ending our game exactly at the same time." Candy, who had been listening, now approached.

"He's mad," he said to the now puzzled member. He tapped his temple. "He believes that he is born blessed, but in actual fact, he's mad!"

"That," said Torben, "is a matter for discussion. Because, you see, it is hard to define who is mad and who is not." He fixed the club member with a penetrating stare and said: "What exactly is madness? Perhaps you can tell me!"

Torben was, and is, an extraordinary human being. With him in view one would automatically consider such phenomena as intellectualism, the power of the mind, mysticism, things deep, Gurudom even. He had, for a start, long hair and a beard, which in those days were unheard of (we were busy imitating the crew-cuts of Trabert and Seixas) and which lent him the somewhat scary appearance of the son of some grave god. He moved in an aura of private contemplation which I, for one, was reluctant to interrupt. He explored thoroughly the fields of nearly all sensitivities, always distant and thoughtful behind his youthful, hirsute disguise. Pleasantries generally escaped him. All remarks addressed to him would make their way into his head for consideration. I once said to him as he left a court after a match,

"Torben, did you win?"

"No," he said.

"Then what happened?" I asked.

"I simply played in the usual way. It was my opponent who lost," he said.

His delivery was slow and deliberate, each word weighted with consideration. He played the clarinet and tenor sax (very well, when the time was right), immersed himself in the angular harmonies and oblique progressions of new jazz and carried, at all times, a record player and records—Miles Davis, Art Farmer, Mulligan, Terry, Bill Evans, Parker, Powell, John Coltrane. Complicated cadences always drifted out of Torben's quarters, sounds which greatly puzzled Don Candy. His music was more straightforward—a simple set of guitar chords and songs, about John Henry being a "Steel-Driving" man, "Muscles and Blood", "Whisky Bill" and "Home on the Range", which he did with a stetson and a Roy Rogers delivery, sometimes startling everyone with a yodel or two. After putting up with Torben's music for some time, he decided to remedy his taste and bought a record of marches. Armed with this, he broke in on Torben's contemplation of Thelonius Monk's "Round Midnight", turned off the player and presented Torben with the record.

"What," he asked, "do you think about this?"

Torben examined the record carefully, then handed it back.

"I would avoid thinking about it," he said.

"Try it," said Candy, unabashed. "Put it on."

"My machine," said Torben, "would not be able to reproduce it."

"Why not?" asked Candy in a challenging voice.

"Because," said Torben, "this is a machine which plays music. It cannot perform other functions."

"And this," said Candy haughtily, "is a musical recording. It cannot, for instance, be played through a washing machine."

"It would not surprise me," said Torben, "if it was not perhaps better to play that record through a washing machine."

"In any case," said Candy, "I did not come here with the intention of discussing the possibility of having laundry done. I came here to introduce to you a new kind of musical experience."

"I think, Donald," said Torben, "that I would find it more valuable if you told me how to get my laundry done."

A long wrangle ensued, involving the unlikely combination of laundry and music. At last, Candy's persistence won the day. Monk was removed, the marches installed. Suddenly the player began to emit stirring martial sounds. Candy marched up and down the room several times, delighted, saluting and giving Torben an exaggerated "eyes right"! Torben regarded the player with a puzzled expression, as though it had betrayed him. Abruptly the march ended and Candy came to a halt, gave a final salute and stood easy. Then he picked up his record and strode from the room, like someone who had done a trick. Torben was silent for some time, before he raised his eyes to me and said:

"It would be much better if people had never discovered the way to make war!"

Torben's tennis game, too, was heady and profound. He would sometimes become so engrossed in the science of the game, that the winning of it became incidental. At such times he might embark on a series of acutely-angled volleys, each more fine than the last; or lob volleys or topspin lobs; or a round-arm sliced service which bit into the breeze, drifting across the net in a curve, light as thistledown, not bouncing but settling onto the grass with a soft sizzling sound. It was one of these services which had ended up in the water jug under the umpire's chair and left Teddy Tinling waiting with a forehand grip.

Somewhere in my diary I found a little description of a match which Torben had played against Manuel Santana.

What more unconventional, almost occult, tennis match could one want? For several games they try things out—their strokes, the flight of the ball, the quality of the court, the air movement, various slices and spins, like musicians tuning their instruments. Torben ponders immensely between points, strikes prodigious poses, thinks, listens, reflects. Manuel selects his strokes like a surgeon selecting his instruments—but it is Torben who leads 8–7 and forty love. He loses the game and seven more set points before losing the set at 17–15. These situations bring to light a splendid bit of whimsical Ulrich logic. "You know, Gordon," he says to me in the change-room, swathed to the eyes in towels: "Manuel is so good under pressure that it is a dis-advantage to lead forty love. You have a better chance leading thirty love, or thirty fifteen. But forty love is very dangerous!"

Diary Notes: Paris, Summer 1955

Tonight at the restaurant with Abe and Heather Segal, Herbie Flam, Larsen and Hugh Stewart, Herbie got hopelessly entangled with the cheese on top of his onion soup. We were all hungry by the time the food arrived, having had only the frugal "sandwich jambon" at Roland Garros for lunch. Herbie set about his onion soup with far too much enthusiasm and not enough finesse. In his defence it must be said that it was the stickiest cheese ever created. Unbelievably resilient. The first spoonful created a thick thong of cheese from his plate to his mouth and left another minor thong attached to his spoon which, when he returned it to his soup, immediately attached itself to the edge of his plate. The thick thong, meanwhile, stretched into a triangle when he tried to cut it with the back of his knife, and then, when he brought his spoon back into attack, the thick thong stuck to the thin thong, still attached to his spoon and the plate and they both sagged down together and bonded themselves to the edge of the table.

We all watched, absorbed. Larsen began uttering cries of encouragement.

"Come on, Herbie baby, you can lick that plate of soup. Atta boy, Herbie! Now come back in with the spoon. Try a finger, Herbie! You're all out of knives and spoons. That's the boy! Watch it, Herbie, it's stuck to your sleeve!"

Herbie, concentrating grimly, fought the soup for several minutes. At last, caught in a web of melted cheese, he leaned back and said:

"God damn, Abie, get me out of here!"

At which point our waiter arrived with a huge pair of scissors, and, literally cut him loose. Then Larsen began to discuss the possibility of having his rackets strung with cheese: "You get hungry out there, big Abie, and you can eat your gut," he finished.

At times like these, Heather weeps with laughter, copious tears which make her mascara run, and leave her looking like a dishevelled child.

Abie, who had ordered a crab, was appalled when it had to be wheeled in on a trolley. The waiter lifted a huge round lid and there it was. A monster, pink and beady-eyed. Then another waiter began arranging in front of Abie, the instruments which he was to use.

"Jesus Christ," he exclaimed, "a tool kit. God damn, Herbie, you think you had problems with the soup. Can you imagine if this bastard starts with me!"

Larsen was delighted at the prospect of another to-the-death struggle.

"You want me to kill that thing for you, big Abie?" he offered.

Heather backed away when it was finally served. I don't think the French waiters are very impressed with our approach to their cuisine.

I can't think of tennis in Paris without remembering Art Larsen. Abe Segal first told me about him. Abe had toured Europe for a season before I arrived on the scene, and gave graphic descriptions of things or people who impressed him.

"This Larsen," he said to me one day, with the inevitable forefinger prodding my chest, "has got to be unreal. A genius at tennis, for a start. Play him and you think you've got yourself mixed up with that Spanish stuff they had."

"Inquisition?" I asked tentatively.

"That's it, Inquisition," said Abie. "He stretches you about so much you think you've invented rubber! You move one way an' he goes the other. Your shoes wear out an' your knees cave in! An' that's only for starters. Go around with Larsen for a while and you've got to see a psychiatrist—and if you go to the psychiatrist too often, *he* has to go to *his* psychiatrist. I went around with Larsen for a month and after a while I stops and says to myself: 'Hold it, buddy. Hold it a shake. One of us is crazy. Only I can't figure out which one!' So I 'phoned Herbie (Flam) and says to him: 'Hey Herbie, do I sound OK to you, or do I sound like I've gone a little soft?' So Herbie says, 'Keep talkin' a while, Abie. How can I tell how you sound if you only say a few words?' So I talk a bit longer, and suddenly Herbie says, 'OK, that's enough. You sound the same to me. That doesn't mean you're not crazy. Just that you haven't changed. So if you figure you weren't crazy before, then you're OK now!' That's Herbie! He's also mad, mind you! Talk about the deaf leadin' the deaf."

Abe went on at some length about the vagaries of Larsen's behaviour, throwing in phrases about "eagles on his shoulder", "gettin' stuck in doors", or "goin' about tappin' people".

"That's why he's called Tappy," he said, "because on certain days at certain times he has to tap certain things, and only he knows when!"

Although I knew that Abie was given to exaggeration, I looked forward to meeting Larsen.

For once, there was something in what Abie had told me. I met Tappy Larsen at last, in Naples, and he was, it turned out, almost everything everyone had said of him. A natural left-handed player of almost uncanny ability. He had that rare gift enjoyed by only a very few tennis players—a perfect touch, a feel for the ball, an inner knowledge of exactly what was going on between the strings of his racket and the melton cloth attached to the rubber inside of the ball.

But Larsen's tennis was not the most extraordinary part of him. Stories about him were legion: that he had survived a desperate situation in the war when all his comrades had been killed or wounded; that he'd been in a plane accident or a burning tank. Others similar. His superstitions were said to have been caused by these events. Whatever the cause, the superstitions were real enough. He did tap all kinds of people and things. He did, constantly, glance upward and backwards over his shoulder, sometimes even during rallies, watching for eagles.

We played together in the doubles of the Paris championships in 1956. Not the French championships, but the Paris ones, the ones that Budge Patty always used to win. Larsen and I were put together in the doubles, and after many adventures found ourselves in the finals against the wily French Davis Cup team, Paul Remy and Marcel Bernard. I was young and eager, and, apart from being excited about the opportunity to play doubles with Larsen, I badly wanted to win the tournament. Although I am sure that he, too, wanted to win, I think that the urgency of the thing escaped him. Besides, he greatly enjoyed devising surprises during the course of matches and seldom missed the opportunity of ending points with extraordinary strokes—like making sliced drop-shots come back over the net, or turning what appeared to be enormous smashes into the softest of pats. The more important the point, the more excited he became when one of his tricks succeeded, sometimes bowing to his partner, tapping the net with his racket and nibbling at his shirt collar before continuing. I was far too young and nervous to fool about with cheeky style, and ruthlessly bludgeoned even the easiest of sitters, never daring to try clever things. As it was, Larsen's tricks badly scared me on a number of occasions.

"Don't you think, Art," I said to him once, tentatively, "that you should maybe just knock off the easy ones?"

"Don't be crazy, kid," he replied, "we have points to spare. There's no fun going about killing balls like a butcher!"

As far as I was concerned, I *never* had points to spare. With me, even at 5–1, forty love and my serve, I was still barrelling about, looking for things to kill.

The score in our doubles final crept along, dead even. At one set all and about 8–8, the match was balanced on a knife edge. I held my service from 15–40 down and Larsen muttered something about it "never being in doubt" as we changed ends, although he'd picked up an extraordinary half volley from somewhere between his legs at 40–30. We fought to deuce on Remy's service and eventually got a set point at our ad. Larsen's chipped return developed into a flurry of volleys out of which, to my infinite relief, came a mis-hit lob-volley, straight to Larsen. A sitter to end all sitters. With a typical display of Gallic despair, Remy and Bernard turned their backs, dropped their heads and walked towards the baseline. Larsen meanwhile, sensing an irresistible opportunity for a queer kill, began stalking the ball, waving his racket in circles like a sword and baring his teeth with a growling sound. Dumbstruck, I watched the ball bounce, watched him close in for a mighty smash, then suddenly check his swing and, with the end of the handle of his racket protruding beyond the heel of his hand, like a billiard cue, he tapped the ball over for a tiny dropshot winner.

The spectators leapt up with a roar of delight and Larsen waved his racket to them and turning to me said: "Scared you badly, eh kid? Thought I was going to foul it up, eh?" and laughed the happy laugh that he used when things were going according to plan.

On the way to the centre court that day, Tappy got stuck in the door—hung up, really, with no visible obstruction. He just stood there, nibbling his shirt collar and saying: "God damn, buddy, get me through this thing." I had to unhook him from nothing—and finally as I lifted his foot over some last invisible obstruction, he burst free and ran onto court calling to me: "Okay, kid, take it away, swing it wide, baby, and play the net on my service; we got beers waiting!"

He never trained, seldom practised, smoked a lot, drank beer, sat in damp clothes and cold winds after his matches, stayed up all night, slept in the dressing-rooms, and had difficulty changing into tennis gear—often getting stuck in his trousers, when half way up his legs and having to hobble all over the changing-room and chat to people about their matches before the trousers would slide up and fit him. Sometimes his sweater would jam, and he would walk onto the court with only one arm in a sleeve, and the rest of the sweater wound round his neck like a scarf. On the court he would either *have* to step on lines, or *not have* to step on them, and was able to cross over on only one side of the net, usually the umpire's side, where he could give the fellow a tap or two in passing. He had about six cameras, all expensive, including one movie one, and one day each week he would hang all of them around his neck and shoulders and go out taking millions of shots, sometimes peering through the view finder of one, while pressing the button of another.

"This is for colour, this for black and white slow film, this grainy, this fast, etc.," he would explain proudly. "You want me to take a colour shot of you? Sure. Just stand over there. That's the boy. Over there!"

The players loved him to the point of adoration and never missed watching his matches. In Rome he beat Andy Stern 6–0, 6–0, 5–7, 6–0 because he said, a set off him was a "good result" for Andy (which it was) but that he shouldn't "spoil him". Larsen verged on greatness and won many large tournaments, including Forest Hills. His accident was a tragedy and deprived tennis prematurely of one of the great individualists of the game.

In Rome that year, I also met an American called Wayne Van Voorhees, who used to travel the circuit and practise a great deal, but who could never quite get it all together. He was memorable, for me, because one day I happened to say to him:

"Hi Wayne, how are you playing?"

"Nearly great," was his reply. "I feel that my real good game is only about two weeks away!"

To this day I have carried about in my head the image of a player patiently doing the tennis circuits, year after year, with his best game about two weeks ahead of him! And yet, in a way, to get within two weeks of a good game isn't *that* bad. I know many players who haven't even got within *six months* of anything worthwhile!

Around 1955 tennis equipment was in short supply in many European countries. In fact, all sporting gear was hard to get and the selection very meagre. Nearly all the players, except the Americans, used Dunlop or Slazenger rackets. Endorsements were unheard-of. One got rackets and gut free and that was all. In Paris, the good players received Lacoste tennis shirts, and in London, nearly everyone got a few Fred Perry shirts and shorts; also Teddy Tinling's gear was flashed about while he was still making stuff for men. But, basically, good gear was in short supply and expensive if one had to buy it. Especially in countries like Spain, Germany, all the Iron Curtain places, and even Italy. Thus were born the traders of the circuit.

While all of us used to sell the odd item from time to time (I once ate good dinners for one full week in Barcelona from the proceeds of one Maxply), some players traded far more extensively. Like Don Candy, for instance. The lower region of his enormous travelling case was packed with the impedimenta of the game—new stuff, like coils of gut, frames, clothing, wristlets, and sometimes more sophisticated merchandise like golf balls, or Hong Kong cameras and watches. In various dressing-rooms throughout Europe, one would come upon him festooned with his wares, conducting brisk auctions:

"Gut!" he would say, peering about through his spectacles. "Gentleman, I give you gut. From India. Now how much am I offered for gut from India? Did I hear two thousand lire?" (Whether or not a bid was forthcoming, he always invented one to set things off.) "Of course I did. Good thinking." Here he would nod warmly to an unsuspecting onlooker. "Excepting, of course, that this Indian gut is worth much more. It's tough. *Tough*, you see," and he would loosen a strand and give it a mighty tug—"And when it *does* wear out, which doesn't happen very often (only once), you can cut it out of your racket and make very good curry with it!"

He would fix his onlookers with a penetrating gaze and say:

"You understand. Vous comprehend? *A good curry*!"

All sales were made for cash, and all bills were added to an ever-growing roll which was usually kept in his trouser pocket, except during matches when it was put into a well-guarded racket cover. This racket cover was even taken along to the shower cubicle after Donald's matches, so that the inside of the roll became dampish and occasionally had to be aired against mould.

"Don't give me one of your rotten bills," Mervyn Rose once said to him after a poker game. "Give the damp ones to Segal. He won't keep them long enough to spend them anyway!"

While Don ran what he regarded as a "sophisticated trading set-up", involving a "wide range of quality articles", other players were less imaginative. One Polish player ran a straightforward tennis ball racket between London and Barcelona where balls fetched a fortune apiece—at least a dollar. He had *two* mighty suitcases in which a thin layer of clothing concealed hundreds of balls, removed from their packing to take less space and to enable him to say that they were "for practising" if he was searched. He got away with it for months until one day the catch of a case flew open and tennis balls flooded the customs hall. Whistles were blown, policemen with dogs appeared, one of which picked up a ball between his teeth and dashed around the hall, further adding to the excitement. Chaos generally reigned. Above the hubbub could be heard the anguished cry, "They are for *practice*—they are for *practice*!" But it was no use.

Diary Notes: 1955

Alvarez talks to his racket. Sometimes when he's playing badly he throws it on the ground and walks round it in a circle, scolding it. His racket, it seems, is responsible for nearly all of his bad shots. I envy him his alibi. How about going into the dressing room after a match and saying. I *played great! My* racket *was awful!?*

The greatest single trading coup was said to have been performed by

William Alvarez of Colombia—William apparently crossed into Prague with a vast, new suitcase crammed with merchandise. In Prague he played an exhibition match, probably against Drobny, then sold all the merchandise, his own tennis clothing and rackets and, finally, even the suitcase. He then converted the cash into East German cameras and lenses and returned, triumphant, with only his loot and the clothes he stood up in.

Even Abie was a trader. He used to be a partner in a business which manufactured ladies' coats. Wherever we went, therefore, he kept an eye open for new ideas, fashions, or samples which might lead him to his fortune by a shorter route. In Oslo he came upon a store which sold furs; seal, mainly, but with a sprinkling of other varieties—reindeer, fox and other tundra creatures. Abie was ecstatic. He, in the professional voice he used to use when he spoke of objects of his trade, called them "pelts".

"Great pelts, Forbsey," he said to me. "From all those furry buggers they got runnin' about in the snow up there"—gesturing northwards. "Wait till my uncle gets a look at these!" he exulted. "He'll go even further out of his mind. Pussy hair! Wait till he sees this lot."

Abie's uncle, also a partner in the business, was obsessed with fur collars.

"Coats mit some pussy hair around the neck," he would insist to Abie. "Vomen are med about pussy hair. You listen to me! Give them a bit of pussy hair and they pay double mit-out asking vhy!"

So Abie purchased pelts and as was nearly always the case with his projects, he purchased too many. I was called in to assist with transportation.

"Just 'til we get to London, Forbsey," he said. "From there my shippers will handle them. Jesus. Who'd have ever thought that six dozen pelts were so many?"

We reached Paris, somehow, but in Paris, what with Heather's clothing purchases and Abie's further collection of coat samples, there was no way the skins would go into our cases. To make things worse, the other players were reluctant to assist us, muttering things about contamination and confiscation, and quarantine.

"We'll carry them," said Abie determinedly when it was time to leave. "We'll string 'em together and carry them round our necks and over our shoulders."

I viewed the mountain of fur with some trepidation, as we set to work tying the skins into bundles.

"Jesus," said Abie as we finally surveyed each other. "We're like

Trader Horn. One thing. If people ask us where we got them, we can say we traded 'em for beads."

To complete the picture, we were also both wearing fur hats which we had purchased in Oslo.

At Paris airport, the French averted their noses and gave us a wide berth. At London airport we approached customs like two people recently arrived from Alaska. Inevitably the customs men beckoned us over.

"All right, all right," said one. "What's all this, then?"

Abie paused and peered about with a worried look.

"Mush! Mush!" he said at last.

"Mush Mush?" repeated the startled customs man.

"That's right," said Abie, "Mush! Mush! We're trappers. We're lookin' for our team of dogs."

"Team of dogs, sir?" said the customs man.

"Yeah," said Abie. "If you see a team of dogs pulling something along, they're ours."

"Haven't seen no dogs, sir."

"That's very funny," said Abie. "We should have dogs." He peered about again, his eyes low, searching underneath things, saying "Mush Mush", and snapping his fingers.

"Lot of hides you have there sir," the customs man said to me.

"We traded them for beads," I said, a little weakly. I was never quite sure about using Abie's methods, especially when Her Majesty's Customs were involved.

"Beads, sir?" said the customs man.

"We're traders and trappers," said Abie, coming back into the attack.

"Well, I don't know about all this, sir," said the customs man finally. "You better come along with me."

By the time the explanations were made, Abie had promised Wimbledon tickets to half the customs staff, and the skins were examined and passed as clean.

"You got to come up with a story, Forbsey," Abie said to me as we caught a taxi. "Once you got a story, you got a chance. You just stand there bein' nervous and they lock you up for sure. So always have a story ready!"

Story or not, we were back in England and I was glad. It has always been a second home for me, has England—soft breakfasts, hot smells out of the underground stations and white-stemmed birch trees. London Transport. Camden Town, Notting Hill Gate, Clapham Junction, Hampstead Heath, Battersea, Barnes, Bexhill. I liked the sound, sight and smell of it all, and we were back, staying at the Cumberland Hotel, no less, and wondering, as Abie put it, "what the poor people were doing just then!"

5

My first real season on the red European clay had taught me a good many things, including a truer conception of the term "slave labour".

Having learnt my tennis in Johannesburg at an altitude of six thousand feet, I was a true net-rusher and had only a scanty selection of ground-shots, none of which was really well produced, although they were better than Abe Segal's, and on about a par with those of Mervyn Rose's. Rushing the net on a really slow Italian court while using the Pirelli balls of the early sixties was an eerie experience—like being in a movie, half of which was speeded-up while the other half was in slow motion. I was the speeded-up part. I would come barrelling up to the net, only to arrive there far too early, and have to hop about in a frenzy of suspense while my opponent (who often seemed to be Pietrangeli or Merlo) decided on which side to pass me. Desperate anticipatory decisions had to be made at the very last minute, resulting in huge lunges either right or left, staking one's all on guesswork. To make matters worse, even if one did happen to guess correctly, anything short of a miraculous volley simply put the ball back into play and recommenced the whole awful cycle. Lobs were too frightful to contemplate and had to be blanked out of one's mind to preserve sanity. I finally decided, irrevocably, and forever, that certain players could *never* be beaten by net-rushing on slow courts, and made a mental list of them: Santana, Pietrangeli, Merlo, Lundquist, Gardini, Larsen, Drobny, Flam were amongst the "total impossibilities" and then there was a longer list of "almost impossibilities" that included people like Jovanovic, Tiriac, Woodcock, Mulligan, Couder, Haillet, Darmon,

Ulrich, and so forth. There was also a secret list of people whom I privately considered "very hard" to beat, but about whom other players spoke contemptuously, with phrases like "can't break eggs" or "can't beat their grandmothers". These players gave me nasty scares if they cropped up anywhere near me in the draw and had to be treated with terrific determination. Of course, there was also a list of "impossibilities on any surface", but no one ever, on grass, was as frightful to contemplate as "the clay court impossibilities". Grass speeded-up everything considerably, and gave the groundstrokers less time to pause and consider.

Jaroslav Drobny was another master of the art of clay court play. Apart from his usual, fluent game, he had another style of play into which he used to lapse when the mood took him—a method which inflicted upon his opponent a sort of bend and stretch form of torture.

I have often made sceptical faces at reports of players actually using the dropshot-lob technique to *win matches*. Drobny could and did, not only against second-raters, but against players of the stature of Ken McGregor, or Vic Seixas, or people like that. He would start proceedings with soft, feathery little crosscourt dropshots off his left-handed backhand. These floated over to the right-handers forehand, where, if one was very nimble, and had prodigious acceleration, they could be dug out of the clay. Having dug them out, a tremendous application of brakes was necessary to escape fouling the net, and the only safe counter was a deep recovery back to Drobny's backhand. (His forehand was a superb and devilish shot which had to be avoided at all costs.) Having made the recovery and having applied brakes, one then had to hit reverse like a madman, and back-pedal to stretch for the down-the-line lob which one *knew* was coming, and which floated over one's left shoulder to pitch deep in the backhand corner. Again, this recovery shot had to be carefully hit back up the line to avoid the forehand. And so forth. I have seen Drobny subject steady players to miles of this kind of cross court roadwork, and on the occasions when I played him on clay, I managed to avoid the torment of it only by suicidal all-or-nothing smashes at the floating lobs. On grass, which is a much faster surface, one could obviate the dropshots altogether by barrelling up to net at every opportunity.

And talking of remarkable tennis players, what of Orlando Sirola; Why he never became an unbeatable player, I could never quite work out. He was a giant of a man, with huge hands and feet, yet with deft ball control and fine strokes. It was my private opinion that he was a little self-conscious about his size, for he never really seemed to exert himself. At

Wiesbaden, in 1955, he almost casually beat Tony Trabert in straight sets, and Trabert had a huge and rock-like game which could normally be cracked only with high explosive.

With Pietrangeli, Sirola formed the nucleus of an Italian Davis Cup team that twice reached the challenge round, losing to the dreaded Australians—always on grass. He could play tennis all right, could Sirola—there was no doubt about that! But the size of him! He used to hold three balls in a row in his hand and you couldn't see any of them; and he downed plates of spaghetti, literally at a gulp; and, it was said, he could release, at will, Italy's most monumental winds. Once, the story went on, when Drobny was co-opted to train the Italian team, it soon became apparent that he was a late riser. Usually, Davis Cup trainers are supposed to be up early and do brisk things before arousing their teams. Not Drobny. With him in charge of the Italians, the whole camp used to sleep 'til mid-morning, and then it was the team who would have to awaken Drobny.

One such morning, I was told, a member of the Italian entourage, with the accumulated gases of the previous night still unreleased, wandered into Drobny's room, stood beside his bed and let fly with wind like a thunderbolt which rattled the windows and left echoes to die away like thunder during a dry electric storm. Thereafter, Drobny made sure that he was the first to rise, in case the incident was repeated.

Pietrangeli, of course, played superbly. He came very close to being a genius at the *art* of playing tennis; and like Santana, he had that deftness of touch that made the average player look like a bricklayer or blacksmith. In addition, he was a world-class soccer player, and a follower of high society, and the possessor of supreme self-confidence. Nicki, for instance, was the first tennis player to learn to do the twist, an accomplishment extracted from the nightclubs of Rome. He often appeared escorting good-looking girls, and was seldom at a loss for words where ladies were concerned.

We sat at dinner one evening in the Kursaal at Baden-Baden, swapping stories and talking of tennis and suddenly I saw Nicki's eyes focus, and his face take on the rapt look of a bird dog that senses pheasant. A girl had entered—no ordinary girl, but a tall beauty, cascades of hair and the kind of liquid form that gets the blood up—movements under silk. She was on the arm of an older man, bashed-up, to be honest, but rich, with that honed and polished look as though he'd been set upon each day by a team of valets, and mechanically buffed up. On his fingers, rings flashed and he smelt of several layers of expensive smells—as though decades of lustrous interiors, expensive aftershave lotions and cigar smoke had coated him from head to toe.

"Beautiful lady," I said wistfully. "I wonder how that old guy copes."

"He's got his own private winch," said Abie brutally. "Gives it a wind and up she goes. Then he sticks it in splints. Then his butler lowers him into position and gives him a bounce to start him goin'."

"She needs," said Nicki, "a young tennis player."

"Can't be done," I said, thinking of the awful vengeance of the very rich.

"Can be done, Forbsey," said Nicki.

But I, for one, doubted the viability of this claim. Presently the couple got up to dance, moving to the languid German strings in a bored and distant way, the girl resting her chin on the top of his polished head. Nicki's plan of attack was brilliant in its simplicity. First he wrote the number of his room on the palm of his hand. Then he innocently asked Sandra Reynolds to dance, moving expertly into position behind the rich, old victim. With fine timing, he caught the eye of the girl, winked, then showed her the palm of his hand, at which she glanced with imperious eye and a toss of her head. Nicki returned with a gleam in his eye.

"The trap," he said incorrectly, "is struck."

"Sprung," I corrected him. "Ten Marks says it doesn't work."

In the dawn hours that followed, Nicki lay in wait, and at last came the quiet little knocking—tac, tac, tac. I envied Nicki his coup, and for a while afterwards, used to write my room number on the palm of my hand, just in case. But it was no good. The only girl I ever showed it to probably thought it was my 'phone number, because she never knocked on my door. In any case, such schemes must be spontaneous and always fit exactly into spontaneous situations. The ingenuity that tennis brings!

6

Manchester 1955

Manchester was the first big grass court event of the season. That was the year that Teddy Tinling got to play against Lew Hoad. In those days Teddy designed tennis gear for both men and women, and, whereas in the realms of women's wear he was undoubtedly top dog, he had tremendous competition in the men's section from Fred Perry. Both strove to get the best players to wear their clothes. Perry used the green laurel wreath as his emblem, while Teddy had a sort of red rose affair (which sometimes ran into the white of the shirt). That season, to Teddy's profound delight, Hoad had agreed to wear his clothing. And in Manchester, when Teddy arrived for the tournament, he found that if he was able to win the first round, he would play Hoad (the number one seed) in the second. He was, simultaneously, ecstatic and deeply anxious. His first round opponent was a venerable, but wily, English veteran, a Lord-someone-or-other, with whom, in those days, English tournaments abounded.

From experience in county matches, Teddy knew that he would be hard pressed to win.

"I have the better forehand, do you see," he said to me. "But Lords can be damned crafty. Play all day long, you see. Don't have to make dresses for a living."

Yet, to reach the second round, to walk onto the centre court ("I'm certain to be on centre, dear chap," he said to me, breathlessly) with

Hoad, the pair of them dressed all in white Tinling gear, was an opportunity "too horrible to contemplate missing". By the time Teddy's first round match was due on court, word had got round, and although it was scheduled for court seventeen or thereabouts, many players, including Hoad, went to watch. It was a typical Manchester day. Gusty wind, rain clouds hurrying across leaky skies, and British spectators opening and closing umbrellas and looking upwards at the clouds and saying: "Oh, it's bound to clear up after tea."

"Tinling to serve," the umpire called. "Players ready. Play!"

Teddy got the ball well and truly airborne with his left hand, while his right, attached to the handle of his racket, began the devious swing which would, if things went according to plan, bring the head of his racket round in a final sweep to meet the ball on its downward journey. From the very outset, it was clear that the elements were against him. The wind was whistling directly down court so that serving against it, Teddy found himself bent over backwards like a bow, while with it, he would be leaning far in court, struggling to keep his feet in contact with the fair territory behind the baseline while hitting the ball without falling flat on his face immediately afterwards.

With the business of serving over, play became very brisk. Teddy effectively brought his forehand to bear, directing his shots to his opponent's backhand. His opponent, meanwhile, had a good crosscourt backhand, which he employed to get the ball back to Teddy's backhand side, forcing him further and further over to the left. Extraordinary reverse crosscourt rallies developed.

"I spent more than half the match with my backside interfering with play on the court next door," said Teddy later.

Occasionally, diabolical down-the-line direction changes kept both players on tenterhooks. It was a desperate, even encounter.

At set and 4–5 Teddy found himself down 30–40, match point on his own service, with the wind behind him and still rising. To make matters even more difficult, just at that moment a series of terrific gusts shook the court, causing Teddy to miss with his first service. His toss-up had blown so far over to the northwest that he had nearly pulled a muscle getting within striking distance. He paused then, and stood scowling at the one remaining ball in his hand, waiting for the wind to abate. It wouldn't. A tense hush fell. His first toss-up with the second ball blew so far into the court that he walked after it and caught it. This happened three times. On the fourth attempt, Teddy, by now desperate, stepped into the court after the ball, gave it a desperate whack, and served an unlikely and extraordinary ace. Everyone, including Teddy himself, was dumbstruck. A footfault call seemed inevitable, but none came.

"Deuce," called the umpire.

"My dear fellow," said Teddy's opponent, "surely that was a —, I mean to say, surely that was a — well, you know, well, surely —? Mr Umpire, do you wish to call a footfault?"

"Deuce," repeated the umpire with a stoicism achieved only by umpires who are convinced that they are correct.

"Mr Umpire," persisted the peer, "do you wish to call a footfault?"

"Deuce," called the umpire.

"Mr Umpire—" began the peer again.

"I *do not* wish to call a footfault," said the umpire flatly. "The score is deuce."

"That's hardly cricket," cried the peer.

"My dear chap, I quite agree," said Teddy. "After what we've been through, I can't imagine a purer conclusion."

"It appeared to be a footfault."

"I can't comment because I was busy at the time," said Teddy. "Besides, I had nothing to do with the whole incident. In order to hit the ball, I was forced to station myself in the area in which I expected it to descend. An unfair advantage couldn't have been further from my intentions!"

In my opinion, this probably rates as one of the purest tennis arguments in history. Teddy won the match, and took the centre court amidst cheers the next afternoon to play Lew Hoad. Teddy lost 6–0, 6–0. Afterwards, in the dressing-room, he said excitedly:

"I was *mentally* prepared for the match, but mental ability alone was useless. To begin with, one needs to face oneself in the right direction. I spent half the match hitting backhands with my forehand grip, and forehands with my backhand grip. Lew was very polite. He'd call out to me: 'Are you ready, Teddy?', and I'd call back that I was, but I wasn't. Not once in the entire match was I ready!"

Teddy would have felt far less depressed had he realised just how many other players had gone through entire matches against Lew Hoad feeling as though they were "not quite ready"!

At Wimbledon, Teddy dresses himself up in the most superb clothes and moves about, glowing like a beacon. His afternoons are made up of successions of witticisms and pleasantries, while he admires his designs and the players who wear them. Karol Fageros was, in his words, "gold and Grecian", Maria Bueno, a magnificent "panther of a woman",

Heather Segal, "superbly tanned and straight off some glamorous island beach", Angela Buxton, "a vision of purity", Sandra Reynolds, "a pretty picture with a marvellous forehand", Virginia Wade, "a lithe brown animal" with "ice blue eyes".

Some of his remarks were less complimentary—"What little waist she has, dear boy," he said to me of one lady, "is high up under her armpits—almost above her bosom! Even I can't spirit up a garment to suit a shape like that. I mean to say. What *does* one do to a waist that is *above* a bust?" And again, "Too much backside. You have no idea of the vast quantity of fabric and effort spent in concealing an object so large. One can't even *see* the whole thing at once—have to conduct a sort of aerial survey, like making a map!"

He loved music, and especially the voice of Sinatra, from which he extracted some of the inspiration necessary to make fashion pieces out of the figures of tennis girls. Teddy once arrived at the tennis straight from his studio, flushed with the look of the true creator.

"My dear fellow," he said, "I have just had seventy-two straight inches of Sinatra!"

From my point of view, good girl tennis players presented the widest variety of different female forms and mechanisms. Amongst them you could find every conceivable kind. The great-looking ones like Karen Hantze, Heather Segal or Karol Fageros. The ones with style, like Maria Bueno or Virginia Wade. The soft female allure of Sandra Reynolds, Renee Schuurman and the Buding sisters, Ilsa and Edda. The puckish ones, the quiet ones, the ones with laughing faces. The ordinary ones who thought their thoughts and played their games. And the horses; which was the way in which Abie used to secretly refer to some of the coarser grained ones. "The way she walks, Forbsey," he would say out of the corner of his mouth, "you could hitch her up to a cart an' she'd pull it along."

Also, the girls perspired. Some gently, some copiously, while others simply sweated, sometimes giving off rare and amazing smells.

I have often heard men make controversial remarks like: "Tennis girls make bad lovers", or that their "lusts are vented on court". But I don't think that is true.

What is nearer the mark is that tennis girls make lovers of every imaginable category. The fact that many of them behave conservatively during tournaments, or before big matches, doesn't mean that when they put their minds to it, they're not capable of "rare and ecstatic flights".

Sometimes, late at night after the functions that the tournaments used to give, you may have come across one of the tennis girls. Soft with wine, on the little dancing floors you may have found them, and you could put your arms around them while the tenor saxophone murmured its breathy notes.

> "If you wrap your troubles in dreams
> and dream your troubles away."

Suddenly you found that they had tumbling hair and scented cheeks, and that they could whisper things, while in your mind's eye you saw the same hair damp and tied back, and the faces tensed up, waiting for the serve returns. You'd give a twisted little smile then, at the surprise of it, and so would they.

Afterwards you would tumble into taxi-cabs, and let the drivers take you through streets where the lamps made moving shadows, and you both knew that the moments were borrowed ones, pilfered from the mainstream of things, and that the next morning's sunlight might take them away.

In the dressing-rooms men players used sometimes to wax unromantic about the supposed sexual prowess of their female colleagues. Snatches of Australian accents used to drift about: "Bloody hell, wouldn't like to be trapped between a pair of legs like that. One squeeze, mate, and you'd be a goner. Lose everything. Just one little spasm of ecstasy and you'd be crying out for mercy! Great pair of legs. That is if you're thinking of climbing bloody Everest!" Or: "Old so and so. Fair old body she's got. Wonder what she'd be like in the middle of the night? You'd probably be just about ready to give it the old up and under when she'd do a backhand practice swing and lay you clean out!"

And yet as loose as the talk was, I can never remember anyone telling of actual *faits accomplis.* These remained private, and no one so much as asked of them or whispered a word, although, to a man, they all sneaked off from time to time to get their share.

In spite of the apparent hurdles discussed in dressing-room talk, many tennis friendships turned into romances and some into marriages. Lew and Jenny Hoad, Abe and Heather Segal, Tony and Joy Mottram, Pierre and Rosy Darmon, many others. Husband/wife mixed doubles teams, however, were potentially explosive relationships, and better left to lie, like sleeping dogs. Jenny and Lew used to have rare old quarrels. Lew's classic remark, however, came when Jenny was playing a singles at Bristol in England. Finding herself engaged in one of those eternal baseline duels that girls often get themselves into, she adopted tactics of running her opponent from one side of the court to the other and, in the process, covering a fair amount of territory herself. Lew was convinced that, while Jenny's opponent was a good "side to side" mover, she was a bad "forward and backward" mover. He edged nearer and nearer her court, getting more and more peeved, until Jenny came to the fence near him to retrieve a ball. This was Lew's chance.

"One short, one long, Fathead!" he growled out of the corner of his mouth.

No one is supposed to give advice during matches. Jenny looked wounded, but obeyed and started to win!

After Manchester, we played the tournament at Beckenham. Here I met up with Jack and Jean who had been playing in England while I had been travelling with the Davis Cup team on the Continent. Jean had been playing extraordinary tennis for her age, and was tipped by everyone as the next Maureen Connolly. She had a superb forehand, and almost magical control on her backhand, which, apart from being deep and accurate, could turn itself into a perfect lob, or deft dropshot with no visible change in style. But she had no service to speak of. Big serves were rare amongst the girls at that time. Louise Brough and Doris Hart had them, but nearly all the rest of the girls just used their services more or less to get the ball into play.

In her early teens Jean had already won many major South African tournaments. Now, in England, she seemed likely to repeat her performance. At Queens Club, the week after Beckenham, she beat three of the Wimbledon seeded players, Dorothy Knode, Heather Segal, and Darlene Hard, before losing to Louise Brough in the final.

Then the uproar broke out. At fifteen she was too young to play at Wimbledon and her entry was refused. The British press were very indignant. She was on all the front pages—pictures of her standing wistfully gazing up at the Wimbledon scoreboard, biting her lip. She has a beautiful puckish face—just the kind that the English like to take to their hearts, and make a cause of.

Jeannie. No one ever knew what went on in her mind while she played. She had such genius as a very young girl—and suddenly it went away. Overnight, almost, the magic left her. And yet her game appeared to be the same. One could hardly notice the difference, just that before she had won, and afterwards she struggled. I was sad and baffled, and though I questioned her sometimes, she always hid her answers behind her soft nature and deep, inscrutable composure.

"You must go on with your own game," she said once, "and not worry about me. I'll find my game again, some day." But she never really did.

Diary Notes: Summer 1955

Wimbledon again. Marvellous to get into the draw without the agony of qualifying. And into Dressing-room "A", no less! There, Bully, the old attendant, and his men are very polite and call one, "Mister":

"Your shirts are dry and ready, Mr Forbes. Got another game today, sir? You haven't? Then you won't be needing them, will you? Be ready for you in the morning. Good day, sir."

Everything about Wimbledon is like that. The most special tennis club in the world, yet for these two weeks the members and the officials treat us wonderfully well. Even old Colonel Legg, gruff as he is, usually goes out of his way to arrange your matches early if you have tickets for a London show. Basil Reay, David Mills, Peter Bridge and the others, all with that good-humoured, tolerant English reserve. Alert eyes that forever sum you up.

And the pressmen. Lance Tingay, Roy McKelvie, Rex Bellamy, Frank Rostron, et al. With their gentle British questions. Mostly about Jean. The whole family is there—even Jack. He is in the singles too. If Jean had been born a year earlier, there would have been three Forbeses in Wimbledon.

Today I beat Lennart Bergelin in the first round, on court two. He led two sets to love before it dawned on me what to do. From then on I gave him only backhands. No forehands. Directed my whole game to his backhand corner, like a ray-gun. When players have one favourite shot, it drives them mad if they never get the chance to use it. Of course he ran around a lot of backhands, but then left big holes on the forehand side, through which, every now and then, I slipped a fast, low one. It was very exciting to devise a scheme which could not be refuted. I feel ruthless and superior and more entitled to ask Bully to have my shoes cleaned for tomorrow.

9–7 in the fifth! Good God!

But in spite of that exuberant diary outburst, it was a tragic Wimbledon for us. On Tuesday, the day following my first round triumph, Jack met me with a telegram. Our father had died. Of all times, at *that* moment, when for him, things must have been so interesting and full of promise. It was the first sign of treachery on the part of the tennis gods. Sodde's Law, with a vengeance. We departed that evening on the long flight back, and I left Herbie Flam with a walkover into the third round. He came up to me at Wimbledon before we left and, in his Herbie Flamish way, shook my shoulders and said:

"Stay with it, kid. These things are sent to try us," and turned away.

We returned. There was nothing we could do except comfort my mother, and stand for a while beside the lonely grave at the foot of the mountain.

It was early July. Mid-winter and freezing. In winter the Karroo goes brown and crouches down against the cold like a wounded game-bird. I spent two months on the farm doing all the old familiar chores, and then moved back to Johannesburg and tennis. When Abie got back from Europe in October, he told me about the Wimbledon I'd missed.

He'd beaten Rex Hartwig with some savage serving and volleying and reached the quarter-finals, and there he had lost to Kurt Nielsen. Tony Trabert had won Wimbledon that year. He was unbelievably "All-American". Open faced, smiling wide, freckles and a brush-cut. And massive ground strokes that came at you like hurled medicine balls. He'd beaten Kurt Nielsen in the final.

"It was like a tank movin' against infantry, Forbsey," said Abie. "Trabert was drivin' the tank. Nielsen machine-gunned him, but the bullets just bounced off!"

So Trabert won Wimbledon that year, more easily than befits such achievements, although, apparently this did not occur to *him*.

Abie said that he just stood there, holding up the cup and, "grinning at everybody, like nothing was happenin'".

7

In 1956, travelling with Jean and Ian Vermaak, I played the European circuit from beginning to end. We began in Italy, at Naples, and wended our way toward England by way of Florence, Genoa, Rome, Wiesbaden, Barcelona and Paris.

The good matches that we had played the previous year, and the dramatic ending to our Wimbledon venture, had made an impression on the tennis people in Europe. Jean and I had become "wanted" players and our black-market price had risen considerably.

On the Continent, the term "Expenses" had been about for some time; perhaps because the Europeans had less feeling for the great tradition of amateurism than the British, who seemed totally preoccupied with the notion that tennis players should be gentlemen and should have no need whatsoever for money. Whatever the cause, the Europeans were far more inclined to flash a bit of the folding stuff at tennis players whom they felt might add weight to their tournaments. Jean and I were considered moderately weighty in 1956. We received, on average, about seventy-five dollars each week, as well as full board and lodging and a travel allowance. Each tournament would have a "settling up" day, on which the secretary got all shifty-eyed and furtive, took one into a small, windowless room, inserted his head into a wall-safe and withdrew a money box. Lips were licked while the box was unlocked, and fat, fresh slabs of money were withdrawn.

The Italians were by far the most impressive in these matters because they dealt in lire. These notes were enormous and the denominations staggering. In Rome one year, Jean and I were handed the entire earnings of our Italian tour in one monumental and pungent bundle of 10,000 lire notes, accompanied by the slyest Italian wink we'd ever seen.

We immediately retired to a quiet spot near court nine to sit down, count our spoils and divvy them up.

The big stars would get fat and secret bonuses from many of the tournaments. The handing over of these would also involve elaborate cloak-and-dagger methods. One day, while watching the doubles final of a major tournament from a little "standing room only" backwater, I found myself positioned close to the singles winner. I noticed the tournament secretary sidle up to him, and with the evil grin which seemed to be standard form in these transactions, I saw him slip a sheaf of bills into the player's trouser pocket. The player then slipped his own hand into the pocket and the pair of them stood there, with their eyes on the tennis though not seeing it.

Suddenly the player nudged the secretary, and muttered out of the corner of his mouth, "You're one short, you know!" Whereupon the secretary sheepishly took one more bill out of his back pocket and handed it over.

I remember thinking then that one of the talents that I would have to develop if ever I was to become a great star, was being able to count accurately sheafs of bills with my fingertips in the secrecy of my trouser pockets!

Diary Notes: Rome 1956

Strange, this tennis life. These cities, once in our history lessons, now at hand. Just narrow streets, hotels that smell of teak oil and the little restaurants that we get to know. And tennis courts. It's all just travelling, tennis and waiting. I practise for hours, and all the time in the back of my mind are the matches that I have to play, lying there, like sharp points of conflict in a sea of passing time.

Tomorrow I am to play Art Larsen; fourth match on court four. That means at about five, if the stupid Italian girls don't lob for hours in the matches before. So I have to pass time between now and then; work out when to practise, when to eat, how much to eat, what to eat and how to play Larsen on slow clay. So it's monotony and patience, building up to this one point of tension. T. S. Eliot wrote somewhere:

> *"The New Year waits, breathes, waits*
> *whispers in the darkness."*

Well, he often wrote of dry and cheerless things, and sometimes that's how the tennis circuit is.

You wait, breathe, wait.

And if it rains in the morning, you wait all over again.

Now I am surprised by this rather bitter little page. I have to think back really hard to recapture that particular mood of the tennis circuit. In retrospect, one is inclined to think only of the fun and laughter. But they were there, those anxious times, always there, following like shadows the players who really cared about winning.

In England that year, on grass, I beat Drobny at Surbiton and Lewis Hoad at Bristol—his second tournament loss that year. My game had formed itself into a very penetrating serve and volley thing, and I was beginning to feel the first inklings of some solid ground strokes.

Defeating Hoad was extraordinary. He was a majestic player, with a superb and flawless selection of strokes, and a court presence as arresting and fearless as that of a handsome god. Blond-headed, contemptuous of caution, nervousness or any mannerisms remotely connected with gamesmanship, meanness or tricky endeavour. I worshipped him then, as only the young can worship, and remember my defeat of him as something which took place in a dream—uneasy, ecstatic, triumphant—the bringing down of an idol. He was off form, I suppose, and I exceptionally sharp, but even the defeat of an off-form Hoad was enough to lift my heart.

To add to the triumph, Trevor Fancutt and I beat Hoad and Bob Howe in the doubles final. I travelled back to London for the Queens Club tournament, convinced that I had the grass court game totally and completely buttoned up.

At Queens Club, I met Rex Hartwig in the second round and he beat me 6–0, 6–0. As we shook hands afterwards, he apologised and mentioned that he'd played the whole match with his eyes closed. I was struck dumb. I'd never seen such a torrent of outright untouchable winners. Neither had Hartwig. We both ordered beer after the match and sat there, shaking our heads. Hartwig was like that. If, while playing him, he struck one of his purple patches, one was best advised quietly to leave the court and order tea. He once led Rosewall 6–0, 5–1 at Wimbledon before running out of purple.

At the Hurlingham garden party that year, Abie Segal avenged himself of all his humiliating losses at poker. Morally, rather than financially, but nonetheless a very sweet revenge.

Beside the courts at Hurlingham is a beautiful eighteen hole putting course, with very long, tricky holes which undulate and fall away in the best tradition of English courses. It was well known to Abie and me that both Rose and Woodcock were keen putters and never missed the opportunity for a game . . . and there always arose the little question of a wager.

On the preceding Saturday afternoon during the finals of the Queens Club tournament, whom should we meet watching the tennis, but Harold Henning, who was at the time with Gary Player, South Africa's brightest golfing star, and recognised as one of the world's best putters. We often ran across Harold in England, for he was one of our staunchest supporters and came to watch the tennis whenever he could. We in turn admired his golf and eagerly looked forward to his company, for he could always be relied upon for high spirits and a good many laughs. We took him in hand, fed him some strawberries, spent the afternoon with him and then discovered that he was staying at the same hotel as we were. That evening at dinner I saw a thinking look come over Abie's face and he asked suddenly:

"Harold, what are you doing tomorrow?"

"Why, nothing special," replied Harold.

"Then you're coming to Hurlingham with us," said Abie firmly, and all at once I began to understand.

We arrived at Hurlingham the next day, greatly at our ease, bringing with us a friend from South Africa who wore dark glasses. As luck would have it, who should we see standing upon the first tee of the little golf course, swinging their putters, also greatly at their ease, but Rose and Woodcock and George Worthington. We approached, whistling, with our hands in our pockets.

"Big Abie," called Rose. "We were just waiting for someone to come along to play with us. Now then; you're an expert putter . . ."

Abie stopped whistling. "Mervyn!" he cried happily. "Well now. We might just have a little game with you. There's Forbsey here, myself and this buddy of ours from back home, and three South Africans together are always unbeatable."

"Forbsey doesn't bet," said Rose contemptuously.

"Forbsey's changed," said Abie. "He's come into money. He'll take a little bit of a gamble if he knows he can't lose."

"Okay," said Rose, looking at me dubiously. "What do you say? Would a fiver a hole scare you guys?"

"Make it ten!" said Abie. "Forbsey says he's a great golfer."

We went off to get our putters while the three of them rubbed their hands and beamed at one another. I felt a twinge of apprehension, never having played golf for so large a sum and whispered to Harold, as we selected our clubs: "Do you think you can play that course, Harold?"

"Leave it to me," he whispered back. "I'm a guide on this stuff. This is *my* territory!"

Nonetheless, I looked at the selection of putters with certain trepidation. They were old, lead-headed affairs with warped wooden shafts and didn't seem to me to be at all the ideal equipment for precise competition. Especially with £180 at stake.

"Are you quite sure," I began again.

"Quite sure," said Harold firmly. "Only don't worry about the first hole or two. We must behave with finesse."

We selected three putters and returned to the first tee. Coins were spun and the appropriate noises made. Their team won the honour. All three of them were reasonable golfers and after several practice swings they made respectable putts, Rose's ball drawing to within three feet of the hole. Then it was our turn. Abie positioned himself with a great show of strength, but with his usual lack of forward planning, so that it was only after he had placed his ball and lined it up, that he realised that he was left-handed, where the putter was right-handed.

"This isn't goin' to be easy," he said.

"Nothing is ever easy, big Abie," said Woodcock.

There were no left-handed putters to be had so Abie re-positioned himself, made a few awkward passes and let fly with a stiff, two handed jab. His jab happened to centre the ball perfectly, and it was still gaining speed as it passed the hole, finishing well placed for a two on the third green, some forty yards further on.

"Too much gun," said Rose reflectively. "Try breathing out as you hit. And remember that the Thames is just over that last rise."

"Fuck me!" exclaimed Abie. "Those little balls really move along!"

Harold, putting next, was all feet and elbows. He seemed unable to swing the head of his putter past the toes of his shoes without fouling them. When it finally did get past, it gave the ball such a feeble tap that it moved only half way to the hole.

"Shortish," said Rose, "but a good line. Should be down in five."

I was next. I lined up determinedly, had a long look at the line which served only to confuse me further, kept my head down, and putted. The ball rambled down the fairway, curving over the little mounds and hillocks and finally finishing eighteen inches from the hole. Silence reigned.

"Jesus," said Abie at last. "For ten pounds Forbsey would walk on water."

I squared the hole with Rose, both of us getting twos. Then they won the second hole with a three, when I missed from two feet.

On the third tee, a remarkable change took place. Harold's feet and elbows suddenly began to sort themselves out. His stance looked good and his putter went back in a very orderly fashion, stroking the ball and following through and directing it towards the hole as though it had suddenly become equipped with a built-in guiding system. It lipped the cup, stopped, then changed its mind and gently disappeared into the hole.

"Dear me," said Rose.

Harold looked up with an apologetic smile, so twisted that the corner of his mouth moved in below his ear. He muttered something about "a very lucky shot" and stepped down.

"Okay, Forbsey," said Abie, "you can relax on this hole."

Harold then proceeded to produce a succession of so called "lucky shots", and by the time we had reached the ninth hole, we were four up.

It was then that I noticed our opponents looking at Harold more closely with suspicious little frowns. Suddenly Woodcock asked:

"What was it you said your name was?"

"Henning," came the reply. "Harold Henning."

There was silence for some time, then Woodcock nudged Abie and said with a rueful laugh which the others slowly joined, "You caught us, hey big Abie, you caught us, you beggar!" And we had to admit that he was right. The smile which appeared on big Abie's face, remained there for days!

Diary Notes: Summer 1956

We're at Wimbledon. Jeannie has drawn Louise Brough and will have to open Centre Court on Ladies Day. The papers are raving and Teddy Tinling has made her a special dress. Fate and her clever little tricks. It is last year that this should have happened, last year, not now! Then, she could have coped; had that extraordinary feel for the game. This year I am afraid for her. She says nothing, of course—tells me to worry about my match. But on Sunday she asked me whether I thought that we could find a grass court to practise on. So we found one at last— a ropey one at Hurlingham, but a grass court, nonetheless. Oh, she plays well enough. We practised for an hour at least, and she kept asking me for backhands. Said she had forgotten how she used to feel when she hit backhands. Didn't know exactly where they were going to bounce. She kept trying to get depth, then suddenly changed to her deft little dropshots. I can't tell whether she's doing them as well as before or not. Afterwards we bought cokes and sat on the grass beside the court, drinking them. Jean, as usual, folded up her legs and sat on them. Suddenly, she looked up at me with her calm eyes and said:

"I wish that I could remember why it was that I used to want so badly to play!"

It is my opinion that she used to want so badly to play in order to please her father. She never knew it, but that was why. Now he's gone and she still plays—but there's no one to play for. And she doesn't know it.

She walked on court that Tuesday afternoon, looking valiant and forlorn in her new dress; stood beside Louise Brough, curtseyed, then turned to face the battery of cameras. I watched from the players' stand with my heart in my mouth. It was one of those slippery, summer days, with a light wind blowing and the grass as fast as lightning. Even in the hit up, she seemed uneasy. Her forehand was solid enough, but not her backhand. She was late on the shot—just could not feel the ball on her racket. Kept on having to adjust at the last minute, and of course there was no time. Louise was superb as usual—graceful and careful, with all the time in the world, and tremendous power. Towered over everything.

I kept hoping for a miracle, but there weren't any. Jeannie simply couldn't cope. Louise pounded her backhand and pounced on the volleys—it was as it seemed, a woman playing a child. Suddenly the child hurt her knee. Sank down onto the grass with her leg bent under her and couldn't get up. Just sat there, with tears rolling down her cheeks. Louise came running round, and so did the St John's people, and eventually they helped her off the court, leaving it quiet and uneasy. Filled, it seemed, with a soft British compassion.

No fuss. A non-occasion. The last-minute cancelling of a wild idea by some unruly young tennis god. Later on in the afternoon, the doctors said that she had torn a ligament and would be out of tennis for quite a while.

I had a reasonably successful Wimbledon reaching the last sixteen and losing to Vic Seixas. Seixas was much better than he looked. He played all the time as though he was in the midst of a high wind, whirling about the court at great speed and making a wide variety of unlikely shots, many of them off the frame of his racket. But his serve and volley game was as sound as a bell, and he had the heart of a great fighter.

Diary Notes: Wimbledon 1956

Lew Hoad won. Everyone expected him to. Not that he is that much better than Ken Rosewall—just that he appears to be so much more of a winner. Scared of nothing.

In the players' enclosure everyone seemed satisfied as they watched him win the final point. Rosewall will win some other time.

So last night at Grosvenor House, Lew had to make the winner's speech and open the dancing with Shirley Fry. As he stood up for the speech there was a dead silence, and his deep Australian voice said:

"Ladies and gentlemen, you are lucky to have me here tonight." Then he paused for what seemed to be about half an hour.

"Because," he finally continued, "by seven o'clock my suit still hadn't come back from the clayners!"

There was a great sigh of laughter and relief.

I forget what he said after that, but it didn't really matter much.

After Wimbledon, Jean went home to recover from her knee injury, and I continued the tour with Ian Vermaak. Frinton again, then Le Touquet, Hamburg, Bad Neuhnahr and the Middle East. There was nothing in my life then, but tennis and travel.

Diary Notes: Flight to Hamburg 1956

The Forbes technique for opening conversations with Lufthansa Air Hostesses (variation adapted from the Segal handbook, 1955 edition).

Selected hostess. Regarded her carefully. Noted red hair and vast quantity of freckles. Devised strategy and waited. Delivered opening gambit as she bent to serve tea.

I: *You must have more than a million.*
She: *A million what?*
I: *Sommersprossen!* (Essentially that the German word for freckles is previously ascertained.)
She: *Much more* (and laughed).

I: *Do they cover everything?*

She: No, not everysing! Some sings cannot be covered wis sommersprossen!

Ice now virtually broken. Only formalities remain; name, telephone number etc.

Ursula Schultz. Common enough. Nothing hard about it. Wholesome female. Exotic women with the scents of savage flowers behind their ears never seem to cross my path.

Yes. Ursula has a Volkswagen and will show me Hamburg.

So today it was, amongst other things, the docks, all bombed and battered. The Zillertal. The Herbert Gasse. The Rieperbahn. Coffee on Der Grosse Freiheit. Das Eros Zentrum, and a boat trip on the Alster. Hamburg sunset. Then back to the Hotel Hauptbahnhof. Her sommersprossen are *virtually everywhere. German breasts like plover's eggs, that match the nose. Even the knees and knuckles—freckled all to hell.*

From a tennis point of view, I did not set the Thames alight in Hamburg. But in Bad Neuhnahr, the following week, I won the tournament and a gold Omega watch. And thereafter, Beirut, Istanbul and Athens passed in a welter of brilliant Mediterranean summer, dusty tennis courts, doubles victories and soft evenings with air like silk.

It was then that the Crossroad gods laid a trap for me. Such a small intersection, it seemed. I decided, after several long minutes of thought, that I badly needed a store of some kind for my old age—a sports store, preferably, all beautifully stocked up with rackets and sweat-suits, and one into which I could wander at about ten in the morning after my practice sessions. I would check the till, swing a few dumb-bells, advise customers about racket grips and attend to the lunchtime rush. The place would smell of varnish and linseed oil, and have a golf net in the back. There'd be a wall of tennis photographs, autographed to me by my friends.

"For Gordon, the best always. Hugh Stewart."

It would never, even remotely, I assured myself, interfere with my tennis career.

So I bought a partnership in an arms and ammunition business, which would, I fondly imagined, become my dream, only with a rack of guns and fishing tackle to add glamour.

I also got married; to a slender and sharply attractive girl called Valerie. She too played tennis—was in fact one of South Africa's most promising young players. She had marvellous legs, green eyes and a fiery temper, which when it came into contact with mine, produced quarrels of terrific velocity. In spite of these, we were very much in love. Before us lay stretched out an eternity of travelling and tennis, of friendship, love and fighting, with forward-planning on neither of our priority lists.

The purchase of the store took up all my savings, and even left me with a bank overdraft, which, I was assured by everyone, profits would soon wipe out. I signed and sealed the purchase, paid over the cash, and Valerie and I left almost at once for our permanent tennis honeymoon.

Just after Wimbledon that year, Jack called. The store, he said, was in trouble. On the verge of insolvency. I was to return at once, he suggested. That was all there was. There were no bangs, only some whimpers, and those, my own. Our freedom was at an end. Reality was at hand.

I will never forget those first months of our newly-acquired life. The alarm clock at six-forty-five, the little flat with its rented furniture, the sleepy eyes, the dry toast and weak tea, the bus rides. At seven-forty-five I would open the doors, check out the arms register, clear the till, and try to organise the stock. In the afternoons Jean took time off from university to do the typing and help me with the books. We'd sit and puzzle over cash books and ledgers and sundry creditors, and I would serve the customers under the watchful eye of my Polish partner, who scared the wits out of me by forever telling me that the bank, to which we *always* owed money, was about to close us down. It was boring, desperately boring and, simultaneously, tense. The nine-hour day.

Even the gun shop dished up a few laughs. I was desperate to maintain contact with my world, so I invested in a dozen or so racket frames which I hung up amongst the cartridge belts and hunting knives and which I occasionally sold to loyal friends. My colleague behind the counter was a genial and bookish man called Mr Saphra. He enjoyed demonstrating the various revolvers and automatic pistols which we stocked—especially the large calibre ones with their safety devices. One of the makes had no less than three devices, all of which had to be activated before the pistol would go off. During the Sharpeville riots when there was much panic and consternation, many people decided that guns should be urgently acquired. Our quiet, little shop was suddenly inundated with customers waving money. Bedlam was the order of the day and I was in a constant state of nerves, making sure that no one stole any stock. Help was recruited, including both my sisters, Jean and Jenny, a big German called Gerond and a Greek immigrant called Scoutarides, who used to amaze us all with his graphic demonstrations. Like all Greeks, he was fascinated by guns, excitement and the general idea of a revolution of any kind.

The minute the excitement began, he left the café that he owned next door to us in the care of his wife, and quite voluntarily came to assist us, selling only the biggest and most expensive of our range, and doubling the prices if he thought that he could get away with it. For the premiums they paid, customers would get instructions on fast draws from shoulder holsters, shooting from the hip and dropping to the ground should fire be returned. In the midst of blasts of instructions in mixed Greek and English, he would sometimes become so carried away that he would fall full length to the floor behind the counter, cautiously rising and presenting only his eyes to his startled clients before continuing with his sale. Detailed descriptions of what bullets did to the insides of people kept us (and the customers) permanently agog. Often he sold throwing knives to people as accessories, in case their guns jammed or ran out of ammunition in the face of hordes of oncoming savages. For country-dwellers and farmers, rifles, shotguns *and* pistols were recommended and often he would discuss the correct length of barrel to be left, in case a customer decided to have his shot gun "sawed off".

"Shotterguns with-a short barrel make one-a hell-of-a-mess," I heard him telling someone. "I-a had-a uncle in-a Athens, who had-a such-a shottergun. One-a day he clean-a the gun and she-a goes pouff! Blew-a hole like that (he held his arms in a big circle) in-a the new ice box of my auntie." He paused and chuckled to himself. "Was she-a mad. Oh a-boy! She-a empty the-a bucket of slops on-a his head and-a she shouts at him, 'I spit-a on your shottergun!'" He paused, beaming, and then went on: "This-a gun, if-a you cut-a the barrel, will blow-a such a hole in-a an ice box!" He was an enthusiastic salesman, was Scoutarides.

Of course, Mr Saphra maintained that it was Scoutarides who had left the cartridge in the gun and was thus responsible for the disaster. Scoutarides denied this to the end. At any rate, *someone* had left the gun loaded. Of that, there was no doubt. Mr Saphra, proudly demonstrating the safety device of a .45 calibre ex-army U.S. Colt Automatic, had got through two of them without incident, and was explaining the third.

"And only then," he told the fascinated customer, "when those two are in the 'fire' position and the palm of the hand depresses this lever on the butt, only then will the pistol actually fire," and pointing the gun upwards, he demonstrated by pulling the trigger.

Colt .45's make terrific bangs, especially in small shops. This one was no exception. The explosion that followed shook the whole building and hammered our eardrums with a hot blast of cordite. Scoutarides hurled himself to the floor with a mighty shout, convinced that revolution was finally at hand. Customers screamed, and I turned with my heart in my mouth in time to see my racket frames literally leap into the air and fragment, as the huge bullet neatly tore the shoulders out of six of them, bounced off the concrete ceiling, holed several cans of gun oil, swept away a row of golf balls, and finally came to rest on the office tea tray—with a clatter of broken china. A dead silence ensued. Mr Saphra stood like a statue, the smoking Colt held aloft.

"Bloody thing was loaded!" he said at last, quite unnecessarily.

"Of course, loaded!" said Scoutarides from the floor behind the counter. "Otherwise she never go pouff!"

He raised himself gingerly and began plugging the leaking oil cans with paper, muttering "Damn-bloody-a-dangerous," over and over. We all agreed, but Mr Saphra was furious and felt he had been betrayed.

I remembered very little of those years, and neglected to keep a diary. Not that there was much to record. I kept up my tennis as best I could, playing week-end tournaments in Johannesburg and during the Christmas holiday, the windy South African coastal circuit.

In 1958, Gavin Duncan was born, blue-eyed, unexpected, and much adored, and his arrival at that particular point in time made further international tennis travels seem even more remote.

But in 1959 I won the South African title for the first time, in spite of my precarious position in the arms trade, I was persuaded to travel to Europe with the Davis Cup team again. It was a short, uneasy little tour, during which my Polish partner, who hated tennis, refused to pay my salary, so that I spent most of my time in a state of tension, worried about saving money to send home to my wife and baby son. As team members, we received eight dollars a day, half of which I religiously saved up for this purpose. I was tentative and moody, and hardly played a worthwhile tennis match in two months. In the Davis Cup Competition that year we lost to the Italian team in Florence. Pietrangeli and Sirola again. I have hardly any recollection of that uneasy trip, save for a few disjointed diary entries in an old black note-book. One in particular brings back particularly sharp memories.

Diary Notes: Summer 1959

Florence. Super old city. No! Painting of a city! Full of sculptures. The classical music festival is on and the Modern Jazz Quartet is playing several concerts! Unbelievable luck! The first time that a jazz group has ever been this honoured. The Florentine society people are very serious about their festival—attended by the great orchestras of Europe. Everyone in black ties, with opera glasses, moving about like figures in Lautrec paintings. Abie and I have to hire suits to go. Those, and the tickets, cost a fortune but Abie still has his shippers! He's always paying bills for me, then saying, "Don't worry about it, Forbsey, it's only money!" Which enables me to hire a dinner suit, go to see the MJQ and still send home twenty-five dollars a week.

We arrive, all spruced up and mingle with the Lautrec figures. They're all a little haughty and self-conscious about being at a jazz concert. Not quite the thing. But curious—damned curious. Wouldn't miss it for worlds. Half hoping for a debacle, or at the least, something low-brow! They tuck the programmes under their chins and suck their teeth. Last night it was Ivry Gitlis and Sibelius, tonight, Milt Jackson!

Abie and I take our seats. Even Abie is silenced by this lofty, reverent place. My heart is pounding away. The Modern Jazz Quartet! I can hardly believe it. Know all their recordings off by heart! On the stage is nothing but a white grand piano, a set of shining drums and the vibra-harp.

"Good God, Forbsey," says Abie. "They're gonna need more than just four people to fill this place with sounds!"

He's right. Nothing happens for ten minutes or more—just elegant, Italian Counts and things, filling up the seats. We are absolutely in the best place—"If we're goin', Forbsey, we're goin' first class," says Abie.

Jazz has fascinated me for years. On the farm gramophone we had played Artie Shaw's "Deep Purple" over and over, and the Benny Goodman quartet recordings. Then George Shearing, Errol Garner and the big, fat tenor saxophone sounds: Coleman Hawkins and Lester Young. Finally, the exquisite agonies of Charlie Parker.

In Paris that year, I'd abandoned the *Place Pigalle* and spent three dollars each night to sit in *The Blue Note* on the Rue d'Artois, listening to Bud Powell and Kenny Clark. Powell in his twilight world, stumbling over his unbelievable chords, and once, ending a mammoth performance of *Cherokee*, by doing a double-handed run to the top of the keyboard and then, just keeping going, falling slowly off the stool onto his side and just lying there! Torben Ulrich had introduced me to Gerry Mulligan one night at *The Blue Note*. It was a brave world, that modern jazz world of the late fifties!

Diary Notes: Summer 1959

At eight, exactly, the quartet emerge. John Lewis in black, the others in white tuxedos, calm and aloof. Percy Heath is smaller than his bass. They take their places and sit motionless. Dead silence. Not a single sound. John Lewis' first chord comes out of the white piano like a solid living thing, all angles, like a sculpture. It's "Django"—absolutely simple—each sound separate in these acoustics. Cascades of notes from Jackson's vibes; Heath's bass, plunging and lifting against the metal cymbals. Webs of sound, spun together, lifting off the stage like mobiles, balanced on silence. The audience are caught and held, half-way between surprise and disbelief. The theme is stated and suddenly the true rhythm emerges, insidiously, anchored by the bass and drummer's brush work. The sly jazz phrases of Milt Jackson. Lewis' stately piano, walking along behind.

At last the tune ends. The last notes of the vibes hang quivering, and then again, the eerie silence—which is suddenly, violently, torn to pieces by a wild applause as the black-tied people jump up.

It is one o'clock before we leave, walking softly. For once even Abie is quiet. "Damn Forbsey, I mean, how do they do it, those guys?"

In 1961, when the Sharpeville riots came, we sold out our entire stock of firearms in less than a month. I seized the opportunity to sell my share of the company back to my Polish partner and, with a boundless sigh of relief, celebrated my return to tennis by winning the South African open title for the second time.

8

My only reservation about envying the lives of the rich, young tennis professionals of today, is the fact that very few of them will ever know what it is like to be locked into an eight to five desk job. Very few of them, therefore, will ever realise how extraordinarily fortunate they are to be able to follow the lifestyle allotted to them by the Destiny Gods. Like being the son of someone very rich, and then trying to imagine what it is like to feel the shock of realising that there is not enough money to pay the rent!

In 1962, there was still no real money to be made out of tennis. Nonetheless, I returned to the freedom of the circuits with utmost eagerness. With a selection of well-timed sideways movements, a few dollars could be squeezed out of the amateur officials, and the summer sunlight was available to everyone.

To add to the excitement, Abie and I were back on the Davis Cup Team. The third member was a young newcomer, Cliff Drysdale. For some time he had been alarming us with some very mature tennis; then he suddenly accepted a scholarship to Lamar Tech. in Texas where he studied for about a year. We met him at Geneva airport, as our first match that year was against the Swiss team, to be played in Lausanne.

Diary Notes: 1962

At Geneva airport, we wait for Drysdale, whose plane gets in two hours after ours. Abie is on the move again and very excited. Beers are ordered while we wait.

"And thank Christ we're playin' the Swiss," he is saying to me. "Even you're not goin' to get nervous playin' the Swiss. Glorious bloody holiday. Those Swiss can't play for sour nuts. Too many mountains. They're so used to slopes that when you give them a flat surface they can't stand up straight. Come in to net leanin' over to the side! All you have to do is pass them down the side they're leanin' away from!"

Abie hasn't changed. If anything, he's got worse. At his insistence, we are both wearing jackets and ties.

"You dress like a peasant, you get treated like a peasant," he says. Looks in the mirror, straightens his tie, gives himself a smile and says: "Jesus! I wonder what the poor people are doin' today?"

Cliff's plane eventually arrives. The swing doors open and there he is.

"Holy Hell," says Abie, "look at Drysdale!"

There's no doubt about it. To put it very mildly, he looks dishevelled. Lamar Tech. tee shirt, crumpled mackintosh, cotton slacks soiled with several layers of airplane cooking. Two rackets, wrapped in a towel, a split open suitcase out of which more towels are oozing.

"All he's got is towels and a raincoat," Abie mutters.

Cliffie approaches with a wide smile. He has extraordinarily good looks.

"You gentlemen look eminently affluent," he says. "I assume that we're on the same team!"

"He assumes we're on the same team," says Abie. "Idiot! Let's get out of here before they stick you in quarantine!"

The drive to Lausanne is superb—a soft, brilliant, spring afternoon. Cliff sits in the back, all young and dirty, paying no attention to Abie's ravings about "showin' a bit of class". He has, he informs us, only one jacket and no ties. Tonight in our room Abie informed me that he thought it was going to be "one hell of a problem gettin' Drysdale into some kind of shape"

The fact that before the week was out he'd spat a mouthful of water onto Budge Patty's shoes, added weight to Abie's opinion. Budge had been appointed referee for our match, as he was living in Lausanne at the time. I, personally, was delighted by this news, as he had been one of my early heroes, and I had secretly admired the marvellously debonair way in which he dressed, spoke and generally presented himself. Budge had also been one of the game's great opportunists, with the almost occult ability to produce winning shots exactly when they were most urgently needed. He had an excellent service and forehand and perhaps the best forehand volley of all time, but the rest of his game was unimpressive, with some unorthodox goings-on on the backhand side. Nonetheless, he'd won the French Championships on clay and the same year beaten Frank Sedgman to win Wimbledon, and he seemed to me to be a very illustrious referee to have for our match against the Swiss.

To this day I am unsure of the exact duties of a Davis Cup referee. They have to be of neutral nationality and they sit in a chair at the foot of the umpire's stand, looking grave and wise. I have also always suspected that they are all-powerful and able to overrule, as a last resort, any decisions made by the umpire or linesmen. However, in none of the Davis Cup matches I've played, have they ever overruled anything; merely agreed with everybody after brief consultation, before returning to their seats to look wise *again*.

Against the Swiss nothing controversial happened. We won quite comfortably and Claude Lister decided to let Cliff play the final singles to gain experience. This he proceeded to do with great skill and Abie and I realised that he was soon to be our best singles player. During change overs, between games, Cliff had developed the American habit of rinsing his mouth out with water, then spitting it out onto the court. This he proceeded to do, but added a technique of his own which comprised a tremendous gargling exercise, followed by head-shaking and an enthusiastic expectoration of fair velocity and erratic direction. It was one of those blasts that drenched Budge Patty's Guccis. Budge hardly reacted really, just looked pained and tucked his feet under his chair, as though it didn't surprise him in the least that any player as carelessly got up as Cliff would spit on his shoes. But it annoyed me to have one of my heroes spat on by our junior member. Abie was also displeased.

"Jesus, Forbsey," he said to me. "We're goin' to have to explain to Drysdale that he is not in a friggin' American university any more. I mean, we're gonna have to spend a week or two civilizin' him."

Not that Abie himself didn't have a little habit of his own which involved irresponsible spitting. He used, on occasion, to make rumbling noises deep down in his throat, then arrange his face into a thoughtful look before suddenly turning to one side and emitting a blast of something that resembled a dubious oyster at the foot of some tree or shrub.

"At least I don't do it on people's shoes," he said cryptically when I reminded him. Then we both began to shake with laughter, remembering the time when we'd driven from London to Bournemouth in a little Mini Austin which Abie had hired. Sitting beside Abie on the front seat, I'd detected the familiar rumbling sounds and then seen him surreptitiously unroll the window. I knew that a blast was imminent, and was thankful that he'd remembered to roll down the window. At the precise moment of expulsion, a man in an open red sports car had shot past him without hooting. Abie's oyster must have got him fair and square, because he swerved wildly before righting himself and turning to alternately wipe his eye and shake his fist at us.

The week in Switzerland was a particularly happy one for me. I'd escaped the entombing atmosphere of my arms shop and been granted a week of mild tennis in one of the world's most civilised spots. Moreover, I was equipped with a new and special pair of Zeiss sports-framed spectacles which at long last produced for me a clear and sharply-etched tennis ball. Life was bright again.

Gavin Duncan was safely ensconced with Jack on the old farm, and I was to meet Valerie in Paris.

I was twenty-eight years old.

Diary Notes: 1962

Rome again. The Foro Italico. Nothing here has changed. Emerson singing in the shower, Woodcock practising serves, Pietrangeli moving about in a very superior attitude. He is playing beautifully and has invented a new method of helping linesmen make favourable decisions on close calls. This consists of placing a ball on the spot where he would like the linesman to believe the ball has bounced. Here in Rome, where he is regarded as at least a god, the method invariably works to perfection. Two new Yugoslavs on the scene called Jovanovic and Pilic. Jovanovic is dark and stocky and Pilic tall and distinguished-looking in a cruel sort of way. Also a sprinkling of Russians and Rumanians. Sombre fellows, with heavily-loaded minds—filled, no doubt, with dark red thoughts. Who knows what goes on behind that iron curtain of theirs?

I had begun writing again—tennis articles, mainly for Gladys Heldman, who was then in the process of building her magazine, *World Tennis*, into a super publication. Tennis articles are generally boring and difficult to write, so that, in an attempt to brighten them up, I used to search for unusual ways to describe tennis wins and losses.

My players used to "get flattened", "razed to the ground", "hammered into the turf", "ground to powder", "ravaged", "pummelled", "badly mauled", and sometimes "put to the sword", or even "fire and the sword". Sometimes nautical terms like "swamped", "sent to the bottom", "scuttled", or "harpooned" would creep in. When Ray Moore beat Emerson in Johannesburg, he "holed him below the waterline", and Emerson "floundered" at five three in the final.

In the same tournament, Christine Truman (later Janes) "by being British and remaining at her post under fire", held Maria Bueno to three sets, and one would expect to find written at the foot of her score sheet the words—"killed in action". In another tournament, Christine had "waded indomitably toward the title, waist deep in volleys". This was after Maria had "gunned down" all comers on the way to the final, not bothering to remove "the bodies of her opponents" from the court.

In one of my articles a young player got "crapped upon from a dizzy height", but Gladys Heldman cut it out. She was a callous cutter-outer, was Gladys. Generally speaking, when writing her articles one had to be brief and do away with players swiftly and mercilessly. She disliked "fine writing" and ruthlessly carved her way to what she considered to be the crux of the matter. Detailed stories were often stillborn in one's mind—like the time Warren Woodcock played Jovanovic in Rome, that year.

All the players went to watch, of course, and as the match lasted all afternoon, one could watch it in a sort of serialised form; besides which, it was during one of the periods when Woody's service was acting up, making it, in his own mild words, "very trying to get the ball into play". At these times, it was as though a spanner of particularly evil character had got into the works of his service—works which, at the best of times, appeared to contain at least one or even two spanners. Things took place completely at random and it became, for Woody, a matter of intense effort and concentration to get the ball aloft and have it rendezvous with his racket, the head of which arrived at contact point only after a tortuous journey through an unexplored region behind his back.

"Sometimes," Woody explained to me philosophically, "I have to throw the ball up *first* and *then* start my swing, and at other times, I have to start my swing *first* and *then* throw the ball up. And the worst of it is, I don't know when or why!"

His service remained, apparently, a permanent mystery. At the time of the Jovanovic match, a further complication had crept in. Suddenly, for no apparent reason, the throat of his racket had begun to make contact with the back of his head—not on every swing, but often enough to create tension.

"It's very disturbing," he said in his grave, serious way, "not to know when you're going to get hit from behind. It makes it very dangerous to go for an ace!"

"An ace!" Abie Segal rejoined with derision. "What's an ace, Woody?"

"I sometimes serve aces, Abie," said Woodcock with dignity.

"Yes, aces," said Abie, "your opponents wait so long for the ball to arrive that they think the point must be over and so they cross over! Then the ball arrives and passes them, and you think you've served an ace!"

Boro Jovanovic, Woodcock's opponent, also had a poor service—one which used to remind me of someone digging an overhead trench—if that were possible. Both players, therefore, relied upon steadiness, guile and determination to carry them through. The result was a sort of prolonged trench warfare. Both were expert gamesmen, both determined to win, both willing to stop at nothing. Inevitably, the match went on and on. Single points lasted for several minutes. The court surface, red and heavy, became tilled, ploughed up, until one felt that potatoes could easily be put in. All close line calls were disputed on principle and every conceivable trick was used. A steady, insidious tension built up, softened by a strange dignity—the granting of each to the other a grudging status.

In Rome, the courts are laid out in pairs and between matches, courts are dragged, then drenched with hoses similar to those used by firemen. At 10–9 in the fourth set, with Woodcock serving for the set, the match on the court adjacent to that on which Woodcock and Jovanovic were playing, ended. In a flash, the groundsmen went into action unreeling their hoses and turning on the water at full blast. Tremendous tongues of spray and spume leapt about the court. Simultaneous to this, Woodcock commenced his service game, so intent upon getting the ball into play without hitting himself on the head that he hardly noticed the flying spray on the court beside him, simply treating it as another distraction to be endured and overcome. Jovanovich, high and dry at this end, said nothing, merely playing out the points, probably wondering at Woodcock battling the elements so stoically. The game ended dramatically when at Jovanovic's advantage, a carelessly directed tongue of spray drifted across on the wind and Woodcock, having missed his first service, tossed the second into the mist, hit himself on the head and served a double which bounced on his own side of the net before it got to Jovanovic.

The umpire called the score: 10-all, Jovanovic to serve. Woodcock looked very grave. Jovanovic gathered himself together and got ready. As he took the balls to serve, the groundsmen began to hose his end of the adjacent court. Jovanovic paused in mid-swing, caught the ball and appealed to the umpire.

"Tell them," he said, "not to hose this end of the court while I serve."

The umpire obeyed and the groundsmen obediently turned off the water. Woodcock was thunderstruck.

"Boro!" he said, "you *have* to let them hose the court!"

"Why?" asked Jovanovic.

"They hosed when I served," said Woodcock.

"I can't serve with water flying," said Jovanovic.

"I had to serve with water flying," said Woodcock.

"Maybe you like water," said Jovanovic—"I can't play with water."

"You've got to try," said Woodcock. "If there was water for me, there has to be water for you!"

He walked up to the umpire in his loping way and tapped the chair with his racket.

"Mr Umpire," he said, "make them spray while Jovanovic serves!"

The umpire gave a start and conducted a brisk conversation with himself in a clatter of Italian. Then he turned to Woodcock and said in a formal voice:

"They spray-a next-a game, after the-a service of Jovanovic."

"But then," said Woodcock in a pained voice—"they'll be spraying on my side again!"

"Then-a," said the umpire laconically, "we talk-a again!"

With a wounded look, Woodcock returned to his post. The game was once more on.

After Rome, we made a little excursion into Germany to play at Dusseldorf and Cologne. Whereas in Rome the atmosphere had been spaghetti, stucco, caramel custard and pandemonium, Germany was the land of the spiced sausage, new and orderly tennis clubs, dark coffee, kirschkuchen, and the smell of brown cigars. In Cologne, the club was on the Rhine. Barges moving and the smell of river water on the wind. German waitress girls with puffed sleeves and bodices spilling out little glimpses of breast. All smiles. We would sit back in our chairs, sip apfelsaft and watch the river, and I could lazily jot down little paragraphs about the things that amused:

Diary Notes: Summer 1962

Warren Woody has equipped himself with a lovely new wife called Dagne, out of whose womb, not very long ago, there appeared a baby. Dagne. Scandinavian, and the image of Woodcock himself. I have a strong theory that self-centred people, such as tennis players, often choose mates that look the same as they do. So Woodcock now has an entourage. Dagne seems to be exactly as dreamy as Woodcock. Occasionally they even temporarily mislay the baby, each thinking the other has it. Then there's a great hue and cry, with all the other players forming a search party to look for "Woody's baby". When it has been found, it often lies in its carriage next to Woodcock while he plays poker. Sometimes he shows it his cards and discusses them with it, in whispers, with his lips right next to its ear. It lies there, quite good, sucking its fingers and staring up at full houses and straights and wild aces. The bottom end of the carriage is filled with bottles of various kinds, and all players have instructions that if they come across the baby being restless, they are to insert a bottle.

Yesterday, Abie and I arrived at the courts at ten o'clock in the morning, all set for a good, solid work-out. About two and a half hours, Abie said. After about half an hour, Woodcock meandered into the grounds, pushing the baby in its carriage. He arrived at our courtside, watched us for a few minutes, and then said:

"Abie, would you watch the baby for a while?"

Abie, who was doing streams of backhand volleys said "Sure", without losing concentration. Woodcock wandered away. After about half an hour, the carriage began to wobble and make funny noises. Abie, poised for a serve, stopped.

"What's happening to Woody's pram?" he asked.

"Probably the baby," I said.

"And where the hell is Woody?" asked Abie.

Woody wasn't about. We stopped playing and, approaching the pram cautiously, peered inside. The baby was eating its foot. It took one look at Abie and emitted a terrifying bellow. I grabbed a bottle from the selection at hand, and inserted the tip. Immediately the bellowing stopped, and vigorous sucking ensued.

"Holy Hell," said Abie shakily. "I didn't realise you could just plug up a baby like that! God damn! Just look at that kid go! Like a vacuum cleaner!"

He paused and looked about nervously.

"Now, where the hell is Woody? I mean, a man just can't go about leavin' babies lyin' around where people are tryin' to practise!"

I looked at my watch. It was eleven-thirty in the morning. At three, a taxi drove up and Woody and Dagne alighted. By then the baby had done everything even remotely conceivable for someone so small: inexorably drained all the bottles; bawled powerfully for half an hour. Done one large motion and several small ones and then, when the napkin supply was exhausted, wet Abie's tennis shorts: and at last, exhausted, it had fallen fast asleep about ten minutes before the arrival of the Woodcocks.

Woody walked up to the pram, looked down at the sleeping baby and beamed at us.

"Hasn't woken up yet, I see," he said.

Abie turned to look at me, very slowly.

"Forbsey," he said, "say something to Woody."

"It has been awake," I said, brilliantly.

"You're sure it's actually been awake?" asked Woody.

Abie looked at me.

"He wants to know if we're sure the baby has been awake," he said.

"It wet Abie," I said.

"Dagne," said Woodcock, turning to his wife. "Did you hear that? Forbsey says that the baby wet Abie."

"You mean wet him?" said Dagne.

"That's right," said Abie. "Wet me."

"It drinks anything you give it and converts it into widdle," I explained.

Abie had a wild look about him, which reminded me of an unexploded bomb.

"I can't stand it," he said to me, still in a most genial way. "I'm dreamin'. I've got to be. Forbsey, listen. 'Phone down to room service an' order breakfast. That way I'll wake up and know I'm dreamin'."

"It's the afternoon," I said.

"Where in the hell have you been?" Abie asked Woodcock.

"Having lunch with Dagne," said Woody.

Spontaneous combustion is a rare phenomenon, taking place only when selected ingredients are present simultaneously in exactly the right proportions. For Abie, conditions were near-perfect. His particular explosion, when it occurred, reminded me of one of those fireworks which can't quite decide when to go off—fizzling, crackling and hopping about and emitting odd blasts of varying intensity. Phrases like "driven moggy", "chokin' to death", "ran clean outa milk", "bloody bottles don't work", "changin' nappies full of crap", kept popping out of his mouth, while he walked up and down swinging his racket.

"You can't be well," he said to Woodcock, several times. "You are a sick man. We gotta call a doctor. A specialist, maybe—"

His explosion lasted all of ten minutes before, with a final blast of: "Fuck you, Woody!" he turned and made for the clubhouse. I followed. We had a men's doubles at four. As I walked away I heard Woody say to Dagne:

"That's very surprising. Heather assured me that Abie loves children!"

After Germany came our Davis Cup tie against Rumania—an event which, whenever I considered it, caused a certain hollow feeling in the pit of my stomach. Although Ilie Nastase was not yet on the scene, Ion Tiriac was mean and hungry and hardly ever missed a ball. To make matters worse, we had no idea at all about the strength of the rest of the Rumanian team. For all we knew, they may have cooked up some diabolical plot to overthrow us.

Abie viewed the whole expedition with immense scepticism. He'd read up bits about the tyranny of communism, the Russian secret police, Siberia, the Salt Mines, the NKVD and Iron Curtain, in some of his magazines and scowled darkly whenever the trip was discussed.

"That guy Marx," he said to me while we were changing, "couldn't have been for real. They should have locked him up. I tell you, Forbsey, we're gonna have to keep our heads screwed bloody well on. It's not impossible that the whole lot of us disappear for good. What's one tennis team, specially South Africans, to that bunch of fanatics; *nothin'*. Absolutely nothin'!"

And he did up his tennis shoes with a jerk that half lifted him off his seat.

We embarked at Zurich on a grey, Russian jet with droopy wings that immediately set Abie off again.

"Bloody thing's unstable, Forbsey," he said as we climbed the steps. "They don't care too much about safety, these commies—they make these things real tough to fly, then they sell them to the Chinese."

I asked Abie where he got his information from, to which he replied cryptically: "You don't read the right books, buddy!"

At Bucharest airport they took our passports away and told us that they would be returned on our departure. This actually *did* make me uneasy. Abie muttered something to Claude Lister, our captain and trainer, about "disappearing without trace".

From the moment we landed in Bucharest, Abie changed completely. He turned up the collar of his raincoat and kept a cigarette, mostly unlit, in the corner of his mouth, which made his sentences even more curt.

"Our rooms'll be bugged for sure," he said, "so don't shoot your mouth off."

"I don't actually know anything secret," I said.

I was, in fact, surprised and subdued by the dreary greyness of the place as we drove from the airport through the city. It was like a film in black and white. The people hurried up and down the streets, hunched into their coats against the fine drizzle, featureless, anonymous. I was depressed and worried about the pending match as I always was about pending Davis Cup ties. We stayed at one of the best hotels, a tall building which towered above most others. Abie and I were shown to a room on one of the upper floors—comfortable enough, with a bathroom attached.

"Hey, Abie," I called out, relieved, "this place is a—"

"SSssh," he hissed, with a finger to his lips.

I froze in my tracks watching him. He was frantically busy setting up the portable record player he always carried, opening it up and arranging the electrical connection. Miraculously, it began to work. A record was installed and suddenly the room was full of Sinatra with *London By Night*. Abie turned up the volume.

"What's that you were saying, Forbsey?" he asked.

"I was going to say that this is not a bad hotel," I said lamely, but by then Abie was moving around the walls peering behind the pictures, pressing an ear to the panelling, tugging and tapping. In the centre of the room he stopped and stood gazing at the light pendant.

"You know how you can tell when a light is bugged, Forbsey?" he asked.

"No," I replied.

"It flickers," said Abie. "Something to do with the volts." He moved to the door, turned on the switch and we both eyed the burning light.

"Seems OK," I said hopefully.

"Could be," said Abie. He moved into the bathroom.

Now Abie has a fixation about bathrooms. The time he spends inside them is very important to him and if, by some chance, he has a room without one, he gets demented and broods about it, sitting upon the edge of his bed, picking his toenails and scowling like the devil.

Certain things are ritual. Each morning he wakes at about seven with two immediate objectives always in mind. The first—a bath. The second, a session on the toilet with the newspaper. He runs the bath while he sits on the throne and the session is under way. Now Abie has the most unbelievably regular and explosive lavatorial habits I've ever known. Against a background noise of rushing water would come a series of blasts and rumblings which sometimes shook the room, and often used to remind me of the sound track of a war film on TV. The variety of his sound effects was unbelievable. Sometimes he produced a series of evenly spaced, heavy raps. At others a sharp, tremendous bang tapered off in a series of grumbling noises, while sometimes the grumbling noises led up to the bang. After a can or two of prunes, followed by doses of salts that he sometimes took, savage sounds ensued, like sheets being ripped. Once, in Paris, I remember a particularly enthusiastic assault had raised a cloud of pigeons from the eaves of our hotel. Severe gas attacks usually accompanied his performances, adding to the realism, and assuring him of privacy during his bath. It was Abie's opinion that if he flushed the toilet before rising, the gas would diminish. It wasn't valid. When this measure failed he would sometimes stand in the doorway and violently swing the door back and forth, creating draughts of dubious odours to eddy about the place. With a brimming bath at hand, he would then do his press ups and sit ups, swing his racket a few times, run on the spot and generally tone up before collapsing into the bath. Thus his mornings.

His other bathroom habits involved bathing immediately upon arriving at his hotel after his journey. Thus in Bucharest that afternoon, when he finally made for the bathroom, I knew what to expect. I, meanwhile, busied myself unpacking and selecting the bed best suited to cope with whatever nocturnal excursions my subconscious might drum up.

("You gonna be so nervous Forbsey," said Abie darkly, "that I hate to think what's gonna happen at night. We may have to chain you to the bed!")

After five minutes of puzzling silence, Abie's voice reached me from the bathroom. "Hey, Forbsey. Come and take a look at this."

I found him standing with a towel around his waist, contemplating the most extraordinary plumbing arrangement I'd ever seen. A maze of pipes, U bends and elbows connected the various taps, shower, toilet and bidet, and valves and faucets sprouted at intervals for no apparent reason. The bath was a shortish affair with a tremendous inlet, served by two valves that appeared to belong on some Jules Verne submarine.

"And what's more," said Abie scornfully, "with all these pipes and things, there's no water. Not *one drop* of water."

"Have you opened the right ones?" I asked.

"I've opened them all," said Abie. "Even the big one under the bath."

I checked, as I wasn't sure whether Abie knew which was open and which was shut, but sure enough, he'd opened every visible valve and faucet.

"That's it then," I said.

"What do you mean, 'that's it'?" he asked indignantly. "I've got to bathe. You know I can't think straight 'til I've bathed."

We were standing there, nonplussed, contemplating our dilemma when suddenly we heard a far-off rushing sound, like a tube train approaching at high speed. It appeared to be coming up from below us, and began to get louder and louder at an alarming rate.

"Jesus," said Abe, as the pipes began to vibrate and one of the taps began to emit a resonant, threatening hum, like a church organ only half warmed up. With a mighty blast, the water arrived. In a flash everything came on at once—the shower gushed, the toilet flushed, the bidet began filling, the basin taps gave staccato coughs and snorts, mostly steam and a gout of water leapt into the bath, filling it to the brim in an instant with ice cold water. We made frantic adjustments, and finally with the floor awash to the depth of an inch or so, everything stopped flowing with the exception of the toilet. Nothing we could do prevented it from flushing continuously and copiously. Abie eyed it warily.

"And in Italy last week, would you believe it? I couldn't get the toilet to flush at all. Had to buy a plastic bucket and pour bath water in. Jesus. Now we've got a built-in fountain. I can't stand it. I just can't stand it!"

In spite of the expected terrors of Bucharest, my nocturnal activities were remarkably placid. Only one short, but oddish, little event sticks in my mind—and this, I still claim, was caused by the particularly severe gas attacks to which Abie subjected me that week.—*He*, in turn, blamed these gas attacks on the Bucharest diet, saying that the masses of fresh strawberries and sweetish wine which accompanied every meal used to combine and effervesce, and build up inside him such abnormal pressures that even he himself became alarmed at the violence of his morning sessions. Door swinging became essential and all windows and doors had to be flung open, to prevent the paintwork from peeling.

In the dark hours of the night before our doubles match, it suddenly appeared to me that the room was full of noxious gas and I was being suffocated. The shortage of air was so acute that *immediate* action had to be taken. There was no time at all for consideration. I leapt out of bed, seized a tennis racket and darting to the nearest window, knocked out a glass pane with the racket handle, and breathed for my life through the hole in the broken glass. After half a minute of this I began to realise that perhaps the situation wasn't as critical as I had first imagined. I withdrew my nose cautiously, sniffed the air inside the room, realised that I'd been mistaken, then turned to look at Abie, hoping fervently that he had not awoken.

He had.

He was sitting up in bed and watching me with the odd sort of expression which he now adopted for use during the onset of my madness. A monologue, apparently seemed called for.

"Forbsey's makin' his own holes for breathin' through," he said to himself. "I mean, some people are quite happy to open the windows. Not Forbsey. He's got to make his own private holes." He looked up at me. "What's the problem, buddy?" he asked. "I didn't realise we were that short of air!"

It took me some time to explain to Abie why it had seemed necessary to "make my own private hole", and even then he wasn't fully convinced, and for a while seemed genuinely put out.

"Imagine if they are actually buggin' us," he said as we plugged the hole with a towel. "They wouldn't know what the hell to think. Maybe accuse us of releasin' a pigeon or something. Goddammit, Forbsey—"

"Abie," I said firmly, "we are not being bugged. Besides, nobody in their right minds would knock out a window pane to release a pigeon."

"Whose talkin' about people in their right minds?" he asked. "Just supposing the police arrived and asked you what you were doin'. 'Puttin' my nose through a hole in the window,' you'd tell them, and then they'd say: 'And what's so important out there you have to put your nose out?' "

He had a point, I suppose. I felt deflated and sleepy and unhappy about the whole situation.

On our first sortie into the city that evening, Abie had looked in vain for an English movie, or any clubs that had music going. The shops were half filled with thrifty items and only a bar or two showed any signs of life. At last, in desperation, he bought a can of stewed pineapple, marked "Product of Cuba", to loosen himself up after the flight. Not that he needed, in my opinion, any "loosening up".

"You get any looser, Abe," I said to him, "and they'll get a reading tomorrow on the seismograph."

"What's a seismograph?" asked Abie.

"A thing that measures earthquakes," I replied.

He laughed at that. "Better than a pressure burst," he said, shortly, "which is what happens if I seize up!"

We returned to the room, where he set to work with a pair of scissors. Putting the scissor point to the can, he gave them a welt with the palm of his hand, whereupon the can exploded with a prolonged but violent hiss, and took the shape of a football, sending out a jet of nectar which almost filled his shirt pocket. Comment at once poured forth, mixed with phrases like, "booby trapped" and "blowin' up innocent people".

"Jesus, Forbsey," he said as a final word. "Those Cubans are bloody savages. Herbie (Flam) told me. That Castro's something else altogether."

"Somebody else," I corrected him, but he ignored me.

"I mean, when a country gets down to buggin' stewed fruit, where can a man go?" And he moved off moodily into the toilet to check out his system.

That evening at dinner Abie finished his food, as usual, twice as fast as anyone else, pushed his plate away and regarded the assembled team.

"I knew it," he said with the air of a long-suffering scientist who has suddenly verified a private obsession.

"Knew what, Abie?" asked Claude Lister, in his British way.

"The light in the toilet's bugged," announced Abie.

"Oh, come on, Abie," said Cliff Drysdale, the junior of the team. "Do you think the Rumanians want a recording of your farts! They'd be smarter to install a gas detector! The toilet!" and he gave a hoot of laughter.

Abie turned to Claude Lister with a look of extreme exasperation.

"He's only been around for eighteen years," he explained, "and most of that time he's been rattlin' his brains together to make sure they're still there!" He turned to Cliff: "Idiot!" he said. "Don't you understand that they'd bug the toilet just because idiots like you'd figure they'd *never* bug the toilet!" He turned back to Lister and said triumphantly, "Right, Skip?"

Claude Lister was the fairest man I've ever known,-cautious in even the most mundane arguments where his players were concerned.

"I doubt whether they would go as far as, er, bugging, as you call it, the, er, toilet," he said.

"You guys are gangin' up on me," was Abie's only further comment, as at that moment his dessert arrived.

We all forgot about the incident, but Abie, apparently, brooded about the scepticism of his friends. The next morning he awoke especially early, feeling the call and entered the toilet, carrying *Time* magazine. Half asleep, I suddenly heard him give a grunt of satisfaction. In a flash he had emerged in his underpants and shot out of the room, returning in a minute or two leading, or rather dragging, a tousled and bewildered Claude Lister by the arm. I awoke immediately. He dragged Claude into the toilet, set him down on the seat, thrust the magazine into his hands and said:

"Right! Now, Skip, what do you see?"

"My dear chap, I can't get my eyes open!" said Claude plaintively.

"Well, get them open," said Abie.

Claude opened his eyes and found himself seated on our toilet, dressed in his pyjamas and staring at a copy of *Time*.

"Light's flickering like a bastard," said Abie. "You can't even read the magazine."

"You mean we're being bugged?" asked Claude.

"Sure we're bein' bugged," said Abie. "They've got everything we've said down on tape!"

In spite of Abie's forebodings, Bucharest was relatively uneventful. We won the match and were allowed to leave without being imprisoned. But Abie sank into his seat in the jetliner with a heavy sigh.

"We made it, Forbsey," he said. "But you can have those Iron Curtain deals. Boy! They're like bein' in a horror movie."

It soon became clear that Cliff was destined to become one of the best South African players. That year we reached the semi-finals of the European Zone, defeating Switzerland, Rumania, France and Germany before losing to Sweden. All the matches were close and, as Abie said fairly often, I had "plenty of things to shout about in the night!"

Cliff played his first major Davis Cup singles match at Roland Garros in our match against France. Their team consisted of Pierre Darmon, Gerard Pilet, and the new and untried doubles team of Jean Claude Barclay and Jacques Renevand. We had Abe, Cliff and me, and of course the steadfast and long-suffering Claude Lister who had to cope with us and to put up "a good show" with the rather mixed battery of strokes and strategies that, between the three of us, we could muster.

Davis Cup ties consist of five matches—four singles and one doubles, spread over three days. Order of play in the singles matches is decided by drawing the names of the players out of a hat.

In the match against France, the draw stipulated that Cliff play Gerard Pilet in the first match, and that I play Pierre Darmon in the second. The following day, Abe and I were to play Renevand and Barclay, and on the final day the singles order was reversed, with Cliff playing Darmon, first match, and me playing Pilet in the final match of the tie.

Of all types of tennis competition, I found that Davis Cup ties imposed upon me the most exacting form of tension. Other players with whom I spoke agreed with me. Playing "for your country" somehow emphasised the point of honour thing, and added to your own private tensions and ambitions, the burden of obligation to your country and to your team-mates.

Vital tennis matches are at best filled with tension and a kind of painful excitement, with the thrill of the game itself hidden under many layers of anxiety; fear, almost, of your opponent, of the turns of fortune, of your own ability to cope with cliff-hanger situations, of the feeling of despair when, for all your efforts, you feel the game slipping away from you.

And even when a match goes well, and you build up a healthy lead, there is always the little lurking anxiety that things might suddenly change—because some time in the past you have seen such things happen, or because they have happened to you.

Perhaps the one word which best describes such matches is "lonely". And Davis Cup matches were for me, infinitely lonelier than those in which only my private ambitions were at stake.

Often in my diary I wrote introspective little passages on the emotions of tennis matches. The most succinct entry is written in heavy black, angry writing, and has a page to itself.

All tennis matches are lonely. But:

Moods for Winning:	*Moods for Losing:*
Loneliness plus Courage, *Patience, Optimism,* *Concentration,* *A Calm Stomach, and* *A deep, quiet fury.*	*Loneliness plus Fear,* *A Hollow Stomach,* *Impatience,* *Pessimism, Petulance, and* *A bitter fury at yourself.*

For me, the moods were both in evidence during our tie against the French. Cliff played and won a superb match against Gerard Pilet, a match which lasted nearly three hours, and which contained all the classic ingredients of dramatic occasions—

The Junior against the Veteran, tactics against steadiness, bad calls, fine tennis, attacks of cramp, and the emotions of a stadium full of French aficionados. It was also a match in which fortunes fluctuated amazingly, so that while waiting in the locker room and trying to gauge when the match would end, I went through all kinds of agonies and premature preparations: like having lunch too early; then two bouts of tea to compensate, three warm-ups; a jog in the nearby woods and about fifty glucose tablets.

When finally I walked on court with a remarkably calm-looking Pierre Darmon, I felt full of fluids, irritations and sinking feelings. From the moment that the first ball hit the strings of my racket, I was fighting adversity. There was a swirling wind blowing, and Pierre played a kind of mixed, darting style of tennis that, try as I might, I could not fathom out. To make things worse, he seemed totally at ease, clear of eye and at one with the conditions.

We played and I had to endure the discomfort of losing, coupled with the despair of knowing that my game had fallen apart, but not knowing why.

There was one aspect of tennis which, throughout my whole career, never ceased to amaze me. No matter how well prepared I was for any given match, I could never tell whether I was going to have an "on day" or an "off day" until I actually walked onto the court and began to play!

After the first two singles matches we were thus poised at one match all. The following day Abie and I dealt in a ruthless manner with the untried team of Renevand and Barclay, and completely neutralised what the French had smugly considered to be their secret weapon.

That left us uneasily poised with a 2–1 lead, Drysdale having to play Darmon and I, Pilet, in the final match. We didn't dare hope that Cliff could beat Darmon, and I had grave doubts about my ability to beat Pilet, as he was a net-rusher's nightmare on slow clay—one of the "virtually impossibles" on my list. With this state of truce at hand, we attended a gala dinner, a grand function in the combined honour of our match, as well as the annual lawn tennis encounter between the British and French International Club teams. These teams were filled with noble and venerable names, such as Borotra, Brugnon, Destremau and Lacoste on the French side, and a selection of Britons of the very first order—Mottram, Paish, Barrett, *et al.*

Conditions were absolutely ideal for speeches. They cropped up punctually with the coffee and for two hours literally flooded the room with extravagant clichés. Honours, thanks and good fellowship poured forth. To make things even worse, an official from the South African Embassy got to his feet and after some particularly trite verbiage, solemnly congratulated us on having won the match, having apparently mistaken our 2–1 lead for glorious victory.

We were dumbfounded, and for once even Claude Lister was put out. I returned to the hotel depressed, feeling myself to be in one of those tennis troughs which infect all tennis players from time to time. It vanished without warning during the morning of the next day. I practised with Malcolm Fox during Cliff's match against Darmon and suddenly my spirit lifted and by some miracle everything shifted back into place—like a cinema lens, suddenly corrected. I don't remember much about that match, except the sublime relief of seeing a crisp white ball again, and knowing exactly where it was.

Cliff lost, and I won, and we had defeated the French 3–2. The previous night's gaffe was forgotten, and a party was given for us at the South African Embassy. Here the ambassador, rigidly be-crutched and with his leg in plaster from heel to thigh, the result of a ski-ing accident, and his attractive wife welcomed us as heroes. We overdid the celebration, there is no doubt about that.

About halfway through the evening, Abe began singing snatches of "*The Nearness of You*", and a little later threw in a few soft-shoe routines for good measure. Cliff was going about removing strange ladies' shoes and filling them with champagne. Sometimes he removed only one shoe, filled it up and drank it himself. At others, he would become very gallant and insist that both shoes be removed, filled up, and a toast drunk to the owner of the shoes. The next day, in a more sober mood, he confided to me that one of the ladies' shoes had given to the champagne "a most peculiar taste". We were nearly the last to leave, joining the end of the line which filed past the host and hostess to shake their hands. It was then that Abie, while grasping the hand of the Ambassador, struck him such a blow on the shoulder blades, that his crutches fell out and he stood swaying precariously, like a nearly-knocked-over skittle. He would have gone over for sure had Claude Lister not caught him, as by then Abie had moved on to kiss his wife.

It was a famous celebration! The next morning I found, slashed across a page in my notebook, a poem of which I had only the faintest recollection of having written. I remember being agreeably surprised that, in spite of the influence of champagne, the meter of the thing was reasonably good!

A miracle
A turn of fate. Shout: Ho for Victory!
(Victory Ho)
An urgent
Need to celebrate. Shout: Ho for Victory!
(Victory Ho)
The French amazed
Claude Lister dazed,

Myself surprised,
Abe mesmerized.
Shout Ho for Victory, Victory, Victory,
Ho for
Victory Ho!

The French championships followed the Davis Cup tie. Although I lost in the early rounds of the singles, Abie and I reached the doubles finals, beating Hewitt and Stolle on the way. In our quarter final match, an extraordinary thing took place, which I later found that I had faithfully recorded in my diary:

Diary Notes: Summer 1962

A long, tense match today. Abie believes we have a real chance of winning our first major title. At 9–8 in the third set, we at last got a set point. Abie played a great return and I got an easy one right on the net. It was a perfect set up—an absolute sitter. I got up to give it a colossal nudge and looked straight into the sun. My nudge, struck by instruments, just nicked the ball and sent it straight upwards. There it hung, suspended for so long and spinning so fast that a wild thought flew through my head about me inventing some new kind of counter to gravity. Our opponents began advancing with alarming speed while the spinning ball hovered. At last, with a humming sound, it began to descend. It fell at their feet as they arrived, about a yard inside their half of the court and then, as though powered by some demon inside it, it leapt backwards onto our side before anyone could move. Four jaws dropped.

"Holy Jesus Christ," said Abie, with strong religious fervour, "that was one hell of an extraordinary way to knock off a set point!"

"Relax," I said tensely. "We won the point, didn't we?"

"Relax, he says," mused Abie wearily. "Forbsey says that I *must relax!" He turned to me: "That's right, buddy, we won it, only next time you make a shot like that, let me know in advance so I can take a couple of tranquillisers."*

Later on in the dressing-room, after we had won the match, Abie collapsed on the bench and stared at his feet. "With you," he said, "a man's lucky if he doesn't get that stuff that makes your heart stop."

"A coronary thrombosis," I said, absently. I was tired of the "heart attacks" that Abe was always on about.

"That's right," he said. "A coronary. When I see you go up for one of those shots of yours, I can actually feel a coronary startin' to creep up!"

"They don't creep up," I said perversely. "They strike without warning!"

Abie looked at me and shook his head, and said that one thing about playing with me was that, "there's no way a man's goin' to get bored out there!"

It's been quite a week for extraordinary points. In the plate event, playing Warren Woodcock, I missed an easy volley to give him his ad. and match point. "Bloody pissed off", as the Australians say, I gave the net a whack with the edge of my racket and it collapsed and leapt into a ball in the middle of the court. Woodcock walked up to the umpire and in his slow way said—

"Mr Umpire, I don't think the net is the right height."

We had to wait for about fifteen minutes for the net to be repaired, during which time Warren practised random serves into the fence and made the odd remark to casual onlookers, such as it being, "a very awkward time to have a net collapse", or "there ought to be a rule somewhere covering this", and "play not being continuous". He served a double eventually, and I won the match, which pleased me, but not him.

I eventually won the plate event and Abie and I lost the doubles final to Emerson and Santana and were bitterly disappointed. We had another extraordinary tie against Germany in the next round and won it after being down two matches to love, Cliff beating Wilhelm Bungert in the final match. The tie was played at the Rott Weiss Club in Berlin—a very old and special place, smelling of cigars and coffee.

Thinking back, I am now sometimes appalled by our lack of interest in the great old cities to which we travelled.

We would beat a path from our hotel to the tennis courts and back and would only occasionally sally forth and explore. Fortunately the tennis authorities often organised sight-seeing tours for us in the hope, I suppose, that they might contribute towards the broadening of our minds. In Berlin that year a bus was arranged to take us to see the famous wall.

Now Abie had a deep aversion to group organisation, to the extent that he could hardly be persuaded to stand in line for his players' lunches. On the morning of the bus tour he suddenly announced that he was not going to "sit on a crappy bus all day like a peasant", but that he and I were going to see the wall in a taxi.

"You're off your head," I said, "the bus is especially for taking us to the wall. A taxi will cost a fortune and probably take us to the wrong wall."

"Okay, Forbsey," he said, "you go sit on the bus. I'm takin' a taxi. I want to be back by twelve so I can practise."

To keep the peace, I finally agreed to the hiring of a cab, and we set off.

The driver, inevitably, was a rogue, and took us to the furthest section of wall that he could think of, while the meter ticked feverishly away, rattling up the marks and pfennigs in a way which infuriated me. We reached the wall at last, and stared for a few minutes at a forbidding section of barbed wire and concrete and a half-hidden sentry-box. We then got back into the cab.

"That," I said to Abie, "is your biggest balls-up to date. There's sixty nine D-marks on the meter and we're half way to Russia."

"Look, Forbsey. A wall's a wall. What did you expect? A firing squad so you could see an execution?"

"We could have seen a better piece of wall from the bus."

"An' listened to all the 'horses' jabberin' about their shopping!"

We got more and more heated, until in a fit of temper I yelled: "Stop the cab, I'm getting out!"

"Are you crazy?" said Abie, "we're miles from nowhere!"

"I don't give a damn. I'm getting out."

Faced with my dreadful fury, even Abie was taken aback. Before we could consider our move rationally, and having paid an immense cab fare, we found ourselves standing on the wide and bleak Kaiser Wilhelmstrasse. In the distance was the Brandenburg Gate. The cab drove away.

"Now you've really fucked things up," said Abie. "There's no way another cab's gonna come."

"We'll walk to the gate," I said. "At least I can photograph that."

The scale of the approaches to the Brandenburg Gate is so immense that we found ourselves faced with a walk of several miles.

We trudged and I grumbled, and at last Abie blew his top.

"Damn you, Forbsey," he cried, "you've been complaining for two hours. You want to see the wall? Right, I'll show you the bloody wall! Follow me!"

After some time I realised that he was making for the military establishment near the mighty Gate. Jeeps carrying British soldiers were coming and going, and Abie hailed one.

"Listen, General," he said to the driver who was, in fact, a corporal. "How does a man get to have a good look at this wall?"

"Aren't you Abe Segal?" asked the other occupant, who was a lieutenant.

"That's right."

"We watched you chaps playing tennis against the Jerries," said the lieutenant. "What can we do for you?"

The celebrated Segal luck had struck again.

We told them of our abortive attempts to look at the wall, and they laughed.

"How would you like to see the Reichstadt?" the lieutenant asked. "It's in our zone. We have our main look-out on the top of it. From up there you can see the bloody lot, including the Russkies on the other side!"

We accompanied them, me in a daze, Abie triumphant, and finally obtained the necessary permission, from a captain who also liked tennis, to enter the extraordinary place. Even to our tennis benumbed minds, the experience was momentous. The building was vast. It was also gutted, so that only the shell remained. The lieutenant told us that it had been the ambition of every Russian soldier to place his initials on the walls inside the Reichstadt. It seemed that their ambitions had been fulfilled. The interiors of the great walls were covered with hundreds of thousands of names and initials—written during who knew what moods of triumph and victory. Here Hitler had made his schemes and shouted his fanatical words. Here the seeds of the sickness of war had been sown, germinated, flourished and finally erupted into the most unbelievable series of events that mankind has ever precipitated.

We climbed the endless wooden and rope ladders which made their way upwards, I following Abe, and Abe following a pair of British army boots. At last we found ourselves in the observation post and peered over the sand-bagged ruin. There, stretched before us were the time-softened, but still shattered, remains of East Berlin. In the foreground, the green mound which gave access to the bunker in which Hitler and Eva Braun had lived and died. Across the wired wall and canal was a nest of sombre Russians with machine guns and binoculars. We stared and stared, and for a brief moment I was lost in a world of espionage, escape, and the cold lifeless dangers of times past. When at last I lifted my camera for pictures, the Russians swung a machine-gun towards us and the British corporal told me sharply to "put that bloody thing away", which I did, sheepishly. Our visit went unrecorded, yet for me the memory remains, tainted with the unease evoked by the nearness of a new reality. We were, they told us, the first civilians ever to have visited the post. Perhaps no one else had ever cared to try—for who really wishes to become involved with machine-gun nests, sandbags and the grey and brown austerity of proper armies. Secretly, at that moment, I thanked the panel of gods to whom I addressed my various thoughts and prayers, that I never had to live through a war.

Abe was deeply impressed by his effort.

"A bus!" he said contemptuously, as we finally arrived back at our hotel, having been conveyed by the British Army. "Only bums sightsee in buses. Be with me, Forbsey, an' we go first class! What do these idiots know about seein' the wall?"

We flew straight to London with our victory still clutched in our minds and found ourselves in the familiar club house at Queens Club—old wood and brick, with the aloof management and damp changing-rooms. Roy Emerson, I remember, was singing under the shower when we arrived. This time it was a monotonous fragment of opera to which he'd attached his own words:

"I tried to—
Figure it out, figure it out, figure it out—
But I couldn't
Figure it out, figure it out, figure it out—
So I said to my selllllllf
I-I-I-I-I can't
Figure it out!
Figure it out, figure it out,
F-I-G-U-R-E I-T O-U-T"

But, in spite of his operatic enigma he sounded cheerful enough. Roy was another man with the kind of deeply humorous mind which is difficult to put into words. His manner was one of contained exuberance which leaked out grins and sly remarks, overflowing into laughter and snatches of song at the drop of a hat. Without doubt, Emerson is one of the nicest living people. Of course he played well too—an industrious and ingenious game constructed from enormous enthusiasm and a love of tennis.

Queens Club was the only tournament which took place during the week before Wimbledon, except for the qualifying rounds at Roehampton, and so everyone played there, although "expenses" were not paid at Queens. There, one received lunch and tea tickets, could practise indoors and on fair grass courts and, in the evening, buy warmish English beer at the little pub they had, all pasted around with tennis photographs. And yet I liked Queens; the bashed-up old change-rooms and pavilion, the creaky wooden floors and the indoor courts, and the mysterious "members" who moved about in a conservative, British sort of way, carrying squash rackets and the extraordinary "real" tennis equipment.

In the dressing-rooms, the old attendants used to eye the invading tennis players with suspicion and hand out towels for showering as though they thought the players mightn't return them. Teddy Tinling was always very much on show at Queens, walking about dressed in shiny clothes, measuring people up, having several sessions of tea and, in his mind's eye, fitting sporting fabrics to the several curves of the tennis playing girls.

That year at Queens I played Allen Fox in the first round and, much to his disgust, I beat him. As we came off the court he told me it was because of his oafish body. Allen was (and still is) highly intelligent and used to get extremely cross when his body wouldn't obey his brain.

"I have great schemes," he would say. "Mentally I could win Wimbledon, except my body lets me down!"

Often on the court he would berate himself with terse instructions—"Keep your head *down*". "Keep your wrist firm". "Don't foul things up by falling apart on the volley!" Once, watching his match, I heard him say curtly: "Get your service *in*, Allen". He then immediately missed with his first ball, paused and said, "I meant the *first* ball, dummy!"

"My body misunderstood me," he explained when I mentioned it later. In tennis matches, then, he always had, as a last resort, this rueful "out" if he lost, blaming the whole thing on his inept and clumsy body. But when he played chess against the Russians (when he dared) he writhed in the most secret and diabolical of agonies.

"I hate losing at thinking games," he confided in me, "because, when I do, I can't say to myself: 'Don't worry about it—he's got a better body!' With thinking games, it's all pain and suffering."

Allen was a wry conversationalist. He fancied himself as a bit of the courageous underdog, and presented himself as such, but with a knowing smile. We sat in the stands after one of his matches, I remember, and I told him that I was sorry to hear that he had lost.

"I also only heard that I had lost at the end of the match when the umpire announced the result," he said. "Until then, I thought that I had been winning. I *hate* losing when I think I would be winning. This was one of those matches. I was *really* concentrating and playing well, and every now and again I would think to myself: 'Now I've got to be winning!' and then I'd hear the umpire call the score, and I'd be *losing*! I still think I'm the better player!"

Allen also hated "tall guys with *big* serves on bad grass courts", and "guys who win a lot of points with *greasy* shots". "Greasy shots", I discovered, were those that went for winners off the frame of the racket. "I don't have greasy shots," Allen told me. "All my shots are clean. The guy who taught me to play forgot to tell me: 'Look Allen, don't watch the ball too well because that way you're gonna get a lot of surprise winners—lobs off heavy passing shots and crosscourt volleys that go up the line. Not only do you win points, but you cause your opponent to pull muscles when he changes direction.' My coach said to me, 'Allen, there's a sweet spot in the middle of your racket. *That's* what you're aiming for!'" He paused thoughtfully. "Big Abie," he went on, "doesn't have a sweet spot. He just has a big heavy racket and a huge arm. If he *did* have a sweet spot, and he happened to hit the ball with it, it would just keep on going. Circle the earth and come back round and hit him on the back of the head!"

Years later, also at Queens Club, I sat beside Allen watching Fred Stolle playing Clark Graebner. At about seven all, Graebner served one game which consisted of four absolutely clean aces—the streaky kind that flew past Fred Stolle before he could move. Allen pulled a sour face:

"That's great," he said, "if you don't like long rallies!"

We also had long discussions concerning important points, and players who "choked" on them and those who did not. "Choking" intrigued Allen as, in fact, it did me.

"Define the verb 'to choke'," I once asked him.

"Choke," he began at once, "from the Latin *strangulare*. I choke, you choke, they choke, I would have choked, you would have choked, they would have choked. The ability to become paralysed under pressure. Or conversely, the *inability* to make any kind of shot at all if the score is five all in the fifth, and your ad. You get a kind of nervous spasm which causes your racket to:

(a) Go back very quickly and then absolutely refuse to come forward again—or

(b) To go back very slowly and then suddenly fly forward before you want it to.

"There are three kinds of chokers," he went on, warming to the subject. "Spectacular chokers. Pathetic chokers. And Reverse chokers. Spectacular chokers are the most admirable. On vital points they serve gigantic doubles that miss by yards, or go for drop-shots that float into the back fence. Pathetic chokers are the wettest. They get so tense and careful that the balls just dribble off their rackets, usually off the frame. Then they hang their heads and talk to themselves. Usually give themselves bad news. Reverse chokers are the most interesting. They *make* the most difficult shots, then completely fold up on the easy ones. *Everyone* chokes at some stage in his career. I even had a linesman who choked in one of my matches. He apologised to me later. 'Sorry,' he said, 'I saw the ball correctly, but called it wrong!'"

Then we spoke wistfully about the guys who never seemed to choke—Gonzales, who played his *best* shots on the big points, and Hoad and Laver who were so good that they could choke and *still beat people*, and Bob Falkenburg, who used to take only ONE ball, show it his opponent, then serve an ace with it on match point.

"If ever I did *that*!" said Allen, "I'd get weak kneed at my own audacity and freeze completely. Then, when I went to throw the ball up it would stick to my hand. I'd be standing there with my fingers locked round the ball and my arm going up and down! Imagine, getting a match point, showing one ball to your opponent with a superior look and then have it *stick* to your hand! That would embarrass the hell out of me. I'd have to have a spare ball in my pocket before I tried anything like that!"

Queens Club drifted gently, as it always does, into Wimbledon, by way of the Hurlingham garden party. Here the players put on fine British airs and gently stroll the summer lawns, eating salmon and fresh lettuce and strawberries, and at four, the little cress sandwiches and four-sided cakes. God, how mild an English tea. At Hurlingham, the exhibition matches were fresh and light-hearted, dotted with subtle volleys and mighty smashes.

I, for one, always enjoyed the Hurlingham party—a sort of calm before the Wimbledon storm. If you walked up the grass embankment on the far side of the putting course, you could look over the Thames on the one hand and on the other, the sedate croquet games. After Hurlingham, we would always go to an early movie show, then eat a steak before turning in for some pre-Wimbledon sleep.

When I was younger I used to day-dream quite a lot. I still do, but not nearly so much—because, I suppose, day-dreams are the inventions of young minds which, when they are older, have used up many of the dreams and found them empty; and, if they are very lucky, have made one or two come true. I am not sure whether Rod Laver ever day-dreamed. If he did, one of his dreams came true that Wimbledon. Not that he surprised anyone by winning the tournament—simply that it was his first Wimbledon victory and, as I have said somewhere before, the particular moment of that victory must rate as the great thrill of a tennis lifetime, even one as illustrious as Laver's.

I became very friendly with Rodney during that Wimbledon as he was very fond of my sister, Jean, and we spent a good deal of time together. And also Peter Ustinov, who used to love to watch the matches and who amused the devil out of us by his remarks and observations. In an animated monologue he could carry out an altercation between, say, an Italian player, a French player, a British umpire and a sleeping woman linesman and sort the whole thing out after a heated argument. On the evening of the Friday on which Rodney won his title, we went to Peter's show, *Romanoff and Juliet*, which, like many of his shows, cut into the heart of human affairs and dressed up the wound in nonsense. Rod took a bow during the show when Peter called the spotlights onto him, and afterwards we drank beer at the *Down Under Club*.

Later that year when we arrived at Istanbul for the tournament in Turkey, I heard that Peter was in that extraordinary city making a film called *Topkapi* which was about a robbery of jewels from the Sultan's palace, or something like that. At any rate, there was a great deal of running around on the turrets and roof-tops of some famous building, and laughter in the making. Peter invited some of us to watch the filming of one of his scenes and in return we asked him to the tennis. He duly arrived, together with Max Schell who co-starred in the film. In the evening, when it was cooler, I asked him whether he would like to play a game or two. We found some gear and went down to one of the back courts, where we began our hit-up.

Peter can best be described as a determined and well-anchored player. His forehand comes out from around his middle, the racket head gaining speed all the time, so that by the time contact is made, a shot of considerable velocity is produced. The fact that it sometimes flies off course, like a spark off a catherine wheel, is probably due to the fact that he doesn't practise as much as he should. His backhand is a more modest shot—a short-arm jab, struck with a sulky frown. Mobility is also a problem.

"Getting oneself into position is like moving troops," he once said. "One has to plan well in advance!"

He kept referring to himself as "one". "One should lose weight if one wants to indulge in this sport." Or: "One must watch the ball. Even if one can't get to it, one should at least *watch* it!"

Max Schell sat on a bench at the side of the court, chuckling away to himself. Peter frowned at him periodically and gave him his famous sulky looks.

"One doesn't like being laughed at," he said. "Especially by *German* spectators. One would expect them to remain silent during play."

Our warm-up reached the stage where I felt we should play a few games. Peter looked exceedingly dubious at my suggestion.

"Do you mean actually *compete*?" he asked with his mouth turning right down at the corners. "Score points? One isn't accustomed to actual athletic confrontation you know. Damned alarming when you meet it face to face! Oh very well. But you serve first. Then one shall be able to say that, 'games went with service in the early stages'!"

I held my service and we changed ends. Peter gathered the balls and himself together and took up his position on the serving line, standing there like a bewildered Roman commander who is not sure what has become of his armies. For a few moments he stood glancing from the racket in his right hand to the balls in his left, as if wondering which to toss up. I stood waiting, half expecting him to put on some kind of show—an impersonation perhaps, of some famous player's service action. Instead, he began a sort of flouncing and curtseying action, his racket going back in a series of little loops and frills, one to the front, one to the side and one behind him, while his eyes followed the racket head and his knees bobbed up and down in anticipating bends, as though they had not been told which twirl was to lead to the final swing.

Suddenly, while all this manoeuvring was taking place, his left hand, activated by some extraordinary and complex timing system, threw a ball about ten feet into the air above his head where it performed a graceful little parabola before beginning its descent. I, meanwhile, watched open-mouthed and just as I had decided that there was no earthly way that this preposterous swing would ever unravel itself in time to hit the ball, a racket head came flying out of the tangle and gave the ball a crisp whack which sent it whistling past me about knee height without a bounce.

"Good God!" I exclaimed, convinced now that Peter was doing some elaborate send-up of, perhaps, a turn-of-the-century ladies' doubles serve. No one in their right mind, I decided, would consider such a service as standard equipment. "That's the funniest service I've ever seen," I called. "Do another one!"

"One has to," said Peter. "It's the only service one has!"

Hearing funny noises at the side of the court, I turned to find that Max Schell had fallen off his seat and was rolling with laughter. Peter frowned at both of us, sniffed and muttered something about it being "very difficult to concentrate on one's game when the stands were full of unruly spectators."

On finals day, Peter and Max Schell played a set of mixed doubles on the centre court, partnered by Margaret Hunt and Annette van Zyl, and by that time I had alerted some of the players to take note of Peter's service action. His first service game was thus greeted by cheers from the players' enclosure and near hysteria by the spectators.

"I seem," said Peter to his partner, "to be some kind of Turkish Delight!"

The little middle-eastern circuit left lasting impressions: Beirut, Istanbul, Athens—the hot, dry capitals waiting by the side of their tame sea, each with their own ingenious inventions. Beirut, old and festering, rutted by winding streets; nothing orderly, no true planes, no verticals, a city sagging, leaned over by time; the accumulated layers of a thousand years of hoarding, conniving and merchandising, crowding its markets and bazaars. In its stores the artifacts accumulate and settle into piles of eastern goods with eastern smells—musty mixes of spices—incense, myrrh, musk—overlaid by coffee, curry and diesel oil. You wander in Beirut and are aware, above all, that you are Anglo-Saxon. From the West.

There is a road that unravels from the honeycomb and sifts through suburbs and open lots with piles of fruit and melons and, finally, makes its way up the mountain to Broumana. There it is cooler, purer, if you like, with dusty breezes carrying the smell of pine and eucalyptus from the mountain slopes. And there, on half a dozen sun-baked tennis courts flanked by a school, the tournament was held. The players were billeted in the deserted dormitories and food was served in the school dining-room—cuts of lean mutton, chicken, white cheeses, olive oil, goats' milk, piles of fruit and huge sheets of tough, unleavened bread. In the morning, Torben Ulrich grumbled about the absence of newspapers.

"Read your sandwich, Torben," Roy Emerson instructed with his mouth full. "I've read mine and I am now eating the sports page!"

"I am unable to digest many of the world's latest events," replied Torben, typically.

Sometimes in the warm evenings, we sat on the verandah drinking light, sour wine and eating goats' cheese and figs; or talked one of the lazy taxi drivers into taking us down the mountain to the sea. On the moonlit beach we would eat melons, then swim out into the limpid sea—float weightlessly and dream. One such evening I lay upon a deserted bathers' raft with Ilsa and Edda Buding and we decided that the Mediterranean was a good sea for romance. Especially with the moon the way it was that night.

9

Diary Notes: Hamburg 1962

Filled with forebodings I walked moodily through the fading light of a Hamburg dusk. A thin drizzle had been falling down since dawn. There were pools on the concrete apron, shining coldly under the blue-white glare of the arc-lights. Ahead, emerging from the mist, stood the Pan-Am jet, stark and sombre.

I huddled deeper into my great-coat, and let my mind return to the events of the previous evening. The note, enclosed in a plain white envelope, had been thrust under the door of my room at the Hauptbahnhof.

"Imperative that I see you. I will wait in the lounge at 8 precisely." It was signed, simply, "Lister".

I met him there. He wasted no time in getting to the point.

"It's a new assignment for you, old lad," he said quietly. "America." He paused then and waited.

In spite of my months of training, I started imperceptibly.

"Yes," he said, with a thin smile. "It will be no picnic. We both realise that. But it must be done and you're the man to do it."

"What about Segal?" I asked in a flat voice.

"We're afraid he might crack," said Lister. "Besides, he talks too much. No, Forbes, there's nothing for it. It must be you and you only."

I smiled briefly, and met Lister's eyes.

Air Vice Marshall Sir Claude Lister, now seconded to Intelligence. I'd been through a lot with Lister, but never anything like this. The American mission was suicidal—a desperately slender hundred-to-one long shot. He knew it and I knew it, and he knew that I knew it, so there was little doubt in my mind that we both knew it.

"Depend on me, sir," I said firmly, with a confidence that I was far from feeling.

He took my hand warmly then, his fingers trembling imperceptibly in spite of their steely grip. "This will be the last one, Forbes," he said quietly. "Complete this thing and you're in from the cold. Nice warm desk in Whitehall for you, old lad."

I smiled again. Lister, I noticed, had carefully avoided mentioning the alternative. Instead he was talking of the mission. "You'll have Drysdale, of course," he said, "not much experience in crisis, but he'll be there, notwithstanding."

"Drysdale!" I laughed inwardly at that. At nineteen he was barely out of diapers. "Drysdale!" Good God! But I said nothing. What, after all, was there to say?

For five hours Lister briefed me, and then we retired, exhausted, for a few precious hours of sleep. At dawn, America. There could be no turning back.

I reached the great jet at last, and hurried up the stairway, settling myself into the window seat to which the stewardess directed me.

America: I shivered slightly, and, ordering a double Scotch-on-the-rocks, I went over my instructions for the umpteenth time.

I had obviously been reading Alistair MacLean a good deal about that time. Nevertheless, the entry, although tongue-in-cheek, reveals the impact that my first tennis trip to America made upon me.

You could either play the middle-eastern circuit in those days or venture across the Atlantic to play the American East Coast tournaments which lead up to the United States National Doubles event in Boston and then Forest Hills—the fourth leg of the four major tournaments, known as the "Grand Slam", namely, Australia, the French and Wimbledon. At that time only one man in the history of tennis had ever won all four of these tournaments. The man was Donald Budge. Of the other players who had tried, Lew Hoad had come closest in 1956, losing Forest Hills to Rosewall with the other three titles in hand. Other great players might have done it, could have done it, had planned to do it, or had dreamed of doing it. But only Budge *had* done it. And now, in 1962, with three titles already won, Rod Laver was poised to make his attempt.

In 1962 I received an invitation from the USLTA to participate in tennis events in the United States. I had never before been to America, for the reason that the USLTA were particularly thrifty with their invitations and I could not afford the cost of a private trip. Such was the state of tennis in those days that, although I was rated in the first twenty players in the world, I rarely saved more than one hundred dollars a week, some of which had to be saved to pay the bills for my little family at home.

The American invitation offered me travel, accommodation, and two hundred dollars per week for five weeks—good by any standard then, and for America, excellent. I played the German championships at Hamburg and boarded my flight to New York with a certain amount of apprehension. The very thought of America had always diminished me somewhat, and the tales of hordes of huge American college boys with mighty serves on bad grass courts gave me tennis elbow in anticipation, as well as a mild case of the dreaded sinking feeling.

In addition, I had been playing indifferent singles for some weeks, and for the American stint I had lost my doubles partner, Abe Segal, and was to play with Cliff Drysdale, whom I still regarded as an irresponsible minor, with no idea at all of the gravity of my situation.

I landed at Idlewild, which it was then called and which name I loved, and by a series of what I could only explain as miracles in that vast place, I found my luggage, cleared customs without a hitch, and suddenly found myself taken by the arm with a voice saying: " Mr Forbes! We've been expecting you. We have a car ready to drive you to Southampton."

I gave a sigh of relief. I am one of those people who worry secretly (but not obsessively) about being forgotten and left to wander the streets of New York alone, holding my suitcase and tennis racket. We drove down the Long Island peninsula that hot afternoon and the journey became for me one of those moments in life that remain forever in the mind—sharp little nudges of the memory simultaneously happy and sad.

The car radio gave frequent weather, temperature and time checks in the best American style, played Errol Garner recordings, a song called, *It's my party and I'll cry if I want to* over and over, and suddenly announced that Marilyn Monroe had died, while the endless landscape of roadhouses, gas stations and flashing signs floated by. The driver of the car deposited me and my baggage at the entrance to the Meadow Club. There, on a motley of grass courts, were my huge Americans with their enormous services. It was a Monday afternoon, matches were in progress everywhere, and I had the strange feeling that I might at any minute be called upon to *play a match*!

The whole scene, in fact, looked singularly uninviting. The courts, or most of them, were literally laid out upon a meadow. On the back courts one fully expected domestic animals to be grazing, or at the very least, a few stools of fresh dung into which the huge services might fly on big points. Daisies grew in fair profusion and the grass, though not actually waving, quivered in the breeze. Against this pastoral scene the athletic abilities of the sweaty players and their American profanity seemed particularly ominous.

I presented myself at the players desk and they said:

"Gordon Forbes! We sure have been expecting you. Why don't we just show you to your quarters where you can freshen up. You have a match at four!"

A match at four! I felt as though I'd been travelling for days and had the vague idea that for me, with the time change, it was about three in the morning. With enormous relief, I saw Fred and Pat Stolle and Cliff Drysdale approaching. Things began to brighten considerably. Fred was the eternal optimist and Cliff, although alarmingly confident at all times, presented a welcome return to a world which I knew. After cheerful greetings, I told them that I was feeling tired and was scheduled to play someone called Roger Werksman in the first round.

"Roger Werksman," said Cliff.

"Roger Werksman," said Fred.

"Yes," I said, "Roger Werksman."

"Can't mess about with Werksman," said Fred. "Got to get in and play it tight. You'll beat him, of course, but you'll have to play it really tight."

"Oh, you'll beat Werksman all right," said Cliff in a very positive way. Except that he'd said the same thing when I played Lundquist in our Davis Cup match against Sweden, and against Martin Mulligan in Hilversum.

"Only don't pay any attention to what he says," Cliff had continued. "He talks a lot."

I'd long ago decided that it was useless to ask one's fellow competitors about players whom you didn't know, but against whom you found you had to play. Because if one's fellow competitors *did* know them, they usually scared you badly by saying ambiguous things like:

"He hits a lot of balls. Boy, does he hit a lot of balls! But you really shouldn't have any serious trouble!"

Or: "He has a hell of a serve, but if you can get that back, you're home and dry." Then add: "Big forehand, though. Must keep away from the forehand. Bloody frightening forehand!"

If they had not heard of them, one found alarming thoughts about "Dark Horses" flashing through one's mind. There is little fun to be found in the early round matches in America. The population there is generally of very athletic bent—and Americans are taught from birth to display an air of terrific confidence at all times. They *never* hide their lights under bushels. Cliff accompanied me back to the large wooden beach house where we were staying—one of those summer houses for which Southampton is famous. Not as fabulous as Gatsby's house, but well established, expensive enough, and smelling of holidays, canvas chairs and surf boards. What was more, there was a French maid, whose name, inevitably, turned out to be Françoise. She met us at the front door and carried my racket and coat. She was unbelievably French, with wide-set eyes, wider mouth, still wider hips and strong calves, and possessed the kind of looks which spent their time balanced on the knife edge, between "very ugly" and "very beautiful". I could see that Cliff had already summed her up completely. When it came to girls, Cliff was a lightning mover.

"She has a friend," he told me in a matter-of-fact way, as I unpacked my gear, "also French."

"Good Lord!" I said. Two French maids sounded twice as promising as one, and in a distracted sort of way I made a mental note to find out more about her when the time was right. But the four o'clock Werksman encounter loomed large. I was sharply aware that William Clothier had persuaded the United States authorities to issue my invitation and I didn't want to let him down. To make matters worse, Cliff told me that out host had backed us to the tune of five hundred dollars as the likely winners of the men's doubles event.

The dressing-room, when I entered, seemed to be full of towels. Americans have a thing about towels and aren't really happy unless there are dozens close at hand. One towel to an American is the same, basically, as one glass of wine to a Frenchman, or one cup of tea to a Briton. Hopelessly inadequate.

I changed and made my way to the referee's desk. It was just four o'clock—Werksman hadn't arrived. By five past I began to hope fervently that he'd been let down by some form of transport. There are few feelings so good as those evoked by the news that one's opponent hasn't arrived for a match which one has been secretly dreading. At four-fifteen, just as the term 'default' was being bandied about, Werksman arrived—or rather, exploded upon the scene.

My first impression was one of relief—he wasn't a huge American—in fact, he looked a little weedy. A closer look, however, revealed that he'd definitely played the game before. His racket grips had that well worn look about them, his shoes were streaked with grass stains which seemed to creep upwards onto his socks and towards his knees; and he carried a tennis racket headcover full of stuff—salt tablets, glucolin, elastoplast, sweatlets, a few dollar bills and so forth. He also had the type of short, sturdy legs which should be slow but which are, in fact, as fast as the devil. Besides, he'd just come off a practice court, and stood hopping about from one foot to the other and telling a friend that his game had "come good just at the right time!"

We made our way to our allotted court, with Werksman followed by a little knot of supporters. One hears a lot of snippets on the way to one's court. "—Great serve and volley," someone was saying to Werksman, "but a nothing backhand. Can't break eggs", referring of course to me. And someone else said, ". . . South African. Supposed to be good on grass, but doesn't really look as though . . ." And: "Forbes and Werksman. This I've got to see . . .". By the time we'd reached the court, I had heard several bits of information about myself which I had not heard before.

The warm-up was enough to let me know that I had a problem. There is a solid, compact way some smaller players go about their games that spells trouble. It didn't look to me as though Werksman missed too many balls. I was even less impressed by his service (on which, like most Americans, he took about fifty practices)—one of those low, flat affairs which come off the grass at ankle height and curl round at you. So I clenched my teeth and set about the business of becoming accustomed to grass again in three minutes, and getting my backhand to break eggs.

Tennis balls fly off grass faster and lower than off hard surfaces and the curved balls keep going—never kicking back. I liked to play on grass, especially true grass, as it suited my game and levelled things out to a certain extent. But, nonetheless, it took quite a bit of getting used to. And I wasn't used to having to cope with daisies in the grass.

We held serve in a conventional sort of way until about five or six all in the first set, at which stage I broke his service in a way which I considered to be quite conventional—one backhand passing shot aimed crosscourt which went off the wood up the line, and a neat net cord at 30–40. Werksman, however, seemed of the opinion that my efforts had been tinged with a dose of good fortune. He had the habit of muttering things to himself and not quite under his breath, so that one caught snatches of things like: "—a foreigner! A thin man from Africa! And you're struggling Werksman!"

Or: "—if you weren't such a big, deep asshole, Werksman, you'd be towelling off by now, *having won*!"

The monologue which took place as we changed ends after that set was far more extensive.

"You are losing," he muttered fiercely, "to a man who has arms and legs like pretzels! If you weren't paralysed, you would be able to *break* them off and serve them with beer! He *cannot* play, and you *can* play, and he's winning and you're losing—so get your tail out onto the grass and *play*!"

I was tired and irritable and not amused, and secretly began to wonder if there was any truth in what my opponent said. I lost the second set after a bitter struggle, but broke his service in the second game of the final set and quickly took a 4–1 lead. At this point he muttered something about my having a head like a pineapple and that he should be chopping it up and serving it with cocktails. He then proceeded to play superbly, restricting his utterances to things like—"Now! You've got him!" or "One more break and his backhand's got to fold!"

I found myself leaving the court having lost 7–5, feeling utterly dejected, but surprised by the many sympathetic remarks from even casual tennis acquaintances. So I drank three beers with Drysdale and Stolle, slept for eighteen hours then awoke and found myself left only in the men's doubles, but with a week to get some grass court practice, and to investigate the talents of the two French maids.

The beaches at Southampton are long and sandy and the weather that year was particularly warm. Françoise obediently produced her friend, a tall languid girl with a straight sheaf of dark hair which half obscured an eye and fell to an angular point beneath the line of her chin, like a Vidal Sassoon sketch. Where Françoise was big-boned and happy, Nicci was introspective, had a semitic profile, a slightly grainy skin and smiled instead of laughing out loud. She smelt of France—peppery perfume and a hint of garlic and everything about her was lanky—legs, waist, hands and throat—like a newly-born giraffe. Her legs wobbled at the knees. I find girls with long legs that wobble at the knees very attractive in an oblique sort of way. To my surprise, I found that she liked beer.

And so, on most evenings, we watched television and drank beer, eating the hamburgers which Françoise created in the kitchen. Afterwards, with a white Long Island moon at full strength, we would walk down to the sea and hit the water with mighty leaps and shouts.

The beach, the shining sea with its mild waves, and the moonlight, reminded me of the famous love scene played by Burt Lancaster and

Deborah Kerr in *From Here to Eternity*, a film which had left a great impression on me when I had first seen it. With this in mind, I tried a long shot, and tentatively told Nicole that she looked a little like Deborah Kerr. She gave one of her rare chuckles and said, "Ah, mon chéri, but no more than you look like Burt Lancastaire!" Unromantic fare, but nonetheless, the seed had been sown. We walked arm in arm, wading ankle deep in the surf and talking in whispers and at a suitable spot, fell to our knees with the waves breaking around our thighs. True to form, we finally achieved a horizontal position on the sand, locked in a tender embrace.

Fate can play savage tricks on amateur romantics. Disaster struck in the form of a freak wave. We were suddenly overwhelmed by roaring water which rolled us over several times towards the shore, shook us briefly, then hauled us seawards in a swirl of liquid sand, before leaving us lying there like two pieces of driftwood. Both my ears were filled with sand, Nicole, who finished up underneath, was in a far worse plight, with almost all her orifices silted up. We struggled to our feet.

"You and your romantic notion," she cried, half laughing, half sobbing, "such a thing would never 'ave 'appened to Lancastaire!"

She was probably right, although if it had, I suppose they would have done another take. We would never have *seen* Burt Lancaster rolled over and have *his* ears filled with sand! It took some considerable sluicing off in the water to clear ourselves of sand and seaweed and, in retrospect, we both agreed that the whole business of embracing on the water's edge by moonlight, was overdone and best left lying in the mind!

French maids' company must be good therapy for men's doubles. Cliff and I formed an unlikely, but effective, combination and reached the final round without undue desperation. On finals afternoon, Bill Clothier arrived and I was determined that we win the tournament. I had even spent some time the previous evening persuading Cliff to have an early night, and also to *knock off the sitters*—as he had a nasty habit of trying clever and Larsen-like shots off the easy ones, which caused flurries of activity at a moment when I felt the umpire should be calling the score in our favour. There is nothing as bad as being in a tight match, getting an easy one, not quite killing it and having your opponent recover it and send up a high lob, which you suddenly realise is going to drop in, and saying to yourself, "Oh Jesus Christ, now I have to do the whole thing over again, and I should be towelling off and sipping coke!"

Our final was scheduled at four in the afternoon, against some couple like Whitney Reed and Eugene Scott. Chuck McKinley and Dennis

Ralston, the current United States doubles champions, were not playing at Southampton that year, leaving a mixed bag of American teams, all good, but not *that* good.

Cliff and I hit some practice balls at about two thirty, and then he announced that he had to return to the house for some or other reason. I watched the singles finals for a while, then remembered that I had forgotten to bring my spare rackets. I returned to the house and opened the front door in time to see Françoise and Cliff disappearing furtively into our suite. I ran up the stairs and opened the door.

"Oh no, you bloody well don't," I cried and for once Cliff looked sheepish.

"It's quite good before doubles," he said. "It clears your eyes. Before singles, it's a bit ambitious."

"Your eyes are clear enough for doubles," I said grimly, "and I am not interested in your theories about singles. I am not leaving for the courts without you!"

We won the finals and received silver water pitchers and the congratulations of Clothier. I was delighted with Cliff as a doubles partner—he had excellent reflexes and particularly damaging service returns, and he obviously enjoyed playing with me.

I made the journey across the Sound to Newport in a light aircraft, feeling far happier about playing in the United States. The tournament, held at the Newport Casino, was run by the great American innovator and enthusiast James van Alen.

As mentor, founder and general factotum of the Newport tournament, van Allen insisted even then that the nine point sudden death tie-breaker be used in all matches, if the games' score reached five-all. In the first round there I came within a hair's breadth of being done in by Clark Graebner who led me one set, five-all, and four points to love in the tie-breaker. To win five consecutive points, two of which were on his service, against Graebner on grass, was a miracle by any standards and so rattled him that I won the third set quite easily.

There has always been a great depth of competent players in the United States. You could be sure that even number thirty-four on the National Grading List could play well enough to add a few grey hairs to visiting foreigners. Even if they weren't the standard big serve and volleyers, they were always other things—diabolical forehand hitters, lightning net rushers or neggety devils who dug in on the baseline and hit heavy groundshots; and all of them behaved as though it was simply a matter of time before they would become the world's best tennis players.

To breeze through the early rounds of any big American tournament, one had to be an almighty player, fully equipped with everything, including a sense of humour. After Graebner, I beat Larry Nagler in another third set tie-breaker, and after him, someone else whom I can't remember.

Chuck McKinley in the semi-final was too hard to handle. On court he behaved like a rubber cannon-ball which had been fired into a walled enclosure, bounding about and hitting everything at a hundred miles an hour. Against him I kept feeling that he was about one point ahead of me, so that by the time I had completed my point, he was already half way through the following one. By the end of our match, which he won in three sets, he had begun towelling off and I was still busy playing the last point or two when I heard the umpire call the score. It was very disconcerting. Cliff and I lost to McKinley and Dennis Ralston in the semi-final, also in three sets.

The United States men's doubles championship took place in Boston in those days, during the week preceding Forest Hills. The doubles combination which Cliff and I had drummed-up made the event far more interesting and I arrived at the tournament filled with enthusiasm.

"You'll be staying," they told me on arrival, "with the Furcolos. Rod Laver will also be there and you will be sharing the guest suite."

I was excited. Foster Furcolo was the ex-governor of Massachusetts and lived with his family in a superb old house not far from the club. Besides, Rod, tremendously famous always, was at that time at the height of his fame, as he was about to compete at Forest Hills for the last leg of his grand slam. We were firm friends by then, and I knew we would have an interesting time. My faithful friend, Clifford Drysdale, was consulted and relegated to more modest digs, while I made ready to move into the luxury and culture of Bostonian society.

The house was beautiful. It had a hall with a wide and elegant stairway which divided into two on the landing, before giving way to the suites above. On the wall above this landing hung a great sail-fish, a trophy, I think from some heraldic deep sea fishing trip of days past. After climbing the section of stairway beneath the sail-fish, one reached the upper floor and turned immediately left into the suite which Rod and I were to occupy. This elaborate description all seems irrelevant now, just as then it did to me. Only later, after that night, had I cause to examine the topography of the place more carefully.

Rod had already arrived. He was sitting in the bedroom upon one of the beds, surrounded by piles of new tennis equipment. Most of the better players of the circuits were well provided with tennis gear, but I never got used to the quantities and varieties showered upon Laver. He looked up as I entered, with typical Laver-like casualness.

"Hello bastard," he said, although I hadn't seen him since Hamburg. "Look at all this bloody gear. Enough gear here to start a store. And that's only half of it. There's no way I'll ever be able to wear all this lot, unless I change my bloody shirt after every game!"

I felt happy and at home with Rod—he had a mild manner with a sense of humour which often played on understatement. He'd understate almost everything, especially his remarkable successes and superb tennis ability; like the unbelievable, impossible shots he sometimes pulled out of a hat when they were least expected and badly needed. These he would scrutinize soberly, before remarking:

"Not a bad little bit of an old nudge, would you say?" or: "Rare bit of old arse, that one, don't you think?"

When Governor Furcolo gave us a Cadillac for the week, Rod gave it an appreciative look. "Thanks Governor," he said, "now we've got transport!"

Now, sitting on his bed, busy lacing up a tennis shoe, he waved a hand at the extravagant surroundings and said. "Choose a bed. It's not much, but it's home!"

There was only one other bed apart from the one upon which he was sitting, so I established myself upon it and began unpacking. Rodney told me that he and Fred were top seeds for the tournament, and that Cliff and I would meet them in the quarters.

"Who do we play on the way to the quarters?" I asked him warily. He had a bad habit of judging other people's abilities on the strength of his own, thus carving away the mere possibility of losing before the quarters, at least.

"Oh, teams," he said vaguely. "Dell and Bond. Hoogs and McManus. Eugene Scott and somebody. People like that. Just got to keep the ball in play and give the loose ones a bit of a nudge."

"I see," I said. "You mean just coast through the early rounds."

He nodded, not even recognising my slight sarcasm. Competitive tennis, I realised, was a very simple matter for Rodney George.

I began unpacking and as I did so, an uneasy thought struck me. Rodney was, as far as I knew, unaware of my erratic nocturnal behaviour. It was true that Abe Segal had frequently raved about, "Forbsey belonging in a strait-jacket at night," or other such remarks, in various lounges and dressing rooms, but it was equally true that Abie himself was considered highly unreliable as a source of factual information and, in fact, an imminently eligible strait-jacket case himself—moreover, not only at night.

I conducted a quick consultation with myself about the wisdom of even broaching the subject with Rodney. I'd hardly done anything unusual for weeks, discounting the odd outburst or two and the fact that Cliff informed me one morning that I had pulled him out of bed the previous night and coldly instructed him to get on with the match, as play had to be continuous—an accusation which I felt to be groundless, as I usually had some vague memory of my more positive actions, whereas, on this occasion, I'd had none. Still, Laver was Laver, and I baulked at the idea of taking him completely by surprise, so I decided to mention the thing very casually.

"In case you hear me moving about the room in the dark," I said, idly examining one of the racket grips at which he continually scraped and whittled, "don't worry. Just put on the light." He looked at me thoughtfully.

"What might you be doing?" he asked.

"I er, sometimes, very occasionally, well, you know, I, er—."

"Start a revolution," he interrupted. "Don't tell me big Abie wasn't just raving on?"

"Abie exaggerates enormously," I said. "At worst I usually walk quietly round my bed, or give one or two instructions."

He said no more, besides giving me a penetrating look and muttering, "My bloody oath," under his breath once or twice, in a very Australian way.

The Furcolos were a great family, epitomising the warm, but casual hospitality, the lack of pompousness, yet the proper dignity of the true American. We had dinner and a game or two of table tennis before turning in. It was as well that I had warned Rodney. Sometime during that first night, in the light of the moon which poured in through the window, I saw a thin, smallish and vicious-looking animal leap onto my bed and run up the covers towards my face at an alarming rate. Laver or no Laver, action had to be taken. In the nick of time I leapt up, rolled the creature up in the bed covers and, kneeling on my bed, I was busy squeezing the rolled bed cover violently in order to throttle the creature, when Rodney awoke. He sat up immediately.

"What's happening?" he asked, not unreasonably.

"I've got the little devil in here," I cried.

"Who is he?" asked Rodney.

"A thin little bastard," I replied.

Suddenly I threw the rolled up cover on Rodney's bed.

"Have a look if he's dead yet," I commanded.

Rodney backed away. "You have a look," he said.

I began to realise then that something passing strange was going on, but was still in the grip of the dream. Gingerly I unrolled the cover and by the time it was open, I had fully awoken.

"I warned you that I sometimes did things in the night," I said sheepishly. "You should have switched the light on."

"Sorry about that," said Rodney, typically. "Came as a bit of a shock though. Didn't know what you had rolled up in there. Wasn't sure whether you'd managed to kill it. Thought it might jump out. For a moment there I really thought you had something!"

"So did I," I said fervently and quietly thanked my stars that the incident was over and that it had not been worse. Also, to my great relief, I began sleeping like a log, so that it seemed that my night-time performance had been a flash-in-the-pan.

I practised each morning with Rodney—rigidly effective Hopman type practice which forced you to make every shot with a purpose in mind—not the comfortable, free swinging hit-ups which were so tempting and which made you imagine that you were beautifully in form, and playing like a sort of improved version of Donald Budge.

Ten minutes of forehand cross courts—ten of forehand to backhand, up the line, ten of backhand to forehand, ten of cross court backhands; then all four repeated twice over with alternate players volleying. All that added up to two hours, leaving thirty minutes for practising overheads, services or any special weaknesses. A half-hour practice set completed the three hour session which Rodney insisted we follow. By the end of the week I had never played better, and often in retrospect, I have thought of those far off sessions and said to myself wistfully, "If only! Forbes, if only!"

Cliff and I continued our efficient combination, edging out the American teams by the odd service break—all that is needed in grass court doubles. In the quarters we found ourselves faced by Laver and Stolle, having beaten Donald Dell and Billy Bond in the sixteens. It was strange that, having begun my doubles link-up with Cliff in a state of some uncertainty, we now found ourselves in the quarters of the United States National Doubles, actually discussing positively the possibility of beating the first seeded team.

The evening before the encounter, the four of us drank a few beers together in a mood of good-natured banter. Fred Stolle warned Cliff against hitting, "Those arsey shots off that crappy double hander", and Cliff in turn said that Fred should, "Watch his tramline and not serve too many doubles."

This remark carried a slight edge to it, as Fred never pandered to caution on his second ball, serving it virtually as hard as his first. This resulted in a restless time for the receiver, but also, on Fred's off days, a good many double faults. Rodney said very little except that he thought the four of us should be able to, "Move the ball about a bit out there on fast grass!"

Rodney and I turned in early that night. And I remember clearly that the thought of any unforeseen activity did not even enter my head. I was tired and fell asleep almost at once. Our room was so arranged that the wall which backed up against the stairwell consisted of a long built-in cupboard which Rod and I shared. As Rodney had chosen the bed furthest from the cupboard, my bed was adjacent to it, at a distance of perhaps ten to twelve feet.

Some time late that night, I opened my eyes to find the room full of moonlight. Standing in the cupboard, quite still, was a man whom I could see clearly through the open door. My heart froze as my mind raced through the possible reasons for his presence, finally fastening onto the obvious one. He was there to "get" Rodney. There was no doubt about it. Rodney was a celebrity and this man, hiding in our cupboard, was an American psychopath, out to do him in. But my bed was between him and Rodney and the thought that he may not be sure which was Rod and which was me, made the situation even more desperate. The headline, "Laver saved when Assassin strikes Thin South African," flashed through my mind. Action had to be taken at once.

Suddenly a daring and subtle plan occurred to me. The cupboard had heavy doors with keys which turned easily. All I had to do, I decided, was to brace myself, leap up, slam the door and lock him in. There was no time to lose so, tensing myself for the deed, I began the countdown. In a state of nervous tension, one moves like lightning. I counted to three, hurled aside the bed clothes, gave a mighty leap, landed besides the cupboard, closed the door with a slam, and turned the key. As the noise died away, I heard an answering rumbling from somewhere in the house, then silence. I leaned for a moment against the cupboard door, weak with relief and overwhelmed suddenly by tiredness. Such was the depth of the nightmare that I was still tightly in its grip. It was then that I noticed Rodney, standing bolt-upright on the far side of his bed.

"Bit of a hell of a bang," he said shakily. "What's happening?"

"There was a guy in the cupboard," I replied, "who was going to get you. I locked him in."

"Oh, really?" said Rodney.

"We'll get him out in the morning," I said.

I was desperately tired and climbed back into bed. The incident was closed, my mind was blank, yet at that moment as I lay back and closed my eyes, the first nudges of reality occurred.

"It's not possible," I remember thinking to myself. "I *couldn't* have actually done *that*. Not again. Not tonight, of all nights!"

But then there was a knocking sound and I opened my eyes. Rodney was standing next to the cupboard, tapping on the door with his knuckles and holding an ear to it.

"Anyone in there?" he said in an urgent whisper. "Who in the hell are you?"

"It's OK, Rodney," I said loudly and he jumped about three inches off the floor, "there's no one in there."

"You just told me there was," he said. "Could have believed you too."

"It's one of my dreams," I said. "I'm terribly sorry. You should have put the light on."

"No time for that," he said. "Just a bloody great bang. A man doesn't think about switching lights on when he thinks he's in a raid. Anyway, I'm opening this cupboard, just to make sure!"

We both watched in silence as he gingerly unlocked the door and opened it. Immediately inside it hung my raincoat on a hanger. Rodney gave it a contemptuous punch.

"Fooled you, you bastard," he said to the coat. "Thought you were going to get us, hey? Hadn't counted on my friend here, had you?"

Now, thirteen years later, the unreality of that particular situation still occasionally strikes me—Rodney Laver, chatting to a raincoat in the middle of a far-off night in Boston!

We slept, eventually. So badly did I want to disassociate myself from the incident that, when I awoke, I found myself still with the faint hope that the whole thing might yet prove to be a dream within a dream.

"I dreamt I had a dream last night," I said to Rod when he finally awoke.

"Your dream couldn't have been as bad as *my* dream," he said with deep conviction.

"Bad, hey?" I asked.

"Nearly crapped myself," he said cryptically. "Going to pay a lot more attention to what Abe Segal says from now on. Now I realise why he sometimes behaves as though he's got someone after him! Always looking over his shoulder, these days, is big Abie. Now I'm beginning to understand why!"

We went down to breakfast after I had made Rodney promise not to tell of the incident. Governor Furcolo looked up as we entered.

"Morning," he said cheerfully. "Quite a night wasn't it?"

I was speechless, but Rodney found words.

"Something happen in the night?" he enquired carefully.

"God-darned sail-fish," said the Governor.

"Sail-fish?" Rodney looked puzzled.

"Been hanging on that wall for nearly eight years now and last night—down he came. Made a mighty bang, too. We kinda thought you might have heard it."

"You hear a bang in the night, Gordon?" he said.

"Can't say I did," I muttered.

"Broke a piece off his tail," said the Governor. "I'll have to get it glued up."

My private theory was that the banging of the heavy cupboard door had dislodged the sail-fish, but it could never be proven. I consoled myself with the thought that there was just a chance that by some remarkable coincidence, the fish had chosen that particular moment to drop from the wall. Just a very small chance. But we never found out.

Our match was scheduled for about three that afternoon on one of the centre courts. The weather was sunny, the grass fast and from the very outset I had the feeling that Cliff and I might just play very well.

We held firm until four games all in the first set, then dropped service and lost 6–4 in a very conventional sort of way. At about six all in the second set it occurred to me that we were containing the game—that it was not, as I had been afraid, running away with us. If anything, Rodney was perhaps too much the individual to ever be as great at doubles as he was at singles. While he made some shots so quick and stunning that he left everyone, including his partners, with severe cases of dropped jaw, he also sometimes confused things by playing unconventional shots—things like drive volleys, or topspin lobs for service returns or colossal ground shots from the back of the court when he should have been at net. He also sometimes advanced to net behind his own lobs, quite confident apparently of volleying back his opponent's smashes, which he sometimes did.

Men's doubles is a game where certain rules should always be stuck to, and these rules seldom allow for the spectacular, usually demanding firm, if sometimes tedious, positional play while openings are looked for. Rodney, being a law unto himself, firmly believed in making his own openings by sheer weight of shot. The result was hair-raising for his opponents. If he happened to be on form they spent a good part of the match collecting balls and protecting their persons. If not, he was vulnerable to solid resistance. Fred Stolle was a great doubles player, orthodox, intelligent and hard to penetrate. We became locked in mortal combat that day, and played for hours. I remember that Cliff and I won the second set at 12–10 and then, as though annoyed by our effrontery, Rodney and Fred snatched the third out of our hands at 6–2. Rodney's pre-match prediction was perfectly accurate. The ball *was* moving about like lightning. Fred's service led me to believe that he was conducting some fresh experiments in rocketry; Cliff hit tremendous two-handers and Rodney startled all three of us in his usual mercurial way by flashing about in tight circles and pulling every conceivable shot out of his hat. At two sets to one down, it seemed likely that Cliff and I were about to suffer one of our gallant defeats, but to our surprise we latched onto the fourth set and stuck like limpets. At 10–9 for us we found ourselves with points for the set, won a hand-to-hand volley exchange, and heard the score called at two sets all.

By the time the fifth set began, we'd been playing for close to three hours and still the match hung in the balance. With the score at twelve-all in that set, dusk was coming on and a heavy dew had begun to settle, making the court surface very slippery. At fifteen games all in the fifth, with the light fading fast, I held my service after several deuces and we changed ends leading 16–15. As we towelled off, the umpire turned to us and announced that we were to play only one more game, a decision which, I remember thinking, was decidedly strange as it put a lot of pressure on Fred, whose turn it was to serve. On the other hand, to return Fred's service on a greasy grass court in fading light was also not the easiest thing imaginable. We took up our positions in silence. It was one of those occasions when a match catches the imagination of the public. The stands were packed with players and spectators, excited by the fact that the top-seeded pair were in trouble.

Fred opened proceedings with a clean ace to Cliff on the right hand court. He then served a huge double fault to me, the first ball hitting the tape of the net and the second narrowly missing my heel.

As I moved to take my position for the next point, Rodney caught my eye and murmured something about Fred giving his second ball too much of a nudge. At fifteen-all Fred served a flat bullet of a first ball down the middle to Cliff, who apparently anticipated it, for he stepped into it and hit a two-hander down Rodney's tramlines so hard that the point was over before Fred had recovered from his service swing. This time Rodney's murmur was drowned by the roar of applause, but I saw his lips moving and guessed that he was discussing Cliff's 'nudge' with himself. At 15–30 Fred served an ace to me. At thirty-all Cliff mis-timed his two-hander so that instead of a clean return the ball went off the throat of his racket with a wooden clunk, hit the tape in front of the oncoming Fred, ran along the top of it for about a yard, then fell over on his side and disappeared into the grass. Fred rolled his eyes upwards. The crowd roared, the umpire called out the score at 30–40, and Cliff and I found ourselves with a match point against Laver and Stolle at 16–15 in the fifth set, on a wet grass court and in the dark to boot. In absolute silence I got ready to receive.

Fred's first ball narrowly missed Rodney's head and someone in the crowd laughed nervously. His second was so deep that for a fleeting moment I thought he had served a double. But the ball hit the line and presented me with an awkward skidding backhand which I managed to dig out of the corner with a late slice like a nine iron in golf. My shot drifted slowly towards the net, climbing slightly as it went, like a tired bi-plane trying to get airborne, with me closing in behind, while Fred approached the net from his side with a worried look. With a final surprising spurt, the ball cleared the net and settled into the grass at Fred's feet, leaving him an appallingly difficult half-volley. He got it back, but not well enough, and Cliff pounced with his two-hander down the middle and knocked it off. Game, set and match to Drysdale and Forbes—4–6, 12–10, 2–6, 11–9, 17–15.

The actual moment of victory after a long and tense confrontation is filled with different emotions. For me the strongest of these has always been a feeling of profound relief. The exultation and satisfaction I found only came later. There is a fair amount of agony in a finely-contested tennis match. Nerves and body are simultaneously engaged under maximum stress and held that way, and there are few players who can honestly claim to enjoy such intense competition. This match, though, had thrilled and excited me beyond words. There could be no finer sportsmen than Laver and Stolle.

We enjoyed the cheers of the crowd, the cold beers in the dressing-room and the excited post-mortems, but there wasn't time for prolonged celebration.

In the semi-finals the following day against Antonio Palafox and the late Raphael Osuna, the fortunes of the previous day were reversed. We lost 12–10, 11–9, 11–9, and found ourselves only twenty-four hours later sipping beers in the same dressing-room. Only the mood had changed from celebration to introspection. The gods which dished out major doubles titles had not, it seemed, included us upon their lists. And so we went on to New York with a fresh layer of memories to try again.

We arrived at night and at first, from the aircraft window, the city was just a skyline, far-off and soaring. But the next morning was sunny and I rose quite early and walked up Fifth Avenue as far as the park, and that was when the jumble of adjectives drifted through my head. But mere adjectives were only the beginning. Why is it that, in the mind, New York stirs and stuns more than any other city? Creates for itself an image which is untouchable—out of reach of ordinary people? Perhaps the sheer size of it—the geometry of its planes and verticals, which sweep up and fracture the familiar sky. One is anonymous in New York. Totally, absolutely anonymous. I walked the avenue that morning feeling, as I have never felt before, that I was quite alone. Yet there were the names of places and stores, so familiar that I felt I knew them well—Brook Bros., Abercrombie and Fitch, Bonwit Teller, Macys, Tiffany's. At the corner of Forty-sixth street, as I stood waiting for the lights to change, a fat pigeon flew overhead and a large, wet dropping struck me fairly on the forehead and nose. Later, I realised that there must have been something symbolic about the hit, but at first, then, I felt helpless and foolish, and highly relieved when a young girl who turned out to be an Israeli student, produced a wad of Kleenex and set about clearing away the debris. By the time it was gone and we had both agreed that it must have been a very large pigeon, we decided to find a coffee bar to help me recover my spirits.

After coffee, up towards the park, we entered on impulse a superb and lofty church. It was huge and quiet inside with silences hanging about everywhere, in great pools. Suddenly, the organ began to play, rich and splendid Bach, the notes and chords carving away the silences in great slices until the church was full of interwoven sounds. It was strange and unforgettable, that first introduction to New York, and ever since then I have always respected the place and longed, mildly, to become a part of it.

All the visiting players were accommodated at the Vanderbilt Hotel on about Thirty-fourth Street. I was relegated to sharing a room with Cliff Drysdale again, while Rodney was ensconced in the suite of honour where he immediately became inundated again with tennis gear and, in fact, apparel of all kinds, to the extent that, at one stage, it was almost impossible to get into his room. Cliff made a facetious remark about my "rejoining the common people" as I entered our room, but I shut him up immediately by reminding him that I, by being billeted with Laver, had made a decisive contribution to our best-ever doubles win by scaring the wits out of him the night before. Roy Emerson also turned up at the Vanderbilt, having just completed the Middle Eastern circuit. He was as cheerful as ever, spilling grins and greetings all over the place. And so we all gathered for the United States Nationals, at Forest Hills.

It was hot and rainy for nearly a week, at first, and practice courts were at a premium. Besides, officialdom at Forest Hills at that time was about as bad as I had ever known. Players were treated as intruders, necessary evils, and people of low culture and little brain. Lunches, served in a damp marquee were hardly edible, and service at the main clubhouse was haughty and reluctant. Only the faithful white towels were plentiful. The official in charge of allocating practice courts was about a hundred and two years old, half blind, and with a memory which latched only onto odd and random pieces of information. His immediate reaction to any request for practice facilities was that there were either no courts available, or no balls, or neither. The only person whom he could remember was Roy Emerson. The name Emerson, for some obscure reason, had irrevocably lodged itself in his mind, and I soon discovered that the only sure way of getting a practice court was to arrange to play with Roy and then have him ask for the balls. He would walk up to the old fossil, pat him on the back, and with a huge grin ask him for a court.

"Name?" the old fellow would grunt.

"Emerson," Roy would say.

"Ah, Emerson, take court nine. Here are the balls," and off we'd go. When I mentioned this to Roy, he looked at me sceptically.

"He'd give you a court," he said.

"Not a hope," I replied, "I've tried."

"Bet you a dollar he will, bastard," said Roy.

"OK," I said. "We'll go up to him, you ask for a court and tell him you're Forbes and see what happens."

"You're on," said Roy.

We approached the desk and Roy asked for a court in the usual way.

"Name?" enquired the old man.

"Forbes," said Roy. "Gordon Forbes, the famous South African."

"No courts," said the old man gruffly.

"It's all right," I intervened quietly. "He's playing with me. I'm Emerson!"

"Ah, Emerson," he said. "Yes, well, court thirteen is about to come off. You can have that one!"

We took the balls and went off to practise, laughing delightedly.

"You see," I teased Roy, "the *name* he knows, not you personally!"

For some reason, that incident must have impressed the old fellow's memory, for the next day when Roy went to ask for a practice court, giving his name as Emerson, the old man looked up at him sharply.

"You're not Emerson," he said. "You're Forbes."

"Can't be Forbes," said Roy. "Not thin enough to be Forbes."

"What do you mean?" asked the old man.

"You have to be pretty skinny to be Forbes," said Roy. He bent his arm sharply and pointed to his bicep. "See that," he said, "that's a muscle. Forbes doesn't have any of those!"

At that moment I arrived on the scene, ready to practise. The old man looked up at me, then at Emerson, then back to me.

"Who are you?" he asked gruffly.

"I am Emerson," I said.

With a contemptuous glance at Roy, the old man handed me the balls.

"Come on, Forbes," I said to Roy. "Let's go and practise!"

Thereafter, nothing would persuade the old bloke that I wasn't Roy Emerson. Emerson, he regarded as a lowly South African of meagre talent.

"Hope the old bastard doesn't have anything to do with the draw," was Emerson's wry comment. "It's bad enough being Forbes in practice; wouldn't like to be him in a match!"

The weather cleared, the sun came out, hot and steamy, and play got under way on damp, heavy and not-too-even grass courts. Forest Hills can be desperately humid. By the end of the warm-up one is wet through and physically, there, matches are largely a matter of keeping one's body lubricated. Allen Fox used to spend about half an hour before each match, quietly eating salt tablets and glucose; to "hydrate himself".

Rod Laver was by far the best amateur in the world at that time, under any conditions and on any surface. He didn't even need to "hydrate himself". No one has ever played tennis more positively than he. He controlled his matches absolutely; quietly, simply, modestly even, but also superbly, with a control so rigid and purposeful that it seemed that every shot he made was part of an unwavering scheme to win. Other players guided their strokes. Rodney fired his at predetermined points. It was *not* simply a matter, as he used to so often claim, of just "keeping the ball in play and giving the loose ones a bit of a nudge." More accurately, his game was a grand, deliberate and inevitable road to victory.

When he was young, he was a wild and woolly player. Every ball got well and truly hit, and I remember laughing at some of his early matches, watching his forehand and backhands flying, out of control, into the backstop. Yet, never did Harry Hopman, the great Australian strategist, and Rodney's adviser, suggest that he play more carefully. "One day," he said to me, long ago, as we watched him spray balls over a particularly broad front, "he's going to start hitting all those shots in and then, my boy, what a player he will be!"

That year, at Forest Hills, the shots all went in. Rodney won his grand slam and Hopman's prophecy came true. What a player he was.

I find with surprise that I haven't, except in passing, written of Harry Hopman. It is impossible really to contemplate that tennis era without considering him. His influence totally dominated it. Over a period of a dozen years, he presented to the world a succession of champions of such character and class that without him, this section of the game's history would have been quite different. He was a genius at the art of winning tennis; had uncanny ability in the key aspects of producing champions; was able to spot potential in players at a very early age; and, having spotted it he was able to develop it, nurture it, protect it and force it to grow. His methods of extracting the most effective game from his players were enterprising and diverse. He would coax, bully, praise, berate, encourage, inveigle, persuade and sometimes rant and rave. His disciplines were rigid, his sympathy for weakness was scant, his training schedules verged on slave labour. He wanted tough, confident and fearless champions, and he dedicated himself totally to developing these qualities from the varying personalities of the players in his charge. His collective results are undoubtedly one of the great sports-training achievements of modern tennis.

Beginning with Sedgman and McGregor, he produced a series of champions of such remarkable ability and character that nearly all of them have found niches in tennis history. Look: Lewis Hoad, Ken Rosewall, Rod Laver, John Newcombe, Neale Frazer, Roy Emerson, Ashley Cooper, Tony Roche, Malcolm Anderson. Even his lesser players were successes by most standards: Rex Hartwig, Mervyn Rose, Ken Fletcher, Bob Mark. Others too. Of course, it is not true to say that without Hopman these players would not have become champions. What is unquestionably true, is that he profoundly affected their game and their lives. Never in sporting history has there been a line of such noble champions.

I played particularly well at Forest Hills that year. I beat Niki Pilic, Fred Stolle, Alex Metreveli, and Billy Knight on consecutive days, then forgot to hydrate myself properly and lost to Raphael Osuna in the quarters. Osuna lost to Laver, who won, defeating Roy Emerson in the final. During the weeks after Forest Hills I went with Donald Dell to Washington to stay at his parents' house on 5204 Battery Lane.

Even then, Donald was the true law man, always ready for a debate. Always looking for logical conclusions. With him the perfect guide, we roamed about Washington seeing all the sights. Now, of course, as a result of some inspired crystal ball gazing in the late sixties, he has become a tennis millionaire, acquired a blonde wife of rare form, and gotten a little heavy round the middle. But he is still unquestionably the same Donald Dell!

After Washington, Donald and I went on to play a tournament in Tuscaloosa in the heart of Alabama. Devastatingly hot. By means of some cunning negotiations, Jason Morton, who ran the tournament, had obtained as his top seeds, Rod Laver, winner of the Grand Slam, and Whitney Reed, the eccentric American No. 1. Whitney was one of the few players of that particular era who was almost totally unorthodox. For him all the age-old clichés concerning footwork, balance, transference of weight, follow through or controlled backswing, meant nothing at all. His main concession to transference of weight, for instance, was to tuck his tongue into one or other of his cheeks and let his arms, legs and eyes do the rest. For a year at least he was the United States' No. 1 player, and during this period he conducted his life in such an unorthodox way, both on and off the court, that it is fair to assume that many of the more staid USLTA officials fervently wished that he had taken up some other form of sport.

At Tuscaloosa, Laver and Whitney Reed were the star attractions, and Donald and I were brought in as semi-final cannon fodder. We toiled. The heat and humidity were barely endurable and the grass courts brave, but suspect.

I dutifully reached my semi-final against Reed and suddenly began to play really well, defeating him in three sets, while in the other half of the draw, Rodney melted down Donald. In the final, then, it was Forbes v Laver.

"It's a good thing," said Rodney mildly, "that we're not rooming together. If what happened in Boston is what you do to opponents before *doubles* matches, I wouldn't want to go to sleep near you before a *singles* final!"

My form carried through to the final. Although it is perhaps fair to assume that Rodney eased up a little after his Grand Slam victory, we nonetheless played a long and exciting four set match. Moreover, it was simply not in Rod's make-up to lose unless he was forced into it. I won in four sets, playing what was to be the most consistent match of my career.

And won a silver casserole. Which Jason Morton forgot to send home to me.

It was important then, and thrilling, and the papers made quite a fuss, but now it doesn't seem to matter much. None of the things which then seemed so important, now matter very much.

America was all that I'd wanted it to be. Not frightening or sinister or even too impersonal. Just a wide, wide country filled with people who wanted to be friendly and who generally believed in themselves. Good people. A remarkable nation.

10

Diary Notes: 1964

A new and sombre thought has recently crept into my head and lies like a shadow at the back of my mind—somewhere, something is going wrong. My game just absolutely won't "lift" itself that last fraction or two. And whereas always before, there has been a deep, inside feeling that it will suddenly, one day, lift its head, just recently that feeling has been fading. I search for it anxiously, rummage around in my thoughts and sometimes I can't find it anywhere; find instead, a few fresh traces of despair. My tennis elbow, it seems, is now a permanent fixture, and the right eye sees two of everything. These things nag at me, depress me, tie me down.

What will become of me when the game is over? Thirty years old. The time has come to move again. To move again—but whither?

In defence of that little far-off requiem of despair, let me state that in 1964, there was still no sign of real money to be made from playing tennis. Only the handful of greats could turn professional and earn respectable fortunes—and that little paragraph in my notebook indicated that it had suddenly occurred to me that I was not going to be a "great". So, whither?—as I so dramatically asked, was I to move?

The trouble with being a sportsman of the kind that I was, is that you become accustomed to and familiar with the good life. You travel about the world, stay at fine hotels, meet worldly and wealthy people, monied people, international people; and so, unless you keep your feet firmly attached to the ground, you are inclined to *believe*, finally; that you are a *part* of their world and not just a borrower of it. It is a very strange illusion, and if the feet are actually allowed to *leave* the ground (a hard thing to prevent), the actual return to earth invariably produces a fairly heavy thud.

On the tennis circuits there were always a handful of people who followed the players from tournament to tournament. They were fascinated by the aura of the circuit. They wanted so badly to become a part of the inner circle of tennis that they copied, exactly, the movements and mannerisms of the players; dressed, ate and spoke as the players did, and even carried their rackets in the same way. In the locker rooms they would casually mention that their backhands were "coming good," as they'd heard Malcolm Anderson say to Hopman. They'd whittle at their racket grips, as Laver did, wear four sweat bands and talk of serving people wide on their forehands. The only thing they couldn't do was *play tennis*. They'd get on court, spin their rackets the way the champions did, look up for the sun, test the breeze, do a knee bend or two, exhale fiercely, like Darmon did, and choose a racket out of several. Expertly they'd take things to the brink of the game itself, and then everything would fall apart. The whole show would wobble and collapse. Tennis itself could not be bluffed. For years I had watched these people with amusement and a mild sort of contempt. Now, I found the tables turned. Outside the world of tennis, the clumsy athletes were often kings!

It didn't take long for me to discover that I was not particularly skilled at anything except playing tennis. As a tennis player I was wanted everywhere; as anything else, the need for me diminished rapidly. Rich people got distant looks on their faces when I spoke of my fears for the future.

"But there must be *plenty* of opportunities," they would say, vaguely. "Try the big concerns; something in Public Relations, or perhaps the sports business or the petrol companies. They always seem to need people."

I had numerous interviews, all of them arranged for me by my influential friends.

"Certainly, Gordon, old fellow," they'd say to me. "I'll arrange that you talk to the chairman of the group. Old Buster Miles. A great friend of mine, old Buster. Jolly good chap, really. Loves his tennis, too. We ride together, d'you see?" and they'd beam at me as though "Old Buster" would solve my problems.

I would listen diligently and follow up all the leads. They always ended with interviews. I'd wait in lobbies, turning over the pages of business magazines and tugging at my collar with a forefinger. Then get shown into offices and find myself facing polite personnel managers. Tea would be brought in.

"Now, Mr Forbes," they would say, "Mr Miles has said that you might be interested in a position with our group. You're our famous tennis player, I understand?"

"Yes," I would say, "I suppose I am."

"Well, what is it exactly that you have in mind?"

Not only did I not know exactly what I wanted to do, I hadn't the foggiest idea. I wanted *them* to tell *me*. I wanted "Old Buster" to take me into the inside of his big, quiet office, to sit me down in a leather chair and say:

"Gordon, my boy, I have just the kind of thing that I believe you could handle. A completely new venture. And with your name and approach and my business experience, I am convinced that we cannot go wrong!"

"I'm not sure, exactly," I would hear myself saying to Old Buster's tenth in command. "I've never worked for a big company. I've worked in a sports store. I'm good at talking to people, and I write a lot. I thought that perhaps Mr Miles might have some ideas."

"Yes, well Mr Miles has asked me to talk to you. Throw some ideas about, you see?"

"I see," I would say with a sinking heart.

"Have you any sales experience?"

"Not really," I would say. "I've sold sports stuff in the stores where I—"

"Any qualifications? Degrees, diplomas of any kind?"

"No, not really. I passed school and then went farming. Then I played tennis—"

"Yes, we know about the tennis. You have no business training then?"

"I've said that I have no training."

"I see. Well, I hardly know what to suggest. Sales, perhaps. Do you think that you would enjoy selling our products?"

"What are your products?" I would ask.

"Earthmoving equipment," they might say, or plastics, or fertilizers and insecticides.

My stomach would turn and I would sit in an uncomfortable daze, trying to picture myself selling strange-sounding equipment. They would be winding up the interview—

"Contact us in about a week. I will have a word with Mr Miles about you. Perhaps something will turn up. I suggest that you give the matter a bit of thought yourself."

Religiously, after some time, I would phone up, and eventually hear the same impersonal voice:

"Not at this point in time, Mr Forbes. We're in the process of consolidation, you see; however, we have your name on our files. Perhaps at a later stage we may . . ."

They were all the same, those interviews. Some firms were genuinely sympathetic, others patient, all of them polite. Some were refreshingly frank. The man at the great Anglo-American Corporation which I thought *must* have *something* that I could do, listened very carefully to all I said, made copious notes, then looked me fairly in the eyes.

"What you really want, Mr Forbes," he said, "is that we give you a salary, an office and a typewriter and leave you undisturbed?"

I don't think that he ever realised how close to the truth he had come.

"Yes!" I wanted to say to him. "Yes! That is exactly what I want!" But instead I murmured "I do see your point. I'm not very experienced at the things you do in here!"

By the time I'd interviewed a dozen or so firms, it occurred to me that all I was succeeding in doing was getting my name on people's files. I began to realise that I was as far removed from their world of making money as they were from my world of tennis. There were skills required, and I didn't have them. I didn't even know the meaning of things like equities, debentures, options, budgets, sales promotions, mailing-shots or cash flows. After one particularly discouraging interview, I met Abe Segal for a tennis game. I was in a low mood, I remember, and ended my tale of woe by saying, "Bloody cash flows. What the devil is a cash flow, anyway?"

Abie thought for a moment, then said that a healthy cash flow was something that was achieved when his wife went out shopping.

"Ask Heather," he said with a snort, "she'll tell you what a cash flow is!"

But it was Abie who eventually found me a job, that Spring in 1964.

"I got a friend," he said, "who's got a factory that makes lights. I told him that with your name you could sell more lights than he could ever make!"

When I looked a bit woebegone and uncertain, he said firmly, "Look, Forbsey, there's none of those big deals you've been talkin' to who are going to come up with anything except hot air. There are no hand-outs in this life, buddy. You're going to have to take a selling job, so you may as well sell lights. You go out there and talk a lot of crap about beer or petrol and nobody'll know you're alive. You'll be just a number, buddy. This way, when you sell lights, you sell lights, and people will know that you sold them. It's exactly like tennis. Nobody throws away any matches. You gotta get out there and win them. *Then* people talk to you!"

Abie may not have known all about debentures or preference shares, but he did know about life.

And so I began to sell lights—architectural and industrial lighting fixtures, to be precise. I was paid £50 each month, was to receive a five per cent commission on what I sold and was given a customer list, a catalogue and a price list. There are few occupations in the business world as chastising as hard selling. It is not recommended for people with airs and graces. A rueful sense of humour is almost essential, maniacal laughter should only be indulged in after working hours, and tears of frustration should be saved for private moments when no one is about.

Uninteresting stuff. Countless people have had to earn livings by selling things. It was, as Abie had said, just like tennis. A matter of "staying in there". Hanging on and letting the waves break over your head. In any case, he made things a lot easier for me. He knew half the people in Johannesburg and many of them well enough to instruct them curtly to: "Make goddamn sure and buy Forbsey's lights!" And the ones he didn't know, Owen Williams did.

To my surprise, I actually began to get orders—small ones at first, but getting progressively larger. It became quite interesting to add them all up at the end of each month and work out five per cent of them.

Diary Notes: 1965

Today is month-end and the occasion for a wide variety of disasters. For a start, sales budgets have not been reached and Pearson, the sales manager is very nervous. What will the MD say, he wants to know? Time is running out. It's like being down two breaks and thirty-love in the fifth. Turnover must be drummed up. Frantic phonecalls. By five, we're all exhausted, but Pearson is still making shots. One last phonecall, he says, but the telephone girl is gone. Feverishly he picks up one of the two phones on the front desk and dials. Listens. Waits. The other phone gives an urgent ring. He picks it up impatiently.

"Hullo," he barks, with a receiver to each ear. A very funny look comes on his face, and he quietly replaces both receivers.

"I just phoned myself up," he says.

He picks up his coat and briefcase.

"When a man phones himself up for an order it's definitely time to go home!"

We all agree.

My first big contract came by way of an inspiration supplied by Roy Emerson, who was playing tennis in Australia at the time and who was, no doubt, quite oblivious of his contribution to my sales effort. During my last season of tennis, Roy had gone through a period where everything he did was "with feeling". If he hit a great passing shot, it was "with feeling"; if a steak which he ordered was particularly tasty, it had been served "with feeling". Once he even emerged from the toilet with a smile on his face and told me that he, "had passed a motion, with feeling"!

So: I had not been "selling lights" for very long before it was decided that I should handle the mining houses. The reason was simple enough, though quite invalid. I was about the only non-Jewish member of the lighting company and, as the mining houses* were generally very Anglo-Saxon in character, my bosses decided, optimistically, that my nose was the most suitable shape to deal with those venerable establishments. What pleased me most was that the mining industry did, in fact, use large quantities of lighting fixtures. I began calling industriously, pestering every engineer and buyer who was even remotely involved in the purchase of mine lighting and making a general nuisance of myself.

At last I was asked to quote on what appeared to me to be a very large project—the interior lighting for a new gold mining reduction plant. There were hundreds of fixtures involved and I compiled the list with growing excitement. The total value emerged as £20,000, £1,000 of which would be my commission, should I be successful. A fortune!

For days I worked at the tender, accumulating leaflets and drawings and trying to work out the best methods of presentation. At last it was ready and I rounded it off with a covering letter into which I inserted a few extravagant phrases about the excellence of the mining house concerned, and how we valued the opportunity to tender on their requirements. I dropped the fat brown envelope into the tender box an hour before the tender closed, and prayed.

* The name given to the large South African mining corporations of which Anglo-American, Anglo-Transvaal and Union Corporations are typical examples.

The next afternoon I was summoned by 'phone to a meeting to discuss the tender.

"Does that mean," I asked cautiously, "that I might be awarded the contract?"

"Not necessarily," came the reply. "All tenderers are being consulted."

Dubious news. I put on my best suit and presented myself. I was shown into a conference room full of sombre-looking engineers, only one of whom I knew.

"Mr Forbes," said the most sombre-looking one of all, "we have received your bid."

He went on at length to explain that the price and quality of the equipment in my offer were almost exactly the same as my competitors.

"It would appear," he said finally and very sternly, "that some kind of price agreement exists between the various lighting companies."

"I know of no such thing," I said firmly.

"Then can you give us any reasons at all why this corporation should favour your fittings ahead of those offered by your competitors?"

There was a deafening silence while my mind raced about in all directions. The small amount of technical knowledge which I had gleaned by then seemed hopelessly inadequate in the face of the engineering brains which surrounded me. The silence grew longer and even more deafening. I was painfully aware of the fact that intelligent words were imminently expected of me and that it appeared that I had none at hand. Suddenly, out of the blue, I thought of Roy Emerson. I took a deep breath, looked at the faces around the table and said:

"Gentlemen, have you taken into account the fact that each one of our light fittings will be delivered to your stores *with feeling*?"

Suddenly everyone in the room began to laugh. The tension suddenly vanished, and the no longer sombre spokesman said something about my reason being possibly "valid, but of a non-technical nature."

The next day a telegram arrived to say that my tender had been accepted. The lighting gods had smiled on me, and my career was irrevocably launched.

While I concentrated on becoming a seller of lights, tennis slyly changed. Not the game so much as the circumstances under which it was run. It is not possible to pinpoint the exact moment in time when the vast and solid old amateur tennis machine began to shake itself to pieces. It had been vibrating badly for years, that much one could say with certainty. And as the sums of money paid to the "amateur" players, labelled expenses, became larger and more farcical, the vibrations increased. By the mid-sixties, it was quite clear to anyone who cared that the venerable old system was falling apart. But so steeped were the players, officials and spectators in the tradition of amateurism that it died hard. Wimbledon was still open only to amateurs and until it changed, the other major tournaments would hold their ground.

It was a losing battle.

Tennis was entertainment and the players were entertainers, and entertainers in this modern world were accustomed to being paid for their skills.

There was more, besides. It was a great spectator sport; ideal for television; healthy; not too time consuming; relatively inexpensive; sociable; played by both sexes; and it provided an excuse for anyone at all to dress up in glamorous gear, show their legs and run about in the sun. So the money gods took a long look at it, voted in favour and began moving in; and with the money came an entirely new status quo.

Although I was preoccupied with my lights, I was kept fairly well informed, due to the fact that Owen Williams decided to involve himself with the new world of tennis promotion. Apart from being one of my close friends, Owen is a born stager of events. He is also, amongst other things, one of the world's greatest spreaders of news. He is what can be termed a professional leaker of secrets. Any news which he wants distributed, he turns into confidential information and then allows it to leak out. More or less confidential items can be circulated in a week. *Highly confidential* stuff takes less than a day! At a comparatively early age he had stopped playing competitive tennis, had wed the divine Jennifer Nicolson, and had begun building a business career, having declared himself in favour of becoming a tycoon. The large and ponderous sporting goods company in which he had enlisted, however, was neither conducive to mercurial careers, nor famous for making millionaires out of its junior clerks and thus had a poor record in tycoon production.

Owen duly resigned, hired an office with a door, nailed onto it a plaque which said: "Owen Williams (Proprietary) Limited" and acquired a large, if slightly used, desk. He then sat down behind the desk and pronounced his company to be in business and trading. As in many new businesses, the cash flow at first was poor and trading was fairly frugal, combining an unlikely inventory of tennis wear, racket strings and Scotch whiskey with large volumes of telephone calls and a surprising number of meetings.

Even at an early stage, Owen displayed a penchant for meetings. Like many sportsmen, I think he had a secret yen for cigars, financial discussions, confidential reports, private secretaries and big deals—in short, the boardroom. And, unable to immediately indulge in *ALL* the activities of the established tycoon, he nevertheless added the random trappings of tycoonery the instant they become accessible. He soon possessed a private secretary and hand-made shirts, and even smoked the odd cigar, to establish within his office the correct odours—although at that stage in his life, he disliked cigars.

Confidential things began to happen behind closed doors almost from the first day. Meetings took place. Lunches were enjoyed and an air of general expansion and prosperity prevailed. He became possessed of a copious melting pot which never seemed to contain less than two or three big deals, presumably in liquid form. Often when I visited him, he would lead me into his inner office, close the door, stop all calls and in a confidential voice tell me something vital, "between these four walls".

Such snippets could range from anywhere between informing me of a new kind of tennis sock with a built-in cure for athlete's foot to a portable tennis court that would roll itself up into a tight ball at the press of a button if one found one was getting beaten. It was between Owen's four walls that I learned, step by step, of the extraordinary changes which were taking place in the world of tennis and of the part which he himself was to play in this changing world. Gradually but inexorably, control of the game was being wrested from the amateur officials.

This "wresting" process was not as easy then as it now sounds. Almost to a man, amateur tennis officials soundly believed that they were born blessed; men with a power; benevolent men, who selflessly devoted their time to the running of tennis tournaments for the benefit of unruly tennis players.

The fact of the matter was, that although they were reasonably devoted, they enjoyed their powers far too much. They developed grandiose notions and became carried away by their own importance. Or, as the Australian players succinctly put it, they got everything "arse end up".

The process of change then involved a re-distribution of control, a division of power in fairly equal proportions between the players themselves and the promoters who raised the money needed to stage attractive tournaments.

Owen Williams virtually pioneered the promotion of super-tournaments. In 1965 he persuaded the giant South African Breweries organisation to offer sponsorship to the tune of some 30,000 dollars, and used the money to lure the world's best players to Johannesburg. Overnight, the South African tournament became a superb international event and although it was still strictly an "amateur" tournament, it carried all the trappings of the great open tournaments of the future.

The previous tournament committee was thrown into immediate and intense confusion. It held an extraordinary meeting at which nearly everyone passed a motion, and at which no one could doze off. Officials would now have to cope with such things as spectators in queues, Coca Cola machines on court, hot water in the men's locker room, and traffic jams. The secretary would have to count large sums of money without fainting. There were to be bars and hot lunches, and boxes in the North Stand. It was all too much for people who hitherto had believed that the ultimate in on-court refreshment was gin bottles filled with tepid water and served in paper cups!

In spite of Owen's early breakthrough, tennis remained until the late sixties, divided into two distinct sections—the amateurs and the professionals.

Traditionally the playing professionals had been a select group of players who travelled the world playing tennis matches for money. Nearly all of them were former Wimbledon champions or, if not, famous for other major tournament victories. My memories of the great pros. began with Donald Budge and Bobby Riggs and progressed to such players as Kovacs, Kramer, Segura, Gonzales, Sedgman, MacGregor, Trabert and Hoad. All of them were greats, and all of them were barred once they turned professional, from ever again playing the amateur tournaments which had made them famous.

In the early sixties, Jack Kramer expanded the four-man professional tours to eight, or even twelve, selecting from the amateur ranks players whom he thought could play attractive tennis, and who would add variety to his pro. tournaments.

They were brave times, those first pro. tours. Each year one or two new stars would be added to the group, and one by one the Wimbledon champions appeared as "rookies" amongst the seasoned pros. Ashley Cooper, Malcolm Anderson, Butch Buchholz, Barry Mackay, Ken Rosewall, Andres Gimeno and, inevitably, Rod Laver.

Those were the names which pioneered professional tennis. They toured and played in big cities and small; on makeshift courts and city streets; before large crowds at places like Madison Square Gardens or the Albert Hall, or small crowds at other places like Stellenbosch in South

Africa, or Alice Springs in Australia. The standard of tennis which they played was never bad and usually superb, and their earnings were minute compared to the mighty prizes of today.

But they were necessary those pros. Valiant, excellent, necessary and, above all, successful.

In 1967, American millionaire, Dave Dixon created a new professional group called the "Handsome Eight," taking from the crumbling amateur ranks such stars as Newcombe, Roche, Roger Taylor, Cliff Drysdale, Niki Pilic, Dennis Ralston, Pierre Barthes of France and Buchholz. And in late 1967 the LTA of Great Britain announced that the 1968 Wimbledon Championships were to be open to competition to both Amateurs and Professionals.

Amateur tennis had lived and died and a new era was at hand.

In 1966, two important things happened in my world. Julia Ashley, my daughter, was born, and my dearly beloved sister and mixed doubles partner, Jean, married Cliff Drysdale who by then had established himself as one of the most interesting and talented players of the time.

In 1967, in partnership with two close friends, I founded my own industrial lighting company. Although I had been employed for several years, working as a salesman for someone else contradicted every instinct instilled in me by my tennis career. Tennis is not a team sport. There is no post-match slapping over beer, nor any gloomy sorrow-drowning in groups. The triumphs in tennis are personal, the defeats lonely and above all, the decisions are all one's own. From the moment I began selling lights, I yearned for identity.

And so it was that when finally we found ourselves alone in our modest premises, surrounded by the dusty bits of furniture that we had accumulated, I felt, above all the anxieties and apprehensions which such occasions breed, an infinite sense of relief. I was on the move again. And this time, given any luck at all, I had a good idea where I was going.

Our business prospered from the very first day. The gods who control commercial enterprises didn't seem to me to be nearly as tricky as those in charge of the tennis circuits. They seemed eager, in fact, to dangle in front of our noses endless opportunities for progress. Essentially though, when one analyses it, building a business is very similar to building a tennis career. Both require thought, care and devotion, and in both one improves immeasurably with practice.

We practised and improved, and even in our first year of trading made more money than I had ever dreamed of in all my years of tennis. Enough, even, to get to England in time for the first open Wimbledon.

11

The two airplane tickets which would enable us to board the London bound airliner arrived on my desk in a plain white envelope. I stared at it for some time, filled with the most extraordinary mixture of feelings. The first open Wimbledon! And not only was I to return there for the occasion. To my surprise, I discovered that my entry had been accepted for all the events! It was a very special thing.

Wimbledon has about it one particular quality which the sensitive mind should consider as being positively treacherous. The warmth of the place compels you to regard it as your own—to adopt proprietary attitudes to certain sections of it. Thus locker thirty-one in dressing-room "A" becomes private property, as does your favourite seat in the players' enclosure, or the stanchion in the railings of the players' balcony, where you always lean when you watch the matches on courts three, four and five. The girls in the front office, the man who arranges the cars, the dressing-room attendant and the gate-keepers are personal friends. And the shower under which you have exulted or wept, is your own special shower; and so forth. Or so it seems—until one day you return, unknown, and suddenly all your very special places are not only no longer your own, but completely out of bounds!

The ceremonial return that summer of 1968 then, as a competitor, had parcelled up in it for me about a dozen separate ecstasies, not the least of which was actually to participate. To walk onto those unbelievable grass courts on the afternoon of an English summer and play in the gentlemen's singles. Or doubles. And with Abe Segal, to boot. It was too much to cope with. I was in a happy, lighthearted daze.

London bubbled. She'd changed her mood completely, Abe Segal told me when he met us at the airport. He was driving an old Rolls Royce and wearing a pair of pink velvet trousers and the kind of wide eternal grin which suggests champagne for lunch and the prospect of a thousand hearty laughs.

"Place's gone mad, Forbsey," he said taking my suitcase. "You'll not believe what's happening. To handle a month in London, a man's got to double his insurance an' walk about with a doctor feelin' his pulse with one hand and carryin' a hypodermic in the other!"

The cases were stowed, the Rolls put into motion and all the time snippets poured forth:

"They got these shops on the King's Road, with the music and all, goin' like crazy and everybody's permanent high. You can blow your mind just breathin' the air!"

He'd found a lot of new friends, too.

"Moore's mad." This with total emphasis. "I mean you think I'm mad, and I think a lot of people are mad. But Forbsey, you can think of all the maddest people you ever knew and shake 'em up together, and they'd be sane compared to Moore. I mean, you know that hair of his? Well, he's grown it. I mean, can you imagine? Stands straight up. He's the only guy I know who has his own personal barbed-wire defence system. He doesn't comb his hair. He uses pliers and sidecutters. Then he concretes it into place."

Abie, in certain frames of mind, could pick a random subject such as this and continue for some time. Moore, it seemed, had gathered together a clan of admirers, virtually as mad as himself, who intrigued Abie.

"Harry Fowler," said Abie, "is not exactly what you'd call completely in command of his senses. And Kenny Lynch, black as the ace of spades, an' born in Birmingham. This is his car, in case you're wonderin'." (Which I was.)

Fowler and Lynch were actors—Lynch, more accurately, a singer—who were very funny men.

"Together," Abie was saying, "Fowler and Lynch are worse than Moore. Should be locked up. The other day I met Fowler on the King's Road.

"'Hallo Harry,' I say.

'Hallo Abe,' he says.

'What's happening?' I ask.

'I'm lookin' for a strait-jacket for Lynchie,' he says, 'but they don't make them in crushed velvet.'

'That's funny,' I says to him, 'because I just met Lynchie and he was out tryin' to find one to fit you!'"

Ever since I first met him, Abie had always had a certain leaning towards the production of strait-jackets.

"The world," he used to mutter sometimes, "is goin' out of its mind. A man could make a fortune wholesalin' strait-jackets," or some such remark. And once, when a full-grown litter of boxer puppies had got completely out of hand at his Bryanston house and eaten the best gut out of two of his Dunlop Maxplys, he raved for a while about manufacturing "strait-jackets for dogs", and reckoned that there might be money to be made in those.

London that year gave him his best ever feasibility study for the mass production of strait-jackets.

"Well-cut, of course, Forbsey," he said. "These idiots would never buy 'em if they fitted badly."

The Rolls drove sedately along the motorway while the rows of houses and corner pubs dozed in the afternoon sun.

"Everyone's here," Abie was saying. "Even Segura is here." He gave a snort of laughter. "Seegoo!" he cried. "Jesus. Movin' around on those legs of his hittin' the two-hander up the line and takin' pills.

"'Hey, Segoo,' I says to him, 'this is London, you know. The U.K. This isn't Hollywood. This is where the Queen lives.'

"And he says to me, 'You theenk, beeg Abie, she's gonna want tennis lessons from old Segoo?' he asks. 'Sure she'll want lessons,' I say, 'How you feelin?' an' he says: 'I steel got enough strength to get me to the Club, Abie,' an' he takes another handful of pills. Vitamin B1 to 12. They'll have to lock him up before he completely changes the habits of the English!"

I really liked listening to Abie when he was happy.

"You should see this Newc.*" said Abie. "I mean, Jesus. He just hits the shit out of everything. I mean it's like he's got that stuff you get things against things—"

"Allergy," I said.

"That's right, allergy," said Abie. "It's like he's got an allergy against tennis balls. Hits the shit out of them. Wake Newc up in the middle of the night and give him a tennis ball an' he'll just get up and hit him an unbelievable forehand crosscourt. Meanwhile, he looks like he should be out punchin' cows. Like he's just got off his horse."

* John Newcombe.

He steered the Rolls past Barons Court Underground and into the gates of Queens Club.

"I've got a court booked for five," Abie said, "to get your blood movin'!"

Queens Club! Time rolled backwards. On the front steps, Frank Sedgman, ready for a match, rubbing some embrocation into his elbow. He shakes my hand and says:

"At twenty you don't need these lotions and at forty they don't help you!"

There is no need for a fervent greeting. Everything is back as it was—a tableau frozen into immobility for five years, then set moving again at the throw of a switch.

Lew and Jenny Hoad, Gonzales, Teddy Tinling, Drobny, Rosewall, Torben Ulrich, Luis Ayala, Gimeno, Billy Knight, Emerson, Peter Ustinov, Fred Perry, Donald Dell. Allen Fox, craftier than before. The dressing-room is still damp and smells exactly the same, and the same old man with the same suspicious look hands me one of the same old towels, laundered now to a threadbare grey. Doubles against Alex Olmedo and Segura and afterwards, beer in the same little pub. The world we knew. I kept a diary for those three weeks, simply because I knew that they would soon be past and because I badly wanted to remember them. Parts of it tell the story as well as any other way I can think of:

Diary Notes: London 1968

It's sunny. We're staying in a flat in Putney and if you look carefully through the bedroom window, you can see the Thames through oaks. This morning it's shopping. The King's Road, so we go via Sloane Square and join the crowds. There's madness here. A sort of happy irresponsible insanity. Definite scope for Abie's strait-jackets. The British have found a stage large enough to accommodate a fair proportion of the population so they all join the cast. The result is a temporary loss of reason—a bomb attack on the mind. Gurus meditate on pavements in masses of hairy reflections. Napoleons and Nelsons, hands in jackets, scan imaginary horizons. Lord Kitchener is calling people up; a camel is tied to a parking meter. There are Zulus there and sheiks, hippies, Hindus, the directors of bowler-hatted companies, rajahs, squires, lairds, sultans, valets and jam sahibs. Monks abound, and other robed figures, and the armed forces are well represented; brigadiers, dragoons, commodores and brass. On a corner a bugler sounds a few military notes which bring a gungadin and several legionaries to attention. Skirts are up and underwear out and nipples on view, through the thinnest fabrics. The mood is sensuous, infectious and a little insanitary. We steer ourselves from shop to shop to buy clothes to match London. My South African flannels and shirt are outlandish. In the shops the new music hangs, thick and heavy, pummelling the brain with its beat; kneading at the senses. I squeeze myself into a number of outfits and am transformed into Davy Crockett; a page in velvet and flowing curls; a lean cowboy. A rather weak-looking sergeant major, and a sly character in a black outfit that I don't trust at all. So, at last we buy:

Black and brown velvet trousers;
shirts with great soft collars;
belts, shoes and
some long silk scarves.

The morning softens, dissolves into a mass of images. London has done a trick and we have been taken in.

In the afternoon there are international club matches at Queens. I am to play with Roger Taylor against Richey and Ashe. Ashe has a service which gets away so fast down the forehand side that it leaves me feeling as though I am standing knee-deep in fresh cow dung. Richey hardly has any service at all, but has a high velocity forehand and the most determined jaw in tennis and a sudden unexpected smile, like sunshine after rain. We play. Set all. No decision. I have grown to love matches where no decisions are reached. Draws grow on one as the years pass by.

One of the junior players who had harassed Abie and me in our prime, was a tow-headed fellow called Raymond Moore. He had worked diligently at his tennis since his early teens and his game had developed into a logical if unimaginative arrangement of topspin backhands and forehands, and a not quite natural service action that caused his tongue to creep out of the side of his mouth at the start of his swing, until it almost touched his left shoulder, against which he rested the left side of his jaw during the toss up. I once mentioned this tongue movement to him, suggesting that perhaps he should attach a glucose tablet to the sleeve of his shirt.

"With a little practise," I concluded, "you could easily get your tongue to lick the tablet on every toss up. That would give you a sort of self-energising service; the only one of its kind in tennis!"

"That's right!" said Raymond enthusiastically, "and if I could strap a coke with a straw in it to my chest, I could have a light meal on the way in to net!"

Raymond has the kind of personality which sparked off a certain amount of madness. Talking to him, one felt quite at liberty to fantasize. Although his tennis game was more utilitarian than brilliant, his style of life was ingenious and unmistakable. By 1968 he was a distinct personality on the tennis scene, and in addition, had grown his hair.

As he approached me that afternoon in the Queens Club lounge, my first impression was that I was being accosted by an animated, blonde witch-doctor. His voice, however, re-established him as the original Ray Moore, spilling news and information with every sentence.

"Never mind what Abie says. Laver is the best player," was typical of his utterances, or:

"Arthur Ashe and Diana Ross were together at Wimbledon. She is absolutely something else. I think that Arthur has breathing problems when she's around."

Raymond, too, is full of tales of the escapades of Fowler and Lynch. Only this morning they had taken it upon themselves to infuriate the British public. Harry, prim, supercilious and white, had got himself all dressed up in morning suit, bowler hat and umbrella and climbed into the back of Kenny's Rolls. Kenny, humble and black, put on a chauffer's uniform and cap and drove them through Chelsea. At crowded intersections or bus stops, Harry had rolled down the window, put his head out and shouted:

"Down with the blacks! Keep England white!" while Kenny, his face inscrutable, stared straight ahead.

"At times," said Raymond gravely, "they nearly got stoned!"

And last night they'd eaten at a restaurant where the waitress who served them had a dress made out of a sort of whitish tennis net.

"And no underwear," said Ray, "except a pair of dodgy knickers. Her whole breast came through the top and pointed at my spaghetti, while Harry made humming noises and missed the table when he put down his wine glass!"

London is determined to celebrate its recent escape from the old British reserve. There is a boom coming, people say. "Invest!" they cry. Property, stocks, commodities, copper, wine! It is a very infectious mood and has the effect of making one rush into the nearest store and make an immediate purchase or two.

Diary Notes: Summer 1968

Queens Club. Monday. Lewis Hoad again, on the centre court, after eleven years. I watch, transported. All the impossible majesty of his game flies through my head like a moving picture film. It doesn't matter that the shots that he now plays are off centre. Out of focus. That his service is hampered by a back injury. That he is slower. The style is the same; and with the style comes the memories. At his best, I truly swear that he was unbeatable. Unplayable. Some players do this, and others that. Lew Hoad did everything.

Select, if you like, the best tennis match ever played, and you will find quite unquestionably that Hoad played in it. And then brushed it aside with an understatement. Rod Laver is a carbon copy of the original Hoad. Only lefthanded and without the full majesty. The mighty power.

There is at Queens Club a little man from New York, Bernie Schwartz. A true lover of tennis—an unqualified *aficionado*. Thank God for the Bernies of this world! He watches the matches all day long and carries with him a little plastic bag containing:

A Brownie camera; film;
toffees in a paper packet;
his glasses, a clean handkerchief,
and
the day's order of play.

Each year he comes to watch Wimbledon by way of the Cunard mailships.

"You know, Gordon," he says, hiding his self-conscious little smile behind his hand, "tennis heals people. When people who are ill go to watch tennis, they feel well again!"

His drawl is rich, and so thick that the words ooze out over his lower lip like treacle. He loves talking to the players, and if they are not inclined to talk, he just stands and listens to their conversations. But they know him now and all of them talk with him—which is very good, because hardly any of the players know what it is really like to be small and unknown.

"What do you do in New York, Bernie?" I ask him.

"I'm an investigator!" he says softly and I have swift, unimaginable images, of this gentle man as a ruthless cold-eyed killer.

"I investigate the sidewalks," he is saying. "When people fall in the streets and blame it on the sidewalks, I defend the city!"

Diary Notes: Summer 1968

Raymond Moore has come up with an unbelievable story which he insists is true. He is so excited that he leads me into a corner of the dressing-room, while I am trying to build up concentration for my doubles match. Two totally mad Australian players have acquired a flat, one window of which overlooks the King's Road. The Chelsea models, sensing a source of Wimbledon tickets, beat a path to the flat door, day and night. Raymond doubts whether, by the time Wimbledon actually begins, either Australian will have the strength to change into tennis gear and actually reach the court. In their quest for tickets, says Raymond, the girls will dispense favours of every conceivable variety.

"Will they do it standing up in a hammock?" asks Roy Emerson, who has approached and is listening. Raymond refuses to be side-tracked. One of the girls has been particularly persistent, he continues, and is in addition impossibly kinky. She informs one of the Australians that her ambition is to lean out of the window which overlooks the King's Road, at three o'clock on a Saturday afternoon, and wave to her friends below while he makes it with her from behind. The Australian, momentarily set back on his heels, recovers and agrees. Meanwhile in cahoots with his friend, he hatches a diabolical plot. The event has been arranged for the coming Saturday, and Raymond will keep me suitably informed.

Today, Tom Okker beat Rod Laver. I used to think that Laver was the fastest man alive, but Okker out-ran him. Bursts of stupendous speed—like some mad hopper from science fiction. Bionic Hops.

The far corner of the ancient lounge is full of Russians. They've infiltrated the world of tennis, playing solid unimaginative games, chatting in Russian and thinking inscrutable thoughts. Allen Fox is in their midst, playing chess against Metreveli. He (Allen) goes demented when they discuss strategy in Russian.

"I get claustrophobic and want to rend my clothes," he says. "Russian conversation can make the simplest pawn move look devilish. Yesterday we got down to a king and pawn each, yet I kept expecting something rookish to come up from behind!"

The Eastern bloc is coming to light with superb players.

Diary Notes: Summer 1968

Watch Nastase. The most extraordinary talent. Doesn't seem to concentrate at all, yet the shots simply flow forth. Walks about with the utmost nonchalance, making provocative remarks and swiping at the ball as it comes within reach. Superb swipes. Hardly ever misses. He and Tiriac are a complicated pair and play complicated doubles with some very dicey manoeuvres. Verging on banditry. So many players! You can't move without seeing something wild. On the terrace above the players' restaurant, Emerson nudges me and says:

"Did you see that shot? Who is that guy? Could you do a shot like that? I couldn't do a shot like that! How the hell can he do a shot like that?"

Each day we practise at Wimbledon. You book a court for half an hour and get six new balls. The trick is to have a friend make a consecutive booking so that you get an hour.

Today, Abie and I had the very last court—fourteen, I think. We arrived to find Torben Ulrich upon it, all alone, sitting cross-legged in the very middle of one side. We waited gravely for his "playing" time to expire then walked on. He climbed to his feet in a thoughtful way and began putting on the first of his several sweaters. His rackets were still in their covers, the six new Slazengers, unused.

"What's been happening, Torben?" I asked in a comfortable sort of way, so as not to startle him.

He considered my question profoundly, with the air of a great philosopher, who, while waiting for a bus, is suddenly asked by someone to explain all about God. I half expected him not to reply and was about to retreat on tiptoe when he did.

"I have been emptying my mind," he said.

I was deeply impressed. One doesn't journey all the way out to Wimbledon, reserve a court for thirty minutes, change, collect new balls, then peel off three sweaters, just to empty one's mind. It occurred to me briefly, I remember, that for my part I would much more likely take such pains to *fill mine up*. Abie, unimpressed at the best of times with anything smacking of the supernatural, conducted with himself the inevitable private conversation which occurred when he felt himself confronted by a totally preposterous situation.

"Torben's emptying his mind," he said. "I mean, Jesus; here I'm looking for a grass court to get a few returns goin' an' Torben's sittin' on one for thirty minutes, emptying his friggin' mind."

"Hey, Torben," he said suddenly. "How do you know when it is empty? Does your mind have a dip-stick, or what?"

Torben favoured him with a long-suffering look, completely devoid of malice.

"It would be very difficult to explain it all to you at this very moment," he said. "It might be better for you to practise some returns!"

He left then, with the air of a man with a mind unfreighted with clobber, walking with a measured tread.

I got ready for a heavy practice session, wondering vaguely how one set about refilling an empty mind. And with what? Later that afternoon I hunted Torben down, and unencumbered by Abie's bull-and-gate methods, urgently asked him for an explanation. Poor Torben! He has spent a great deal of his life explaining things mystic and sensitive to thick-skulled tennis players!

"It's the Zen method, you know," he said. "They believe that you can only successfully embark on a new enterprise if your mind is emptied of previous enterprise. So you sit cross-legged for half an hour, looking at a point one meter in front of you and thinking of nothing. After ten minutes, your body begins to become weightless, in a heavy kind of way. After twenty minutes, the marrow in your bones is fluid and soft. Your body rises gently off the grass. Your mind is ready to accept new challenges!"

Again I was deeply impressed. Perhaps *that* was what had been the matter with my game all these years. I had been trying to play with a full mind! I was appalled.

"Do you *have* to sit on a grass court in order to empty it?" I asked Torben, cautiously.

"That is not necessary," he replied. "It was simply that I had the court reserved, and my opponent did not arrive. A football field would do just as well!" This he said with a twinkle in his eye.

I decided at once to tell Allen Fox about Torben's system. Allen accepts *any* advice on how to play better and this advice will intrigue him to a degree.

Diary Notes: Summer 1968

Enormous serving today by Clark Graebner. Absolute devastation. Fred Stolle in ruins. Bernie Schwartz is so impressed that he eats a whole bag of peanuts during the match without noticing. Allen Fox beat one of the Russians at chess today and for some time is speechless. He goes about wanting to tell people, but before he can find words, they've gone away! Pancho Segura has a new type of pill which he claims gives him enormous strength. He is still tennis's greatest living legend, is now coaching simultaneously a stunning mother and daughter in California. He calls them his "package deal". Abie is definitely impressed, but hides it by biting his thumbnail.

Tonight we all went out to eat at Provans and I told Raymond at some stage during dinner that he was a great liver of life. He replied that he was also a lover of life; then Abie said that he would rather be a great lover than a great liver, whereupon Raymond said that whereas he loved to be a liver, Abie lived to be a lover. Then Harry Fowler, who was studying the menu, looked up and announced that he was a lover of liver, and that was what he was going to have. That broke up the conversation. Later on, Harry squirted sneezing powder all up and down the room, and the place collapsed in a hurricane of sneezes. London's mad!

On Queens Club finals day, it rained. Steady London rain. Clouds down to window level and the tube trains smelling damp and warm. And talking of tube trains! Today I boarded the tube at Earl's Court for the short run to Queens Club. The coach is fairly full and I settle myself down. Raising my eyes quite innocently, I find my attention riveted to the extent that it is some time before I am aware that my entire side of the carriage is equally transfixed. Directly across from me, decked out in the shortest of mini-skirts, is a perky blonde. She is wearing absolutely no knickers of any kind at all, and seems totally oblivious of it. There, four feet from my eyes (nose, if you like) is this neat blonde, furry little niche. At least twenty pairs of eyes boring into it. There's nothing to be done about it. Barons Court looms in literally seconds and I am forced to disembark upon the platform. Wits have to be collected and my raincoat donned before I proceed, with nothing to look forward to, but tea at Queens Club. Here the club house is jammed to bursting point. Positively creaking. Outside, the soft, grey drizzle. Inside, the tea queue. Teddy Tinling, in defiance of the drab weather, is magnificent in a striped purple shirt, white collar, extravagant cuffs and a marvellous shirt which glows as though it has been plugged in to some portable power source.

"Filthy luck, dear fellow," he says to me over the heads of short girl players like Rosie Casals or Nancy Richey. "I mean, how dare the weather gods?"

His eyes, meanwhile, roam the room as though he cannot get enough of the sight, sound and general atmosphere of rooms full of tennis celebrities all crowded together: Fred Perry, permanently tanned, smelling of exclusivity, halls of fame and expensive pipe tobacco.

Gonzales surrounded by listeners, is wearing a black track suit.

Gladys Heldman, Burt and Jane Boyar, Michael Davies.

The British types, Messrs. Taylor, Cox, Stilwell. Everyone talks and watches.

Cliff Drysdale and Niki Pilic arguing, arguing. They've taken over a corner table and sit there like two hounds gnawing at a bone—their argument held between their paws. Cliff presents himself as the more philosophical, Pilic as the belligerent, although he would prefer to be the philosophical one. Between them, in the very corner, Jean, now Cliff's wife, observes. Tables are at a premium, so throughout other players drop in on them, using the table for their cakes and strawberries. Bernie Schwartz has drawn up a chair on the outskirts.

"My dear Niki," Cliff is saying in his provocative, light, expansive way, "you must by now realise that your opinion of your game is higher than anybody else's. We all think you play at this level, and you believe you play at *that* level."

He uses his hands to demonstrate the difference in levels. They have been discussing recent defeats, victories, records. Cliff sits back with a bland little smile as though only half his attention is required to verbally engage Pilic. Pilic's face is arranged into an expression of the profoundest disdain, his nose lifted as though Cliff represents a sewerage disposal works upwind from him.

"I have game for *any* level," Pilic says, "and also I can break eggs with volley!"

"Does that imply that my volley cannot break eggs?" enquires Cliff.

"Not only eggs!" cries Pilic. He feels he is winning the exchange. "And not only volley. You have only one big shot!"

"And you, I suppose," says Cliff, "are blessed with a flawless game! What about that backhand that you have to dig out from behind you?"

John Newcombe, who has paused at the table and overheard Cliff's last remark, throws an exploratory spanner.

"He's right, Niki! You've got a bloody terrible backhand. You couldn't pass your grandmother with that backhand!"

"Purpose is not to pass grandmother," says Niki. "Purpose is to make good shot on big point."

By now, Ray Moore, Owen Davidson and Torben Ulrich have also paused to listen, as well as the players at the next table. Cliff turns to the audience.

"Have any of you guys *ever* seen Niki Pilic make a great backhand on a big point?"

"Only forehands," said Moore. "Niki misses most backhands. That's why he loses a lot of matches."

"Misses a lot of forehands too!" murmured Davidson.

It is too much for Niki.

"Screw you guys!" he bursts out. "I have game for big matches!"

I have always been intrigued by the fire of Niki Pilic. On court he walks about like a pressure cooker that is stressed to its limit and about to erupt. But the argument has suddenly deflated itself and Niki, still a bachelor, is musing about his exploits with women.

"I have new girl in Rome," he says. "Countess and model. She call when I pass through. I have time for lunch only. She wear through-see dress, and she have body. Unbelievable; all heads turn. At table she must keep changing seat so all can see. I have to keep moving. 'Go ahead', I say finally. 'You move about. I finish lunch.' "

"Models," he says with a wise look. "I can handle easily. I have no problems with women. I listen to what they say with one ear only!"

It is not the narrative which is important—it is simply another stage in the construction of the Pilic image—international, intellectual and decidedly grand. Of all the travelling tennis players, it is Pilic who is, through and through, the great cosmopolitan.

Cliff Drysdale is either unaware of, or unimpressed by this elaborate Pilic.

"Tell me, Niki, dear chap," he says in a patronising voice, "how did you begin your tennis career?"

"Accident," he says at last, rather shortly. "One day in Split, I pass club where they play; I say to self: 'What is that?' 'Tennis,' they say. 'You want to try?' So I watch the ball and win 6–3. First time I hold racket!"

"No Niki," I say, "that's not possible!"

"Possible!" cries Niki firmly, and he casts a glance at Drysdale who gives a snort of laughter.

"Of course possible!" cries Niki angrily. "Drysdale is capitalist. Never had to fight. I have tough time in youth. I have fight for everything. I beg money from my mother for racket. I sweep snow off court to play . . ."

One has brief visions of fur hats and the brothers Karamazov, and a small boy striving, striving.

"I was nobody, so I fight to be somebody."

"Then you're not a true communist," says Drysdale.

This starts an interminable argument of infinite dimensions.

"Look at you," says Drysdale. "How can you be a communist?"

"Why look at me? Look at you!"

"I'm not a communist!"

"That's what I say."

"What do you say?"

"You can't tell communist by looking!"

"You didn't say that. I said that . . ."

"Not you, me, you dumb bum!"

And so on, Niki Pilic. A colourful product of the world of tennis, and a student of the dying art of conversation.

By evening, the rain is still falling steadily. No chance of tennis. Ray Moore arrives, bearing an expression which suggests unbelievable tidings bursting to emerge. He catches my eye, draws me into a corner of the bar and unleashes his story. It's the Australians in Chelsea. Between them, they have pulled off the most extraordinary coup. Raymond is agog.

"The girl arrives at two fifty," he tells me, "and by three o'clock, she is leaning out of the window overlooking the King's Road, and waving to random friends passing by. Her upper half is demure in a white lace shirt, her lower half is not. Behind her, the filthy Australian gets under way. After ten minutes of this remarkable activity, there comes a knocking on the apartment door.

"Don't move," says the Australian. "It's me bloody room mate. I'll send him away. No time right now for bloody room mates. Stay at the window and I'll be right back with you!"

He disengages and goes to the door. There waiting is the *other* Australian, fully prepared. They change places. The *other* Australian takes over without a hitch, saying cheekily in the accent of his friend that "Bloody room mates can be very inconvenient at times."

Meanwhile, the *first* Australian runs down the stairs, out of the back entrance, around the block and comes walking up the King's Road underneath the window and waves at the girl! For a second or two she actually returns the waving—then her eyes get wide, her jaw drops, and she ducks back into the room. Raymond is delighted at the joke.

"And what's more," he says, "she didn't mind at all. Probably delighted once the surprise wore off."

Burt and Jane Boyar are here, busy with a new book about tennis. Their first book, *Yes I Can*, is about Sammy Davis Jr., and is a bestseller. Davis is in London doing *Golden Boy*. He's Abie's and my number one entertainer. Tonight, Burt and Jane invited us to see the show and afterwards to have dinner with the great star himself. Unbelievable excitement. We eat at the *White Elephant* and the place is alive with film people. Altogether too much for a farm boy.

Diary Notes: Summer Sunday 1968

More rain, but not enough to dampen the spirits. Today it's champagne at Frank Rostron's; conversations are held at gale strength. Brian Fairlie, the young New Zealand champion, downs his glass of Dom Perignon, then allows a happy smile to cross his face.

"Narce warn," he says with feeling. "Arh could handle another glass of that with ayse."

I come face to face with James van Alen, who is on the seventeenth amendment of his simplified serving system. He explains it to me, but with all the champagne about, it is too complicated to follow. Bob Carmichael is telling me of a doubles match in which he played:

"Absolutely abominably. Couldn't hit my hat. So I said to my partner, 'Hey, wait on, mate, hang about a bit. I can't get any worse'; and I was right. I didn't get any worse! But I didn't get any better, ayther!"

After Frank Rostron's, Hurlingham again. The same little golf course; Lea Pericoli in Teddy Tinling's ostrich feathers and her own superb Italian legs. The lighthearted exhibition matches. Tea at four, and afterwards, a comfortable Sunday evening. The first open Wimbledon begins tomorrow!

John Newcombe, the 1967 champion, will open the centre court today against Owen Davidson. The first round is peppered with great matches. Gonzales against Krishnan, Emerson against Holmberg. Abie plays Ken Rosewall. The place is humming with excitement—but, it is still raining. British weather has no respect for great occasions, so it is the player's restaurant again. In the far corner, Ray Moore with his friends Fowler and Lynch, planning some new and private devilry, no doubt. They never miss the opportunity of teasing Abe about his age. Standing behind him in the tea queue, they begin:

"I do believe," says Fowler, "that that is Abe Segal."

"That's Segal, all right," says Lynch. "He once played a great match against Don Budge in '38."

"Budge was a junior at the time."

"Segal's good for his age. Plays doubles with Forbes."

"Their combined ages are ninety-five."

"Ninety six. Forbes just turned thirty-five!"

Bernie Schwartz stands near by, chuckling to himself and eating toffees. He loves listening to the conversations. Usually he just listens, but today he suddenly joins in.

"No one really knows how old Abe Segal is," he intones in an oratorial way, "but they say that when Columbus first landed in the USA, Segal was there to meet him. 'Hi Chris,' he said, 'I've entered us for the US doubles.' "

As usual, Abie is driving everybody mad in his quest for Wimbledon tickets. He has promised tickets to a large and miscellaneous cross-section of the London public—film people, models, people in the garment industry, a few assorted noblemen and millionaires. His friends get accosted hourly—

"Christ, Forbsey, I've got Twiggy and her friend comin' in at two, and I've only got one seat!"

To make matters worse, he wakes up with a start at dawn, trying to balance out his supply and demand situation. At six-thirty he runs in the park. On his return, he goes to the john, has a bath, reads several papers, swings his rackets and does twenty press-ups, then consults his watch. It is still only seven forty-five in the morning. In spite of this information, he feels that his friends must, by now, be awake. So he 'phones them up.

"Raymond!" he cries, hearing Moore's sleepy grunt. "Have you got the tickets?"

"I don't know," says Raymond.

"What do you mean, you don't know?"

"Abie! I don't even know who I am."

"Listen, idiot," Abie raves on, "where are we eating tonight?"

"I'm still busy with last night," says Raymond.

"Well, listen hacker, there's no way you're goin' to be in shape for your match at two if you sleep your brains out all morning!"

Moore and Fowler, badly put out by Abie's early 'phone calls, are determined to plan revenge. Their opportunity comes, quite unexpectedly, several nights later.

Diary Notes: Tuesday

One wanders about this extraordinary Wimbledon bemused by the sensations which rise up in droves and flood the mind. First, the question of time—there is simply not enough of it. Whole blocks of conversations, friendships, tennis and laughter go to waste. Like a colour film, rife with images, crammed with humour, magnitude and pathos of this remarkable circuit; a film which can't be stopped; simply rolls past, numbing the mind.

In the player's restaurant, all at the same moment, Gonzales is saying something vital about the evolution of tennis. Peter Ustinov is imitating Niki Pilic arguing with a linesman. Fred Perry is predicting the eventual men's singles winner. Pancho Segura is talking about a new kind of pill for the over forties, that is guaranteed to "Get you through the night, keed!" Fowler and Moore are discussing Abe Segal's weight in relation to his age, while Abie, within earshot, is trying to listen to Hoadie telling him about Jenny's purchases at the "Way In!" Diana Ross is having tea with Arthur Ashe. Teddy Tinling is on about the tigerish movements of Virginia Wade. Kathy Harter is just sitting there, all pony-tail and legs—unbelievable. And two girls unknown are standing in the tea queue, wearing transparent net blouses and causing the loss of more conversational threads in the course of male conversation than could be readily totted up. And that's only inside!

Outside, Newcombe has lost the first set to Davidson, Guzman is beating Bobby Lutz, Rod Laver is set all with Eugene Scott, and Alex Olmedo is playing the same lithe, crouching kind of game that he played in 1959 when he won the tournament. On the stairs I encounter Teddy Tinling on his way from somewhere to somewhere, rigged out in the most extravagant finery. All cuffs and scarves and the wildest handkerchief.

"My dear Gordon," he says in the tones of someone stretched to their limit, "I'm tearing myself to pieces! I need several more pairs of eyes and ears. I am trying to station myself permanently in half a dozen different places at once!" And on he hurries.

I lose a close match to Mark Cox, after actually leading by one set and 7–6 with set point in the second. Typical of the tennis gods. They allow me a whiff of what would be, for me, a victory, and then snatch it away with sly chuckles when Cox hits a crosscourt backhand passing shot which seems decidedly flukey; on set point, in the second set, no less! Which would have given me two sets to love which would have . . . I find myself playing the game so often indulged in by defeated tennis players. The tantalising and hypothetical game called "If only".

Diary Notes: Summer 1968

Go to the centre court and watch Ken Rosewall, the surgeon. He moves about with a racket sharpened to a razor's edge, and carves his way through cumbersome opponents, leaving large slices of their games lying about on the grass. He is a precision instrument, a splitter of hairs, a specialist. Watching his backhand, one feels involuntarily that that is the only logical way that a backhand can be struck!

Tonight we are to try a new restaurant. London is full of these new 'in' places, very modern and upstage. Provans, the Hungry Horse, Au Père de Nico, The Spot, Angelos, Alvaros, Aretusas, Tiberios, several Dinos, Francos or Carlos. Tonight it's to be a new and remarkable place—manned, says Raymond, entirely by homosexuals. Gay Blades. "But very funny," says Raymond. "Really funny. And good food, really good!" So we go; Ray and Rose, the Segals, the Hoads and a young and earnest fellow who takes life far too seriously and who is always worrying about saving money and the price of things. We seat ourselves around our table, settle our napkins and order our wine, and Aubrey arrives.

"Raymond, darling," he says archly, running his fingers through Ray's preposterous hair. "Ooh dear! So wiry, and full of nice clean sweat! Such a rough, male game you play. I do love rough males, you know!"

"Aubrey, my dear," says Raymond. "How was your weekend?"

"Ooh, lovely weekend, darling! Went to Amsterdam! Got involved with a whole crew of Danish sailors! Very rough, Danish sailors!" A shiver of delight runs up his spine and he shifts his weight from one foot to the other.

"Sit down, Aubrey," said Ray. "Sit down and tell us what happened."

"Sit down, darling!" cries Aubrey. "Sit down? You must be joking!" and he goes off, hugging his chuckles to himself.

Laughter and mischief permeate the place. Only our serious young friend is appalled and is studying the menu with a worried frown. The wine arrives and Harry Fowler pours it, slipping, as he does so, a sleeping tablet into Abie's glass. The meal is hilarious. By the time midnight comes, Abie is nodding off and can't wait for the coffee to be served.

"Holy Hell, you guys, I'm bombed," he says. "I've got to leave. Let's move, Mouse,* before I fall asleep on the table." He leaves some notes to pay the bill and they depart.

For Moore and Fowler, the night is just beginning. First, they must

* Mouse—Abie's affectionate nickname for his wife, dating back to their first meeting.

tease the serious one. The bill arrives. Fowler studies it, then hands it to Moore.

"Are you paying cash?" he asks in a serious voice, "or are you going behind the curtain with Aubrey?"

"I'm short of cash tonight," says Raymond. "I'll go with Aubrey."

He gets up, takes the beaming Aubrey's hand, and they disappear behind a curtain at the far end of the room. All prearranged. Sounds of ecstasy emerge.

"What's happening?" asks the serious one. "What the hell is going on?"

"Aubrey doesn't mind how you pay him," says Harry. "He's very accommodating."

"I don't like it," mutters the serious one. "I've never done anything like this before. This kind of thing can affect a man for life—"

"Well, pay cash then," says Harry. "You don't *have* to go."

"Lot of money," he replies, frowning at the bill. "Damned expensive meal!"

Moore emerges from behind the curtain then, with a broad smile on his face, doing up his trousers.

"How was it?" says Harry.

"Two minutes for the soup," says Ray, "three for the main course, and two for the cheese and coffee!"

"Not bad value," says Harry. He turns to the serious one—"OK, your turn next."

The expression on the serious one's face suggests the most intense mental conflict. Suddenly he gives a huge half sob.

"To hell with you guys!" he hursts out. "I'll pay cash!" and wrenches out his wallet.

By the time we are finally ready to leave, it is just two in the morning.

"Right," says Fowler. "Raymond, it is time that we 'phoned Abie!"

We gather round the telephone at the desk, and Raymond dials the Cumberland Hotel where Abie is staying. At last the connection is made.

Abie's sleepy voice: "What the hell is happening?"

"It's two o'clock," Ray says urgently. "We're all at Wimbledon and Twiggy and her friend are here. Where the hell are the tickets? You said you'd get some tickets."

"Good God," says Abie. "You're joking!"

"Look at your watch, Abe! We're all waiting for you at Wimbledon. Everyone's on court!"

"Good God," says Abie again. "You're right. Listen, just hold it. I'll be right there. Just tell them all to hold it!"

Raymond replaces the receiver, doubled up with laughter. "What's the odds he's jumping about, putting tennis gear into his bag?" he says.

Abie's version of his activities is worth recording.

"By the time I get to the hotel," he says, "I'm so tired I can't see straight, so I draw all the curtains and get into bed and sleep my brains out. Suddenly there's this phone call. It's that idiot Raymond. The curtains are so thick that I can't see too much, so I look at my watch, and sure enough it's two o'clock. I get one hell of a fright. I'm second match on court three, with Forbsey in the doubles. So I get up, shave, throw on my clothes, pack my gear, and take the lift downstairs, carryin' my bag and rackets. I come out of the lift downstairs, and there's not too many people about; but I'm in such a hurry I go up to the concierge and say:

"'Listen, I need a taxi, urgently.'

"'Where might you be going, sir?' says the man, looking at me kind of peculiar.

"'I'm on court at Wimbledon in one hour,' I say to him.

"'I hardly think so, sir,' he says. 'It's two thirty a.m.'

"'*A.m.* or *p.m.*?' I shout.

"'*A.m.*, sir,' he says.

"'It's that bloody Moore,' I say to him. 'I mean Jesus! Are you quite sure it's not *p.m.*?'

"'Quite sure, sir,' says the concierge, 'we do try to keep in touch with these things.'

"'Suddenly the whole thing seems unreal. Here I am, standing in the lobby with my tennis rackets under my arm, arguing with someone about whether it's two a.m. or p.m. It's like I'm dreaming. So I go back to bed," says Abie, "and would you believe it, I can't get to sleep?'"

Ray and Harry classed this particular incident as their ultimate in practical jokes for 1968.

"It was the timing that was so good," said Raymond. "That, and the sleeping tablet. After that tablet, Abie would believe anything!"

Wednesday. Rosewall and Pasarell in an absorbing match. Gonzales loses to a Russian called Metreveli. So extraordinary to see a man of such intense fire and willpower brought down by the mere fact that he is no longer young. How superb he must have been. When one considers sheer strength of purpose, the immense burning desire to win, and only to win, Gonzales must rise head and shoulders above the rest. Hoad's magnificence is in his total mastery of the game itself. Laver's in his flashing talent and the quiet certainty within him of his own abilities. Rosewall's in his precision and artistry. But Gonzales is all fire and passion—exultation in the very act of competing!

Thursday. Abie and I have reached the second round of the doubles, and have to play against Alex Olmedo and Pancho Segura. Fowler and Moore have already indicated that the combined ages of the players will be nearly two hundred years. We begin the match at about three p.m. on court three and by five forty-five, have lost the first set at 32–30. The court is like lightning and no one can return service. Pancho Segura is at his best in such matches. The crowds adore him. At nine-all in the first set, he sniffs doubtfully at the Robinson's orange juice.

"Drink it, Poppa," says Olmedo. "Eet's good. The Queen she drinks eet."

At twenty-all, Segura serves out a long deuce game, then leans against the umpire's stand.

"Don't die on us Segoo," says Abie. "Let's all four of us finish the match!"

Segura looks up with a broad smile, puts a hand to his heart and says:

"She don't stop pumping, keed. She still goes strong!"

It is the hottest day of the London summer. At 20-all I see my first mirage. A distinct palm tree with Slazenger balls instead of coconuts.

At 26-all the umpire runs out of new balls. He calls for more.

"Never mind the balls, professor," says Segura, "eet is better you change the players!"

At 29-all Segura turns to the crowd and says:

"I maybe not make eet to the Club tonight, folks!"

At 31–30, I lose a long service game and we lose the set at 32–30. We realise after the match that it is a Wimbledon record—the longest set ever played, surpassing the 31–29 set played by Sedgman and MacGregor against Trabert and Talbert in 1949. Some odd posterity from the tennis gods!

Diary Notes: Summer 1968

Graebner playing Roche is a battle of ironclads—a locking in mortal combat of tremendous tennis forces. Like two giant wrestlers they meet; quiver; fluctuate; but never give way. The match is decided by the breadth of a hair.

Arthur Ashe has developed a superb brand of super-cool, cerebral tennis.

Lithe movements, a lightning service, and feet with wings attached. Swift, intelligent perfection. Calm intensity. He defeats El Shafei, Newcombe and Okker, but one cannot but feel that this is only a beginning; that there is more to come.

The last four players in that historic Wimbledon were Tony Roche, Clark Graebner, Arthur Ashe and Rodney Laver. I can still remember the feeling of awe which came over me as I watched Rodney dismantle the aura of cool detachment which Arthur Ashe builds around himself as he plays. The match was too short and one-sided to be classed as good, yet the centre court crowd watched quietly until the last point had been played. They were staggered, as I was, by the sheer clinical efficiency of the tennis game of Rod Laver.

We had planned a holiday on the Greek islands after Wimbledon and our thoughts were already racing on ahead. The remainder of my diary notes are interspersed with passages about Greece. I've left them in. There is a great nostalgia attached to the end of things, and the passages seem to soften it.

The night flight from Heathrow to Corfu. It is my friend, Gerondeanos, who has persuaded us to go. For me, even during my previous travels, the Greek islands have always had about them an untouchable aura—reserved as a playground for potentates; sheiks; people with money—the very rich!

Gerondeanos with his Greek forthrightness changed all that.

"The islands," he says, his eyes softening. "They will rinse out your mind. And the sunlight will clear your skin. Come! Come to the islands!"

And so, with the applause still ringing in our ears, and the sonorous voice of the umpire announcing Laver to be the first Open Wimbledon Champion, we are set down in Corfu, in a limpid Ionian dawn. Clatters of Greek as Gerondeanos supervises the collection of our luggage. A softness in the air which could never be England. And in the morning when we awake with sunlight filling our room, it is still impossible to imagine that we have arrived. But the view from our little balcony verifies it all. Serene blue bay with fishing boats; a headland with olive trees and the ruin of a fort; the clip-clop of a gharri by the waterfront. The magnificent sky. We have stumbled into a picture postcard.

It was Laver's Wimbledon. In the final he defeated, quite easily, the industrious Roche, unravelling him in much the same way as he had done Ashe. Afterwards, it was so clear and logical that he should have won.

Even the tennis gods, for once, put aside their devilry and allowed justice to be served and honest history made.

After watching Rodney George play tennis as an amateur and as a professional; after being his friend and scaring him in the night; after partnering him in doubles, losing to him many times at singles, and defeating him once; after all that, I am absolutely ready to concede that he must be as great as any tennis player can be. He has the ultimate characteristics of the truly great—the ability to become stronger as the competition tightens. To play day after day with no fear at all, no sign of strain, but only the positive will to win. To acknowledge the skills of his opponents and to scorn the use of any form of trickery. He astounded the tennis world at Wimbledon with the mastery of his game. He became champion of the world—and true to the Laver style of things, he did so with modesty and a minimum of fuss.

He is one of the best tennis players who has ever lived.

Diary Notes: Corfu 1968

At Paleocastrizza there is no dividing line between sea and sky. Don a diving mask and you can lie on the surface of the bay, suspended in space. Below, thirty feet of translucent water, above, the staggering sky. Never is one so aware of light; pure white sunlight, refracted by the rock walls, splintered by water. Light and water and space, purity of the senses, a total rinsing out of the mind. In this sunlight, fish and wine are new things; the acrid olives a part of the mountain slopes above. V lies on the sand like a seal, her lithe body half in and half out of the water. The sun has burned her to a dark copper. Her hair is like flax across her shoulders. Sipping wine I doze, smiling as the memories return.

Raymond Moore defeating Andres Gimeno, to the delight of Harry Fowler. In the madness of this new London scene, he has fallen into the habit of referring to Ray as "she".

"She'll have to have her hair shampooed for her next match," he says excitedly. "She'll have plenty of TV close-ups to contend with, and we don't want the British viewing public to think that they're at Madame Tussaud's!"

The first round loss of Virginia Wade to a Swedish girl and the tears which she couldn't hide. I watch the match with Marty Riessen, and at one point he says quietly:

"You can't play if you can't see, you know. And you can't see it your eyes are full of tears. So it's not-advisable to cry if you're losing, although often it is very difficult not to do so!"

Who but a player would know of the true compassion in Riessen's lighthearted words?

Diary Notes: Corfu 1968

Take the mountain road which winds almost vertically from Paleocastrizza to Lacones, and sit at the little restaurant cut into the mountain side. The parapet on which my elbow rests drops away to the sea a thousand metres below. Now the bays where we swam are no more than ice-blue coves, the deeper water as deep blue as ink. We eat cheese and figs and drink a cloudy local wine, sharp with the tang of grapes, and afterwards there is baclava and the strong, sweet coffee.

Billie Jean King won the ladies' singles with the same inexorability with which Laver won the men's. They are, in a way, out of the same mould, those two, although of course their personalities differ widely. Billie Jean is the modern American female through and through and a great tennis player. More than great.

I find, in this book, that I have used up all my adjectives on the men players—I suppose because they are much easier for me to understand.

But the girls were as much a part of this section of tennis history as were the men. We watched them, were amused by them, and annoyed when their matches went on too long and held up the starts of our own. We laughed at their funny service actions, and the mighty female swings they made at overheads.

"All arms and grunts and open mouths," said Lew Hoad once, "and then a bloody great swing and instead of a smash, out pops a mouse!"

And there's this mental picture of Roy Emerson waiting in the Wimbledon change-room and idly watching a match on the television set.

"Here's a lob," he murmurs, "and here's a lob, and here's a lob off a lob. And here's a smash that turns into a lob. And here's the lob with the wind, that will lob into the Royal Box."

"What's going on, Emmo?" someone asks.

"Ladies' Doubles," says Roy.

Billie Jean and her colleagues soon changed *that*. Players such as she, Margaret Court, Maria Bueno, Virginia Wade or Darlene Hard could bury overheads with the best of them.

But now, thinking back about all the girl players whom I've watched, I find that there were only a handful who really perfected the simplest and most complicated of all things in tennis—the classic service swing!

Diary Notes: Corfu 1968

The main street of Lacones is eight feet wide and winding. The little shop into which we are lured boasts two superb tame roosters with beads around their necks. Also a half dozen cotton scarves, orange liqueur, bottles of walnuts, olives, pecans, cumquats. Cheese, melons, figs and a rack of postcards. The old Greek owner whips out glasses, pours us liqueurs and stands back with the air of someone who has done a trick. We buy a scarf and feed liqueur to the roosters, and when we leave we are presented with a handful of walnuts.

Afterwards we wander in the quiet olive groves, the air heavy and scented, an aura of peace so pure that we cannot speak, each passing minute a tangible, precious thing. It is the last day, and nearly time to go. Time to move again.

On the very last page of that worn island notebook I found a little scribbled paragraph, which in retrospect appears both cryptic and prophetic:

"They're interfering with our game! Not the fifteen-loves, or the deuces or adds; or even the backhands and forehands. But something more devious. They're tampering with the actual spirit of the thing . . . changing the heartbeats. Synthetics are encroaching. I'm afraid for the old things: wood; gut; grass; clay. I can't even tell whether it's good or bad. Only that it's changing.

'Old T.S. someone' has a line which relates:

"Now I fear disturbance of the quiet seasons," he wrote somewhere.

Well, I fear disturbance of the quiet seasons of tennis. I don't even know why I should. I will hardly be affected!

The poem goes on:

"Winter shall come, bringing death from the sea!" –

But of course that's going too far! I suppose that sometime, on those quiet beaches it came home to me that tennis really had changed; and that the kind of tennis that had been my life had been left behind, and that with it I had left behind a part of my life . . .

Postscript

Wimbledon 1977

Staircase Number One, again: the same seat! Grave-eyed David Mills, the All England Club Secretary, has seen to that. I find the seat and sit there, chin in hands. The sunny court again, with all its simple age and pomp. A year has past, since I sat here, and since those memories came pouring through my head. Well, I've rounded them up now, and got them written down. Trapped between the covers of this book. They were special for me, those days. And this court somehow seems able to recapture the old perspective, if only for an hour or two.

It is two o'clock. The players emerge, and I feel again the heart's lifting, and the irresistible touch of melancholy.

Borg and Connors, superbly modern.

They play. The polished, expensive strokes of two young tennis millionaires.

And while they play, it is easy enough to watch, and to contemplate, in a lazy kind of way, this centenary Wimbledon.

The mood has been festive and the crowds denser than ever. And marvellous tennis. Superlatives congregate, and mill around, but one finally selects Rodney Laver's words, spoken on the players' roof garden.

"A fair bit of old tennis going on down there, Gordon, old sport!" Nothing if not mild, our Rodney.

Abie is here for the veterans' event. He stands in the crowd below the players' restaurant and bellows up at his friends. He never seems to want to speak to the people near him—always someone who's somewhere else, just within shouting distance.

Connors, meanwhile, is winning the first set. He's playing too perfectly altogether—like a complicated machine that has been finely programmed to hit hundreds of risky winners, and then been overwound. Watching him one senses over-kill. Feels instinctively that his best shots would be worth more than only one point. "He can't keep doing that," one mutters. And, of course, he can't.

Gerulaitis, now. He is very much in command of his senses. It's hardly possible to play a better match than he did against Borg in the semis. Fair bit of old tennis there, one could safely say. And if understatements are to be the order of the day, one could also safely say that Case and Masters have played men's doubles before. Definitely put in some practice.

And that Virginia Wade "came good", as the Aussies say, at a reasonably opportune time. Damned opportune. So opportune that one suspects the divine intervention of mellow gods. She looked more handsome than ever before—shorter hair and eyes, eyes, eyes. And then, of course, the legs as well. England has been subjected to a huge collective ecstasy.

And tennis has changed. Come into money and absolutely gone public. One walks about in the players' enclosure, trying to get tea, and hearing things like "contracts", "franchises", "legal representatives" and "twelve point five million by May".

It's the day of the superstar. The superstar, the supercoach, the how-to books, the tennis universities and the tracksuits with the stripes down the side. And a whole new set of people who follow the game. At Queens Club on Sunday they had a sort of combination backgammon—pro-celebrity tennis day, seething with the jet set. Glamorous people, carelessly strolling and emitting expensive smells. Cliff Drysdale, debonair and polished, and Brian Young, the living legend, hitting determined forehands with the handle of his racket stuck, it seemed, in his trouser pocket! Some of the celebrities have terrifically unique styles of play! Jeannie and I furtively joined the strollers, being neither pros nor celebrities.

Oh, there are new kinds of tennis people these days, especially in the States. Social sort of people who have heard that it is "in" to "have trouble with your forehand", or a "touch of tennis elbow". They quickly get equipped with Fila* gear and several rackets, teaching pros and phrases like "topspin lob" and "punch-volley" and "hitting through the netman". And if, after ten lessons, they can't play well with the Wilson

* Fila—The new, super-elegant Italian tennis wear that, in order to purchase, you have to be accompanied by your bank manager.

steel, they can try the Kawasaki graphite, or the Head Aluminium, or Boron X-T or Durafiber or Glaflex. Or maybe take the old road and go right back to wood. And, if they still have problems, *actually playing*, it isn't important, because they have the tennis talk and trappings, and afterwards they can put on "Après tennis" gear, and do fun, "Après tennis" things! But wait!

Borg is starting to win, with his long controlled strokes. Marvellously detached. Inscrutable. Patient. There is a balance in his perspective. calm recognition of the occasion. And he holds the ball on his racket, longer than Connors does, and his topspins pull the ball down and into court.

"This Borg," Abie is going to say to me after the match, "is one hell of an athlete. And what's more, on court, he doesn't come up with any of the usual bullshit."

All the able-bodied stars of former years have been invited to the centenary doubles event. Look:

Pancho Gonzales, Pancho Segura, Torben Ulrich, Sven Davidson, Donald Budge, Gene Mako, Victor Seixas, Rex Hartwig, Frank Sedgman, Bob Howe, Gardner Mulloy, Bobby Riggs, Budge Patty, Jackie Brichant, Jaroslav Drobny. Even Jean Borotra. And, of course, the commoners, Williams and Segal!

The nineteen fifties, revisited, albeit with creaking knees! The event begins only during the second week, so that the first week is given to practice and preparation—a fair amount of the application of knee-guards, ointments, plasters and embrocations, and a determined temporary abstinence from such things as whisky and cigars. Generally, though, they're a fit-looking lot, these over forty-fives, with a great deal of youth and vigour still intact.

They are all taking it as seriously as the devil, because apart from the prestige attached, there are faces to be saved and three or four thousand pounds to be won. The matches get underway at last, with nervousness being concealed by ribald observations, and tactical probes.

Abie, now forty-sixish, is sceptical about Owen's ability to stay the pace.

"I've ordered him a coffin next to the Umpire's stand," he says brutally, "so that if he caves in we can just nail him up an' continue the match." Their first match is against Gonzales and Segura before several thousand nostalgic spectators. Warren Woodcock and I go along to watch.

Abie's service and forehand are still heavy calibre. Owen, nervous at

first
"

three
thirty-s
as six or s
But you w
increase your

Being a bit o
theory into my ow
of myself at seventy-

"But surely, Torben,
matter what you do?"

"Well, of course, *eventua*
become completely immobile.
there is no real excuse for becom

"After all, Gordon," he says sud
really is tennis?" And, when I don't
see. That is all that it really is. Only a g

Connors, meanwhile, is winning the first set. He's playing too perfectly altogether—like a complicated machine that has been finely programmed to hit hundreds of risky winners, and then been overwound. Watching him one senses over-kill. Feels instinctively that his best shots would be worth more than only one point. "He can't keep doing that," one mutters. And, of course, he can't.

Gerulaitis, now. He is very much in command of his senses. It's hardly possible to play a better match than he did against Borg in the semis. Fair bit of old tennis there, one could safely say. And if understatements are to be the order of the day, one could also safely say that Case and Masters have played men's doubles before. Definitely put in some practice.

And that Virginia Wade "came good", as the Aussies say, at a reasonably opportune time. Damned opportune. So opportune that one suspects the divine intervention of mellow gods. She looked more handsome than ever before—shorter hair and eyes, eyes, eyes. And then, of course, the legs as well. England has been subjected to a huge collective ecstasy.

And tennis has changed. Come into money and absolutely gone public. One walks about in the players' enclosure, trying to get tea, and hearing things like "contracts", "franchises", "legal representatives" and "twelve point five million by May".

It's the day of the superstar. The superstar, the supercoach, the how-to books, the tennis universities and the tracksuits with the stripes down the side. And a whole new set of people who follow the game. At Queens Club on Sunday they had a sort of combination backgammon—pro-celebrity tennis day, seething with the jet set. Glamorous people, carelessly strolling and emitting expensive smells. Cliff Drysdale, debonair and polished, and Brian Young, the living legend, hitting determined forehands with the handle of his racket stuck, it seemed, in his trouser pocket! Some of the celebrities have terrifically unique styles of play! Jeannie and I furtively joined the strollers, being neither pros nor celebrities.

Oh, there are new kinds of tennis people these days, especially in the States. Social sort of people who have heard that it is "in" to "have trouble with your forehand", or a "touch of tennis elbow". They quickly get equipped with Fila* gear and several rackets, teaching pros and phrases like "topspin lob" and "punch-volley" and "hitting through the netman". And if, after ten lessons, they can't play well with the Wilson

* Fila—The new, super-elegant Italian tennis wear that, in order to purchase, you have to be accompanied by your bank manager.

steel, they can try the Kawasaki graphite, or the Head Aluminium, or Boron X-T or Durafiber or Glaflex. Or maybe take the old road and go right back to wood. And, if they still have problems, *actually playing*, it isn't important, because they have the tennis talk and trappings, and afterwards they can put on "Après tennis" gear, and do fun, "Après tennis" things! But wait!

Borg is starting to win, with his long controlled strokes. Marvellously detached. Inscrutable. Patient. There is a balance in his perspective. A calm recognition of the occasion. And he holds the ball on his racket, longer than Connors does, and his topspins pull the ball down and into court.

"This Borg," Abie is going to say to me after the match, "is one hell of an athlete. And what's more, on court, he doesn't come up with any of the usual bullshit."

All the able-bodied stars of former years have been invited to the centenary doubles event. Look:

Pancho Gonzales, Pancho Segura, Torben Ulrich, Sven Davidson, Donald Budge, Gene Mako, Victor Seixas, Rex Hartwig, Frank Sedgman, Bob Howe, Gardner Mulloy, Bobby Riggs, Budge Patty, Jackie Brichant, Jaroslav Drobny. Even Jean Borotra. And, of course, the commoners, Williams and Segal!

The nineteen fifties, revisited, albeit with creaking knees! The event begins only during the second week, so that the first week is given to practice and preparation—a fair amount of the application of knee-guards, ointments, plasters and embrocations, and a determined temporary abstinence from such things as whisky and cigars. Generally, though, they're a fit-looking lot, these over forty-fives, with a great deal of youth and vigour still intact.

They are all taking it as seriously as the devil, because apart from the prestige attached, there are faces to be saved and three or four thousand pounds to be won. The matches get underway at last, with nervousness being concealed by ribald observations, and tactical probes.

Abie, now forty-sixish, is sceptical about Owen's ability to stay the pace.

"I've ordered him a coffin next to the Umpire's stand," he says brutally, "so that if he caves in we can just nail him up an' continue the match." Their first match is against Gonzales and Segura before several thousand nostalgic spectators. Warren Woodcock and I go along to watch.

Abie's service and forehand are still heavy calibre. Owen, nervous at first, eventually gets underway, and they win the match. The Panchos are "confounded!"

But Gonzales comes up with the best aside. A Segal forehand flies down the middle of the court, leaving both him and Segura standing.

"Your ball, keed," says Pancho Segura.

"I tell you what we do, Sneaky," says Pancho Gonzales. "You *watch* the ball and I *hit* it, okay?"

There are dozens of these. The crowd is delighted. Ulrich and Davidson win the event, edging past Seixas and Hartwig. Abe and Owen are placed a gallant fourth.

Torben is unbelievably fit.

At one of the evening get-togethers, over wine, I question him about his training methods.

"Do you know, Gordon," he says, all gentleness and enthusiasm, "you need never become out of condition. It is a pity, you see, a pity, to become weak and unfit."

He goes on to tell me of the study which he has made about his fitness, and of the system which he has devised to retain it.

"At twenty-one, you know," he says, "you need to train for perhaps three hours each day. At thirty-one, you will need perhaps four hours, at thirty-seven you need five, and at forty-five, you might need as many as six or seven. The older you get, the more hours of training you need. But you will remain as fit as you were at twenty-one, if you simply increase your training schedule as you get older."

Being a bit of a sceptic in these matters, I immediately project his theory into my own future, and am confronted with the alarming vision of myself at seventy-five having to do about sixteen hours a day.

"But surely, Torben," I say, "eventually, you start to slow up, no matter what you do?"

"Well, of course, *eventually*," he says, with very serious eyes, "you do become completely immobile. Because, you see, you die! But until then, there is no real excuse for becoming out of condition!"

"After all, Gordon," he says suddenly after one of his silences, "What *really* is tennis?" And, when I don't reply, he says, "Only a game, you see. That is all that it really is. Only a game."